Speaking and Listening through Drama 7–11

Speaking and Listening through Drama, 7–11

by Francis Prendiville and Nigel Toye

P·C·P

Paul Chapman
Publishing

Paul Chapman Publishing
A SAGE Publications Company
1 Oliver's Yard
55 City Road
London EC1Y 1SP

SAGE Publications Inc.
2455 Teller Road
Thousand Oaks California 91320

SAGE Publications India Pvt Ltd
B1/I1 Mohan Cooperative Industrial Area
Mathura Road
New Delhi 110 044

Sage Publications Asia-Pacific Pte Ltd
33 Pekin Street #02-01
Far East Square
Singapore 048763

Library of Congress Control Number: 2006936490

A catalogue record for this book is available from the British Library

ISBN-978-1-4129-2968-4
ISBN-978-1-4129-2969-1 (pbk)

Typeset by Pantek Arts Ltd, Maidstone, Kent
Printed in Great Britain by Cromwell Press Ltd, Trowbridge, Wiltshire
Printed on paper from sustainable resources

To Vivien and Sue, our respective partners, who have not only supported us through the ups and downs of writing books, but contributed valuable ideas and healthy criticism from their own considerable professional experience

Contents

Acknowledgements

Thanks:

- to our colleague, Denise Evans, who has supported our work and contributed inestimably
- to all the students we have worked with at St Martins College in Lancaster and Ambleside, particularly the students of 2005–6
- to Gavin Bolton for reading the work and writing the Foreword and particularly as he and Dorothy Heathcote led the way
- to Hilary Cooper, Tony Martin, Steve Moss and Tessa Blair for reading, supporting, and giving unfailing good advice
- to all our colleagues and particularly Cecily O'Neill and Alan Lambert for allowing use of drama ideas that arose from work of theirs
- to Kathy Joyce, Joe Winston, Jonothan Neelands, John Rainer and other drama practitioners who have influenced us
- to all pupils and staffs who worked on these dramas with us, particularly Broad Oak School, Manchester, Hornby St Margaret's School, Lancashire and Parkinson Lane School, Halifax, who allowed considerable videotaping of work and use of photographs
- to Ambleside Primary School and Westgate School, Morecambe for supporting our work and the work of our students over some years
- to all staff in St Martins College, departmental and support staff, who have given us practical help and support
- to Robin Alexander for permission to use ideas from his work on dialogical teaching
- to Barnardo's for permission to use the Edward Fitzgerald photograph
- to Cumbria Record Office, Kendal, for kind permission to use the Workhouse Rules (ref. WD/Cu/78)
- to QCA, HMSO, Ofsted and the DfES for permissions to quote from their publications
- to Helen Fairlie for excellent editorial help in shaping up the book.

Foreword

by Gavin Bolton, Reader Emeritus, University of Durham

At last! – a book on 'speaking and listening' that guides teachers into ways of enriching communication in the classroom. There is now a general recognition among teachers that in spite of the good intentions behind the inclusion of speaking and listening within curriculum skills, the normal culture of the classroom is such that any practice in these skills is limited by the narrowness and rigidity of that very culture: teachers use the language of the teacher in the classroom and listen to their pupils from their position of authority; and, in turn, the pupils respond in their role as 'pupils' and, if they listen to each other, they are attending as one 'pupil' to another 'pupil', their roles defined and confined. An analysis of the language used in the classroom would inevitably reveal a mixture of teacher 'instructing or questioning' and pupil 'answering'. This is not the best context for expanding 'speaking and listening' skills.

Francis Prendiville and Nigel Toye offer a way of moving outside this culture, a way that frees children into temporarily breaking with their narrow 'pupil' role, into more challenging levels of thinking, talking and attending. Prendiville and Toye are lecturers at St Martins College in Lancaster. For many years they have trained teachers, basing that training on classroom practice. This publication is derived from first-hand experience of teaching primary school children. What they offer is well tested; you can tell they know what they are talking about as they share with you the variety of ways in which drama can promote skills and learning.

Drama! The very word, with its theatrical associations, may put you off. But this is '*classroom* drama', rooted in education, remote from stages and actor skills. This is not about 'casting parts', 'dressing up' 'play-acting' or 'learning lines'. This is about signalling an alternative context within which children may learn. In the authors' methodology the teacher, having set the 'frame' within which the drama is to take place, invites the children to take over the responsibility for creating their own drama within the parameters of that frame. But the children are not to 'play parts', for they are required, collectively, to take on a social role, as peasants, scientists, servants, historians, advisers, etc., and to discover the spoken language that fits the fictitious context and their role within it. The authors outline for the reader an amazingly wide range of themes drawn from lessons that have already been tried out in classrooms.

There is a central ingredient, the explanation of which takes up the major part of the book, distinguishing this kind of educational drama. Teachers do not merely *explain* what the context is to be. They themselves take on a role. Thus the class are no longer listening to 'teacher instructions', for they find themselves attending to a dialogue that steps over into fiction, endows them with their role and invites them to step with the teacher into this parallel world.

The authors successfully undertake two major teaching tasks:

1 How a teacher should set about playing a role and, just as important, how to use 'coming out of role' effectively.
2 How to plan a drama session in a way that allows sufficient space for pupil ownership.

Their considerable experience of helping others to teach guarantees the effectiveness of these chapters. I believe any teacher or trainee teacher could learn from these pages and feel comfortable trying out the authors' carefully laid out instructions.

We are given instances of remarkable uses of language expressed by children once they have stepped confidently into the fiction. The teacher–pupil relationship is temporarily replaced by a different culture, from Hans Christian Andersen to *Macbeth*, from a Victorian workhouse to *The Curious Incident of the Dog in the Night-Time*. But of course the achievements by the pupils stretch beyond Speaking and Listening to engaging with a range of subjects from the curriculum – there is a most informative chapter on the teaching of History and the link with Citizenship, for instance – and to matters of cooperation, motivation, empathy, responsibility, stimulation for reading and writing. It is the latter, writing, that can give support to the evidence needed by a teacher in assessing Speaking and Listening skills, for it is now accepted that the experience of creating new dialogue seems automatically, even with less literate children, to motivate towards writing, as if children, excited by their discovery of an alternative world, feel the need to continue to express it in another form.

This book will inspire those of you who have never thought of using drama in your classrooms. The guidelines offered here, opening a new door that could raise the level of achievement of your pupils in many directions, are mapped out very clearly in a way that is protective of both pupil and teacher. For those of you with more experience of using this art form, you will find that Francis Prendiville and Nigel Toye have reshaped, sharpened and refreshed our thinking about the classroom practice of drama.

Introduction

For us drama is the most exciting way of teaching. We see the making of fictions, the joint work of a teacher and class, as the most creative and powerful way of teaching and learning, with all participants involved as both teacher and taught. Pupils learn from the teacher and each other and the teacher learns from the pupils as the piece develops. A new drama will become revealed in its potential and in its current limitations by the class at its first usage.

Those of you who already know our book *Drama and Traditional Story for the Early Years* will know that we portray drama as powerful in its language development for young children. With this book we seek to place the methods we use at the centre of the curriculum for 7–11-year-olds. The basis for learning in all subjects should be speaking and listening and when, as for this age group, the pupil has social skills and language and they can see the possibilities of themselves contributing to the lesson, then we have potential for greater growth in all the communication skills. We can add development in the more reflective and artistic skills because of the greater capacity for self-awareness and creative insight that drama offers.

We have a number of key ideas and themes that underpin good practice in speaking and listening. As teachers we must seek to:

For speaking	For listening
Use Teacher in Role to stimulate and promote response that is natural	Use Teacher in Role to model and support
Build confidence	Allow space for those who are not yet confident
Allow ownership of the work to the pupils through their contribution	Help pupils understand the focus of the work
Help them look at another's contribution to interpret it	Develop empathy and the ability to see the value of others' contributions
Promote the asking of questions by all participants	Value non-verbal communication
Require thinking before speaking	Promote understanding through listening

One of the most important components of personal and social learning mentioned in these lists is empathy. It is a quality that is misunderstood and not as easy to achieve as is sometimes thought. Empathy is vital to produce individuals who are truly part of a community and we consider what that means.

To achieve these attributes, qualities and skills, the work must evolve through dialogue, where the teacher provides structures to stimulate and provide the challenge for the pupils. The pupils must have room to shape and build within the structure so that they own as well as experience. Thus dialogue between leader and led is the stuff of drama. The language you see in this introduction is the clue to our approach – participative, active, interactive, cooperative, creative. The most important tool in this learning style is the involvement of the teacher inside the context, teacher in role. This is not just one of many tools or techniques; for us it is the most valuable and provides the ground-base for all the others.

Our intention with the book is to support teachers in their use of drama by sharing our experience and understanding. Our experience of running courses for teachers supports our approach to drama. For example, at a recent course the teachers' expectations of the day were all in the areas we attend to in this book. They wanted:

Good ideas – literacy learning objectives

Speaking and listening through drama

Promoting self-confidence

How practically to set drama up

Links to PSHE – socially and emotionally aware

Developing intuition

When the sessions were over, the feed-back reflects the effect of drama:

Silence is powerful.

I still like the role of drama to 'hook' children into literacy. It's very engaging.

Showing sensitivity and respect towards my young persons will make it easier for the shy ones to engage in drama activities.

I learned how the technique of drama can take participants to deeper places of meaning and universal understandings.

A different approach to drama especially using characters that are not central to story.

I've strengthened my belief in the power of children being totally involved.

That drama is not just 'acting', costumes and props. It is another way to examine plot, characters and settings.

This approach is similar to other literacy activities where you dig and discuss, but it is so uniquely different when children can interview the characters in the development.

Drama is a form of expression that children can relate to when modelled, with guidance and in a secure environment.

I have learned to take a challenge as a teacher. The drama lesson may not go down path 'A' but it gives the students a chance to form the lesson.

The first section of the book seeks to explore and explain the thinking behind this approach. We have devoted chapters to each of the key elements and given clear reference to and examples from the dramas to support our ideas.

The second section contains the collection of dramas for this age group we offer as material for readers to use. They are usable for readers of all levels; those wanting to gain experience of the power of drama for engaging and motivating pupils will be able to take the dramas as given, whereas those with more experience will be able to adapt and develop the work to suit themselves. There are also ideas for further development and outline beginnings for those wanting ideas for new plans.

It is useful to look through some of the dramas before reading the 'how to' chapters. The chapters refer heavily to the practical work in the dramas and can be better understood if you have looked at them. Look particularly at 'The Governor's Child', 'The Wild Thing' and 'The Victorian Street Children' or 'The Workhouse', which are used in the chapters on planning, inclusion, etc.

Each drama is planned to work for itself and to develop other work based on it, writing and reading.

We hope you enjoy them as much as we have.

Conventions Used in the Text

We use the following abbreviations for convenience:

TiR is Teacher in Role

ToR is Teacher out of Role

OoR is Out of Role

In addition, we use italics for words spoken in dramas. In Part One of the book italics indicate words spoken by participants in the course of the drama. In the outline dramas in Part Two the italicised text indicates where we are giving examples of what a role might say.

Strategies/Techniques for Use in the Dramas

Teacher in Role does not appear in this list, but has a chapter to itself, because it is not just one of a set of techniques. It is the central teaching strategy, which, even if used very sparingly, must be a key element of any drama.

Technique	What?	Why?	When?	Variations
Tableau	Small groups make a still picture of roles in a drama, showing attitudes and relationships, people in an event, an idea of what the material they are working on means	To begin to set up a context To summarise what people think so far To show possible endings	At any time in the drama The timing will affect the nature and depth of the picture	Copy a given picture Add one word/one action Activate and show previous or following 30 seconds Tell story of that event in 4 pictures Triptych – show 3 key moments from, e.g., a life Add captions or speech bubbles Whole class tableau as in 'The Victorian Street Children'
Hot-seating	Pupils question a role, usually TiR but sometimes followed by a pupil role The plain version is that the role just sits in front of the gathered group	Helps build understanding of the role's situation	Needs to be at a point where enough of the context is already clear	Just wheeling in a person to be questioned is limited in its drama. It is better to create more dynamic in how a role is met. For example, when the advisers choose to talk to Hermia in 'The Dream', have them 'on their way' to her room in the palace and 'find' her reading a note. This provides input and a tension, especially when she hides the note
Occupational mime	Creating a semblance of activity and action of the situation	To develop context and belief in the pupils' role	Usually earlier in a drama rather than later	Recreating an event Mime loop – a set of 6 actions is repeated and can be revisited to be updated later in the drama

Technique	Description	Purpose	When	Notes / Examples
Sculpting	Whole class put volunteers into shape of roles interacting	Shows how group see attitudes of roles. Can help reflect on meaning so far	At any time	Pairs sculpt each other. Groups sculpt one member
Defining the space	The outline and contents of an imagined place are given physical representation, using available furniture and labels	Adds context and builds ideas of the role whose space it is	After sufficient knowledge of the role and the situation is established to make it possible to imagine the role's space without it being random	Put one person as a surrogate of the role in that space and use one action/one thought, alternately provided by the rest of the group, to animate the role and use the space
Overheard conversation	TiR is heard having one side of a conversation with an imagined role, who is present or on the end of a telephone	To provide information that the role might not want the class to know	At a time when the information might challenge previously established ideas or preconceptions	
Thought-tracking	Pupils gather round a role and speak the thoughts of the role	To help the pupils empathise with that role	Has to be at a significant moment when the thoughts are focused as a response to the moment	*Alter ego* – where the role has two sets of thoughts, like good and bad spirits, voicing contrary reactions to an event or a decision he/she has to make. Pupils stand to the right and left of the role to voice them
Conscience alley	Two facing lines of participants. TiR walks slowly down between them. One side voices one choice for the role and the other side a different possibility	It explores choices. For example when Maria walked to the soldier to give herself up to save the baby in 'The Governor's Child', some villagers voiced how she was right to do it and others were against it	At moments of decision or difficult conflicting ideas of what another role has done	The two sides can voice opposite opinions of the role. The two sides can represent two other roles trying to persuade the person walking through to take their viewpoint. A walks between the 2 rows towards B, a person they have to meet after significant events, and we hear A's voice, showing the attitude to B. Then B walks away from A and we hear what B thinks about the situation. For example Geb's wife in 'The Egyptians' drama walks towards him knowing he is going to jail. Then Geb walks away from her on his way to prison

Technique	What?	Why?	When?	Variations
Sociogram	Pupils stand round a key role, placing themselves close to or away from the person according to how they feel about him/her	To give a snap-shot of the whole class's attitude	When a role is influential on the community role and we need to see how people feel	
Narration	Teacher tells story of part of the drama	Link parts of drama	At a time where we need to move the drama on and where it is not appropriate, necessary or useful to have a class create the moment	The class can participate in creating the narrative and offer stages of the story of that event – as with the taking of the children by the Pied Piper
Writing input	Note, letter, diary, poster, chants	Can provide a necessary boost to pupil involvement Can be mysterious and demanding or simply give information	Where new stimulus is necessary, e.g. a letter from Lysander to Hermia arranging the elopement	Can be handed to the pupils Can be found by them Can be sought by them as important and which a role seeks to keep from them
Writing output	As above	If written 'in role' it helps develop role, reflect on role	At a time where pupils need to create something from a role, which reflects on what is happening to the role	Can be written by individuals, groups, or the whole class Can be done at the moment in the drama, after the drama or between sessions of the drama
Maps	Picture maps or symbol maps of the place of the drama	Provided by the teacher they help locate place and roles	At any time. At the beginning of the drama they can look to a journey	Can be jointly drawn by class at a point where the physical spaces need to be defined
Role on the wall	An outline of a figure is provided and pupils (or teacher as scribe) write inside words that describe what the role is like and outside the figure they write what they know about the role	This provides a summary of a role and a way of reflecting on the role's importance in the situation	At a point where we have come to see the role and have a relationship with him/her	This can be added to or altered at a later stage when we know more or different things about the role

Forum theatre	An adaptation of the Augusto Boal form, where a class take on a role who has to sort out a TiR, teach the person something, challenge their attitude One representative of the class takes the role sitting opposite the TiR and others stop the role-play to take over in the hot-seat if they see a new approach or the person on the seat gets stuck	Where there needs to be the resolution of an issue or problem	Usually later on in a drama where the problem TiR is most exposed	They take the role on collectively at times where they are inexperienced and lack the confidence to sit on the seat in front of the rest of the class
Collective drawing	A picture of a place or of objects	To give a physical representation of what we are imagining	Depending on the use: At the beginning it would set the scene, for example a map of a village If it has to show what we know of the village then it needs to be far enough into a drama so that constraints are clear and the picture can be focused	
Symbols	The role signifier of each role Key objects in the drama	To represent the role and show when the teacher is in or out of role An object that symbolises an important idea, for example the candle in *Macbeth* showing his death	As stated	A good object can focus a drama and strengthen the authentic feel of the drama, for example the whip in 'The Highwayman' that represents how he treats the horses he rides

Part One:

How to Approach Speaking and Listening through Drama

1 How to Begin with Teacher in Role

Why use teacher in role?

The most important resource you have as a teacher when using drama is yourself. Learning demands intervention from the teacher to structure, direct and influence the learning of the pupils. One of the best ways to do that in drama work is to be inside the drama. Therefore, at the centre of the dramas that we include in this book, is the key teaching technique that is used, namely teacher in role (TiR). This chapter will set out approaches to TiR and give examples of how it works.

Many teachers see TiR as a difficult activity, particularly with older children in the primary school. However, it is our experience that when a teacher takes a role he or she becomes 'interesting' to the children, so that there are less control problems because they become engaged. Many times we have watched trainee teachers with a class of children struggling to get attention when giving instructions in traditional teacher mode. Yet, as soon as they move into role, they obtain that attention more effectively.

For example, a trainee was talking out of role to a class to explain that they were about to meet a girl who was having trouble with her father and needed their help (see 'The Dream' drama based on *A Midsummer Night's Dream*). The class were calling out and not listening properly. She was talking over them and trying to teach without getting their full attention. Then she explained that they could ask questions of one of the roles from the story and that she was going to become that role when she sat down. She picked up a ribbon with a ring threaded on it and put it round her neck as the role signifier. When she sat down as Hermia, they were focused entirely on her and were listening very closely, putting hands up to ask questions and taking turns in a very orderly way. They were interested in her problem, which was her father's insistence on deciding whom she should marry. The trainee was not doing anything different apart from using role and committing to it very strongly. She looked far more comfortable.

The trainee was using the simplest form of TiR, hot-seating the role, where the class meets the role sitting in front of them and can ask questions. TiR creates a particular context and can raise the level of commitment and the meaning-making. It can 'feel real' even though it is not.

You are not effective as a teacher if you do not at some point engage fully with the drama yourself by using TiR. Remaining as teacher, intervening as teacher, side-coaching, structuring the drama from the outside, and/or sending the class off in groups to create their own drama must at best restrict and at worst negate any opportunity for the teacher to teach effectively. It is far more effective for the teacher to engage with the drama form as artist and be part of the creative act.

It is very useful in a Literacy lesson for the teacher to use roles from the text. The very fact that you take on a key role can provide important ways of defining and exploring the text. How does hot-seating open up the ideas and issues of a story to the children? Let us look more closely at the Hermia role. It can be used with 10- or 11-year-olds as a way of introducing Shakespeare or for other objectives.

Negotiate with the class that you are going to be someone with a problem. This can be done by narrating an opening:

The teenage girl with a paper in her hand burst angrily into the room.

Then sit down on the chair and stare at the piece of paper:

What am I going to do about this? How dare he. He can't do what he wants. He's not me. How does he know what I want to do?

Go out of role:

What did you learn about her and why she's angry?

Having discussed the first entry you then give the class a chance to find out whether their speculations about her are correct or not by asking questions.

Here is another way that the role could be introduced. Set it up like this:

I am going to become someone else to begin the next piece of work and all you have to do is look at her and see what you think is going on.

Sit on the seat with a piece of paper in your hand reading it silently to yourself.

How stupid he is. He writes me a letter and thinks I like him and I will like him even more just because he likes me. He knows I like somebody else. I'll never like him, let alone love him. I will have to tell him – again. But he won't listen. Especially as my dad thinks he's really nice and is encouraging him. He doesn't know him.

Notice that the piece of paper means something different in each of the above situations. In the first it is the note from her father, Egeus, outlining her situation (she is under threat of death if she does not follow his wishes). In that case it will have a seal and look official. In the second instance it is a letter from Demetrius declaring his love for her and her blindness in seeking Lysander's love. It will look different and might be accompanied by a little gift, a token like a ribbon or a necklace.

In this case, again, you go out of role to talk about what the class have seen and heard:

How does she seem? What is the situation? Who are all these people she's talking about?

In both cases, when the class have speculated enough, they will have questions to ask Hermia and you have an interesting way to begin to tell them the basic situation at the beginning of *A Midsummer Night's Dream*.

You can then answer the questions by playing the role of Hermia based on the way that the character is in the play. She's obstinate, believes in herself and her love for Lysander, is adamant she won't do what her father wants and will want the pupils' help to influence her father and the Duke.

You can introduce the fact that her father is threatening to invoke the law, to have her put to death if she doesn't obey him. You can set up the idea that in this society a daughter is expected to obey her father. This extreme social expectation and law makes the fiction like their reality but also different from it, something that helps drama create a useful distance, which helps the class reflect on their own beliefs and look at the drama world in a more balanced and thoughtful way.

All of this introduces an interesting set of issues which children at this age are beginning to experience and understand about their relationship with parents and about their relationship with the opposite sex. Even if the main aim of the work is not a study of the Shakespeare play, the role can be used to open up very important areas for personal and social education that the children can identify with. It will motivate them and produce some very strong engagement with Hermia and later, if you introduce them, Egeus, and Demetrius and Lysander, the rivals for her love. (See the full drama set-up in Part Two of this book.)

For another example of the simple use of hot-seating see the Tim the Ostler section in 'The Highwayman' drama. This can show important elements of how the children see the text, what their comprehension of it is. It provides a more stimulating way of approaching comprehension than questions from the teacher. This is partly due to the shift in tense. We are talking 'as if' it is happening now as against the past tense, which so often dominates classroom talk.

Teacher as storyteller

The teacher as a storyteller is something all primary school teachers will recognise. Good teachers slip easily into it and use it frequently. In its most observable guise it occurs when teaching the whole class and engaging them with a piece of fiction. The pupil's role will be dominated by listening and this will be interlaced with questioning, responding and interpreting the meaning and sense of the fiction. The teacher's role will be to communicate the text in a lively and interesting manner, holding their attention and engaging their imagination. In making judgements about the quality of this method of teaching, the critical questions will be around whether the content of the story interests the class and holds their attention, whether the delivery of the teacher, i.e. voice, intonation and interpretive skills, are good and, where relevant, whether accompanying illustrations have impact and resonance. For many pupils the times spent listening to their teacher as storyteller will remain as significant moments in their education. The connection between the teacher as storyteller and the teacher using drama, lies in the fact that they both use the generation of imagined realities in order to teach.

The relationship between story and drama in education is a complex and dynamic one. It means a known narrative can still be used, the knowledge of the narrative is not a barrier to its usage. However, if the pupils are locked into the original narrative it is problematic. It is the negotiable and dynamic elements of the relationship between drama and narrative that liberate the pupils and the teacher from merely retelling the known story. A class can take part in a drama where all of them know the story, where none of them knows the story, or a mixture of both. As long as some fundamental planning strategies are observed, knowledge of the story is not a barrier to participation. Broadly these pre-requisites are:

1 An awareness of those elements of the story that will not be changed – and agreements about these must be made with the class at the beginning or during the drama, in other words, the non-negotiable elements of the narrative.
2 A willingness to move away from the fixed narrative to an exploration of the narrative. The use of drama strategies to explore events and their consequences, to look at alternatives and test them. In these periods the class develop hypotheses, test them and reflect upon them.
3 If narrative consists of roles, fictional contexts, the use of symbols and events then the teacher needs to hold some of those elements true and consistent with the story so far. For example, roles and contexts may already be decided but new events may be introduced, the delivery of a letter, for example. How the class respond to this event is not known and it is at this point that they become the writers of the narrative.

Let us illustrate these ideas with an example from 'The Pied Piper' drama (a drama we designed for 6-year-olds but have used with secondary pupils: see Toye and Prendiville, 2000, p. 225).

The Mayor has got the Pied Piper to clear the town of the rats but has broken his promise of payment and in revenge the children have been led up the mountain. You put the pupils in role as the townspeople making their way up the mountain when they meet TiR as a child coming in the opposite direction. He is limping and carries one of his shoes. (In many versions of this story the child is a 'cripple boy'. This is patently inappropriate and unnecessary. The child who couldn't keep up because he had a stone in his shoe functions just as well in the story and avoids the stereotype of the disabled child not keeping up with the 'fit' children.) This provides the background to a simple hot-seating of the child.

Ask the pupils what would they like to ask the boy. They might want to ask him his name. They certainly will ask him why he is coming down the mountain and what has happened to the other children.

Preparation for the role

In preparing to be this kind of storyteller the teacher must have made particular decisions about this child.

Begin by asking the class out of role what they want to ask the child and the order of those questions. This not only provides the teacher with some security in knowing what is going to be asked, at least initially, but also allows some minutes to refine the planning, so that the teacher can be specific in answering their questions. The questions will, to a certain extent, be predictable because they are largely generated by the circumstances of the drama so far and the role the class has taken, which will be that of anxious parents.

Before the drama session, decide what attitude you are going to take when questioned by the class. You are going to be telling them a story but it will be as if they had just met you and it will not be the voice of the narrator re-telling someone else's story but in the present tense as if it is happening now. There is no book symbolising the re-telling of someone else's words. This is your story re-told in a specific place (coming down the mountain path) at a specific time (within minutes of a significant event) and from the child's point of view, not a dispassionate onlooker or observer of events.

Of course, all these things are possible from the text of a book; however, the pupils will be defining what is important, which are the most important questions to be asked and how to handle the mood of the storyteller, whose views on the events may be very different from those of the audience whom he addresses. Be clear about his attitude towards being left behind, what has happened and how he feels about it.

Then run the hot-seating. The dialogue might go something like this:

Class member in role as parent: *Where are the other children?*
TiR as the boy left behind: *It's not fair!*
Parent: *What do you mean, it's not fair?*
The boy: *Them! They get to go into the fairground and I don't! Some friends I've got. So much for Joe and Kerry. Why couldn't they wait? They could see I had a stone in my shoe and had to take it out. I couldn't keep up.*

Stop and come out of role and discuss what they have found out. Negotiate what they need to ask next. At this point some questions about what the little boy saw will emerge. Then go back into role.

> The boy: *You should have seen it! Lights, big dipper, toffee apples. Oh! the smell of the toffee apples … and all free. He was standing at the entrance shouting 'It's all free. Help yourself. Any ride, any food, anything you want you can have.' It's just not fair!*

This interactive storytelling has an immediacy and urgency and is working at a different level of discourse from the read story, and yet it is still storytelling. It is essential that the teacher stops and comes out of role and reflects with the class on what has been said, but that is also true of the more traditional mode of reading from a book. It engages the class and gives them the opportunity to generate new questions and to make sense of what is happening in an interactive way. They are questioning from within the story, as if they were there. Next we consider this key skill of moving in and out of role.

Teaching from within

Moving in and out of role – managing the drama and reflecting on it

We are describing using role as 'teaching from within' because the teacher enters the drama world, but it is very important to step out of the fiction often and not let it run away with itself. When using TiR, the teacher is operating as a manager as well as participant and must spend as much time stopping the drama and moving out of role (OoR) to reflect on what is happening and give the pupils a chance to think through what they know and what they want to do. This OoR working is as important as the role itself. It manages the role and therefore the drama; it manages the risk, establishes where the class is and helps pupils believe in the drama. It provides time and space for the teacher to assess and re-assess the learning possibilities.

Let us look at an example to see how you as the teacher have the opportunity to negotiate how the role behaves with the class. This also shows a step from hot-seating to role-playing as a demonstration with a small group. As with all of this section of the book, we are using an example from drama based upon 'The Pied Piper' (see Toye and Prendiville, 2000, p. 225).

The class in groups of five have created tableaux as families taking part in bread-making in the kitchen. They then adapt the picture when a rat invades the space. You set up going into role with one of the groups that you know will handle the situation well. OoR you gather the rest of the class round: *You will be able to influence what happens when we stop the action. Otherwise you watch and the members of this family group can role-play. You will find out who I am from what I do and say.*

You negotiate your entry: *I will enter as the rat runs out of the door.* You pick up a rat trap and a notebook and pencil and enter saying, *That was a big one, far too big for these traps.* You write something down in your notebook, before continuing. *That's another piece of evidence to take to the Mayor. I was hoping you could help. I cannot manage what he has asked me to do. There are too many of them for me as the town rat-catcher to catch. I want evidence to take to him to show how bad it is getting. Can you help?* At this point you go OoR: *Stop the drama. Who has entered? What do you know about him/her? What does s/he want? How is s/he feeling, do you think? How do you know. What would s/he look like?*

The whole class is involved in defining the role and can use their imaginations, their 'drama eyes', to help create the appropriate appearance/behaviour and their own understanding. This is in contrast to an actor who has to use acting skills to create the role in its entirety for an audience. We are making a distinction between role behaviour and acting. Both depend on appropriate signing, but whereas the actor must give the non-participant audience the bulk of the signing, a teacher using role can get away with a committed minimum.

The class will see the Rat-catcher as overworked and probably needing help to put his/her case to the Mayor. When you have discussed enough (this process helps the class believe in the role) you can move back into role and take their stories about the problems the rats are causing. You can do this with all of the class or each family in turn. Give the groups time to prepare their evidence before you go into role to receive the input. The Rat-catcher 'writes down' the points and then asks the class/family if they could come to the Mayor to help put the case. We will look at setting up that whole class event later in this chapter.

For another example of using OoR to help establish a role see 'The Governor's Child' drama for the entry of Maria, a travel-weary woman carrying a baby. OoR a blanket is openly rolled up to become the baby and the class describe how they will see the woman – possible answers are: *tired, dusty, bowed-down, tear-stained*. The person playing the role can then simply walk forward adopting a serious tone, holding the blanket, without having to pretend any of those outward signs an actor would have to portray if it were a play being performed to an audience. This is because the class will see it as they have described it themselves. The effect in this context can be more powerful.

OoR is very important as a way of negotiating the intent and meaning of the role and is the way the teacher can best control and manage learning. For the class are both an audience and observers of their own activities. When the drama is stopped they can describe, recap, interpret, think through, consider next moves and understand what is the significance of their work.

It is very important to get the participants to look at and interpret what is going on, frequently by stepping out of the drama. Depth in drama depends on the very clear and regular use of OoR negotiation so that the awareness of the co-existence of two worlds is effective at all times. Children commit to the fictional world of the drama but need always to be aware that it is fiction and to step outside it often to look at what they are doing. Contrary to some opinions, depth is not dependent upon maintaining the fiction all of the time, nor does it depend upon the children losing themselves in the drama. Learning depends upon awareness, not total immersion. In fact, if the latter takes over, children will get an experience but not understanding.

In effective drama, children can actually feel the 'as if' world as real at certain points. The teacher must make sure that if the drama does engage in that way, the pupils know it is a fiction at all times, especially by stopping and coming out of role frequently. That is also a protection.

A class reflect together in order to draw conclusions and consequently can influence each other far more in their understanding. They are in the process of negotiating a group meaning, something that can be held true for all of them.

The relationship developed by the teacher with the class is dependent on the movement between these two worlds. TiR changes the nature of the contract entered into by the class. What is that contract? It is 'the imaginative contract':

- It is not, *I will teach you by telling you what you need to know* – the style of much classroom teaching.
- It is not, *I will present a play before you and you will watch me*, as the actor contracts with an audience.
- It is not, *Listen and I will tell you a story. It is my story and you must not interrupt it.*
- It is, *You will become a playmaker, an author with me and will be a part of the story that I start and we create together*. The result is to make the creative community.

Drama then teaches in the following way. Taking a moment in time, it uses the experiences of the participants, forcing them to confront their own actions and decisions and to go forward to a believable outcome in which they can gain satisfaction. (Johnson and O'Neill, 1984, p. 99)

The requirements of working in role

The teacher, working in this way, is an important stimulus for the learning. It is not necessary to use role throughout the piece of work. It can be used judiciously to focus work at strategic points or to challenge particular aspects of the children's perceptions whilst other techniques and conventions are used to support the work and develop it.

In order to make the TiR most effective, we need to look at educational drama from the point of view of the 'audience', an audience who in this instance are participants at the same time. This will help us shape up the TiR elements particularly according to how the audience is seeing things. Here are two responses to considering the 'audience' position.

Audiences are people who make sense of what they see in front of them. (Year One drama student)

In drama the pupils are making sense actively, knowing their meaning can be acted upon.

You're asking a very complex thing of the group of children. They have to switch from operating as audience to participant and back again often and suddenly. It could be that they find this difficult or, my hunch is, they're very good at it. (Experienced teacher watching a video of a class in a drama)

This is why this sort of whole group drama has so much learning potential. It involves the 'audience' in the process of the play-making, at the same time providing the teacher with ways of influencing directly the situation and the meanings. But that is only most effective if the teacher is skilled in genuinely responding to the contributions of the class members at moments where they take the initiative and make suggestions, those critical incidents where they are teaching themselves and each other.

An example of responding to the critical incident occurred in a session on the drama based on *Macbeth*. When considering the way of showing the overthrow of Macbeth, one of the class of 10-year-olds said, *I want to sit on the throne and stop him sitting on it.* The teacher took this up and put two of the servants on the thrones of Macbeth and Lady Macbeth, with the rest of the servants gathered behind the thrones. He then set up the entry of Macbeth to the throne room. TiR as Macbeth entered slowly and stopped as though taking in the situation. *How dare you sit on the sacred seat of power! Relinquish it at once.* Of course, the pupils sat firm and outfaced him. He froze and one of the servants, picking up the idea of the situation, strode up to Macbeth, ordered him to kneel and took the (imaginary) crown from Macbeth to carefully and ceremoniously place it on the head of the usurping servant. The overthrow was fully symbolised, created by taking and formalising a very powerful idea from a pupil. The class cheered as Macbeth bowed his head and the two pupils stood up, triumphant.

How should a teacher using role relate to his or her class/audience? One of the key issues is seeing them as co-creators. If sufficient ownership is not given to the class, it is possible to turn them into the wrong sort of audience, giving them too passive a role. When they are given opportunities to influence the outcomes, to make decisions, the drama becomes partly theirs.

Disturbing the class productively

Discovery/uncovering – challenge and focus

The ownership also arises out of the way the teacher operates. The teacher's function is to provide challenge and stimulus, to give problems and issues for the class to have to deal with. The drama is developed through a set of activities that build the class role, which is usually a corporate role.

We have to help them into the drama, making them comfortable, and then disturb that comfort productively. The fact that, as in any good play, the class discover things as they go along provides the possibility of productive tension.

In setting up the drama we are doing what Heathcote calls 'trapping [them] within a life situation' (Johnson and O'Neill, 1984, p. 119). The result of constructing the situation thus is that they can then discover what it all means. There, and in the resulting choices and decisions, lies the learning potential, borne out in an exciting challenge.

The key is how children are given information. They can be handed it on a plate or they can be given opportunities to uncover/discover/be surprised by information. In this last case there is much more involvement and ownership, especially if they have to work to get the information from someone who is reluctant to give it (as with Tim the Ostler in 'The Highwayman'), someone who only gives clues as to what is really going on (the central TiR in the 'Macbeth' drama), someone who does not realise the importance of the information (Icarus in the 'Daedalus and Icarus' drama). Hence the skill of the teacher lies in the art of the unexpected.

If pupils acquire knowledge and understanding by working for it, stumbling upon it or having it sprung upon them such that their expectations are challenged, their learning experiences will be more dynamic than simply being told. An example of this occurs in 'The Governor's Child', a drama based on Brecht's *Caucasian Chalk Circle*. The class are in role as a village community helping a woman with a baby, who, unbeknownst to them, has fled a revolution. The villagers discover later who she really is and then have to deal with the consequences.

It is important to withhold information early on, as any good playwright will do. Planning the 'how' and the 'when' of strategies is all-important here.

Responding to your class

The art of authentic dialogue – needing to listen – two-way responses

The class working as a community is the key to the use of drama as a teaching method. This is another reason that the class have more ownership.

This community is made most effective by the teacher participating in role. The art of teaching and learning should be a synthesis from a dialectical approach. If a teacher runs drama without using TiR there tends to be a lack of dialectic because the teacher produces the structure that the children engage with, but the teacher can only manipulate it from outside that structure. The result looks like the diagram in Figure 1.1.

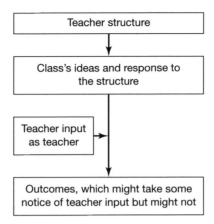

Figure 1.1

On the other hand, if the teacher participates through TiR then there can be a meeting point at which creation takes place because, in addition to planning the structure, the teacher's ideas can operate within the drama and challenge and engage with the children's ideas in a dialectic. The teacher can fully manipulate the structure from within and the resulting activity can be shown diagrammatically as in Figure 1.2.

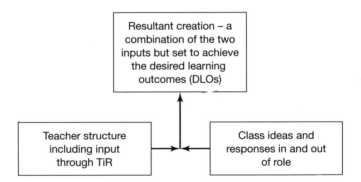

Figure 1.2

The second diagram shows the two inputs as equal, but that is not the case in practice. The teacher gives the impression of handing over the power and does so in a way that allows him or her to teach properly and yet empower the participants significantly. A TiR has to be properly planned and thought through so that the class are presented with an entity to respond to that embodies possibilities for learning.

The more we observe the use of TiR and the more we use it, we have come to the conclusion that if it is set up correctly, it does not require the person playing the role to have the same skills needed by the aesthetic actor. We are making the distinction here between the aesthetic actor and the social actor. The aesthetic actor will have learned skills related to voice, gesture and physicality that are not required by the teacher using TiR. The teacher in role will already have the skills of the social actor that are used in everyday life. These are skills that are learned in the presentation of self in every day life, the skills that demonstrate an awareness of the relationship between who we are, where we are and how we are feeling. It is the ability to adopt an attitude, to behave as oneself 'as if' you were in a particular situation that is required.

Because we work in close proximity to the class there is not the need to project oneself over the distances an actor does when playing in a theatre. The class will use their creativity to see the role in a particular way that has been indicated as long as it has been properly signed to them.

> Whereas the actor defines for the audience the message of the play within the circumstances of the plot, the teacher uses signing as an indication to the audience to join in the encounter, effecting and affecting the enterprise. (Heathcote and Bolton, 1995, p. 74)

As a result of this difference, an actor, using lines written as a script, behaves in a very different way from a teacher improvising within a planned structure, who has to take account of what the class will say in response to the moves he or she makes.

> The audience in the theatre waits for something to happen, but the participants in a drama session make it happen. (O'Neill, 1989, p. 20)

As the class feed back their responses and make possible development of the role's importance the teacher must respond appropriately and therein lies the skill of the 'subtle tongue' and the possibility for authentic dialogue.

The teacher must respond to these responses in an authentic way, honouring how the class see the role. For example, when the servants discover that their king is a murderer in the 'Macbeth' drama, they can respond in two ways: to want to tackle this problem and bring him to justice *or* to see themselves as powerless to do anything. The TiR as the Steward must honour the truth of both possibilities and, in the first case, be the weak and fearing servant who cannot see how this can be done or, in the second, begin to challenge whether doing nothing in such a situation is going to work in keeping them safe. TiR in both instances must make the problems of choice apparent whilst not taking over the decision-making.

At other times the class can be given more input to developing the idea of the TiR themselves directly. The class must be made to work to achieve the aim they have been given in the drama.

Let us look at handling an extended example from the 'Pied Piper' drama (Toye and Prediville, 2000) when the class as the villagers finally arrive at the mountain. At this point in the drama they have accepted the main aim as the villagers of getting their children back from the Piper. Mark the space in front of the class, where the children have been said to have entered the mountain, with two chairs. OoR ask them to describe the mountain in front of them and whether there are any clues as to whether the children have, in fact, gone into the mountain as they have been told. This will give them more ownership of setting the current context.

How are you going to attract the attention of the Piper if he's inside the hill? Work to use whatever idea they come up with, usually a chant or something like playing a pipe. Set them up to carry this out and then retire to the side. When they are not aware of you, slip behind them and when they are carrying out their task 'appear' behind them as the Piper. This simple, theatrical surprise engages the children even more. It is more effective than having a simple hot-seating.

Then as the Piper: *What do you want? You chant my name/play the flute/beat the rhythm that will summon me so you have made me appear.* Consider how you deliver the opening lines. Is the Piper angry or just irritated? Is he amused in a superior way or is he genuinely intrigued to find out what they have to offer him? The dialogue that transpires here is critical to the outcome of the drama.

You need to bring out the key learning area, such as the fact that the Piper is not concerned any more about money: *You can offer me as much money as you like now, but I don't want that; you have upset me by trying to trick me. If you feel that I didn't do a good job then you should have said so rather than insult me with refusing to pay what we agreed. You should never break a promise. It's not about money any longer.*

Go OoR to discuss the Piper's attitude. The burden placed on the class at this point is to offer some way of showing their thankfulness, their sincerity and their trustworthiness to the Piper so that he will accept the apology and return the children. Accept any imaginative offer as long as it is not materialistic but is related more to establishing a human relationship of trust and honour with the Piper.

A different learning area would be to have a Piper who is too full of himself, someone who needs to be taught a lesson about justice and fairness. Hasn't he over-reacted to the original refusal to pay the full amount of money? Isn't stealing the children a much more serious offence than what the Mayor did?

The drama is set up as a framework and is not finished in the same way as a play written by a playwright. In fact, the secret of educational drama is to have the framework, even a tight framework, such that the class feel they have some ownership because of the parts that they are developing.

For example, in 'The Dream' they can create the feelings and thoughts of any character. The pupils can thought-track TiR. It is important not to define everything yourself. If they challenge Egeus and ask, *Why are you making Hermia marry Demetrius?*, the teacher can stop the questioning and come out of role to consider the possible answers to this question with the class.

A drama technique can be used to help them define possible reasons. They can thought-track Egeus about his daughter's opposition or why he must have her obedience. The TiR is not exclusively the teacher's creation. They will know as much about why a father tries to dominate a child, particularly from the child's point of view.

The 'play' we are creating is a joint enterprise and, when the beginnings of a role are in place and we have established the givens, the class will know what we are creating and why and can develop that role by the way they respond and the way they see it. TiR creates an ownership dynamic that is attractive to the participants.

The teacher–taught relationship

In all teaching situations there exists a power relationship between the learners and the teacher. The learners are bound together as a group merely by being the learners and, of course, as there are more of them than there are of you, they hold the power.

If the class decide as a group they do not want to learn and they wish to make your attempts to teach them impracticable, they can do it. The power in the classroom lies with the class. Of course, it does not look like this when the class are responding and contracting into the tasks set by the teacher but should some or all decide not to, the cohesion can be broken. In drama this power relationship is made overt. We must start from the point of view that if the class do not want the drama to work then it will not.

What we have to counter this with is a methodology that, if set up right and handled judiciously, offers interest and engagement to hold the class's attention. So much so that if a minority of the class start to undermine it, the committed will demand they stop; the disrupters are seen as spoiling the enjoyment and it is not unusual to see the majority let them know this fact.

We must begin with the interest level of the class: the plight of Goldilocks will interest the class of 4- or 5-year-olds and a mission to rescue Kai from the Snow Queen, children of 7 and 8. For those aged 10 or 11 it may be the jealousy of Tim the Ostler that gains their attention. The nature of drama makes the interest level a dynamic and flexible dimension. The pupils will, to a certain extent, define a level of interest in a drama by focusing upon the issues that interest them. There is not a hard and fast rule on age groups because we have used Kai with younger children and dramas from our Early Years book have been used with 12-year-olds. It depends upon how you do it.

In the classroom, the pupils enter into an agreement with you the teacher that you are in charge. This may be a tacit agreement, it may depend upon many factors but in it the teacher is in charge and there are certain rights and privileges attached to your role. The power relationship is asymmetric. Of course, in drama we have the possibility of shifting the power when we are inside the fiction because we may choose a role that has low status and has little power. This shift in status and power is very engaging for pupils. It can result in a different kind of dialogue from the usual teacher/pupil one and this can be very attractive to pupils.

So what are the possibilities in terms of power and choosing a role? There are five basic types of role and mostly can be illustrated from the 'The Dream' drama.

The authority role   This is a role like the Duke in the 'The Dream' drama, who is presented with Egeus's problem and has to rule on it. This figure is usually in charge of an organisation and has the class in a role subordinate to him/her. The role is fair, applies rules and governs properly, but often does not know the full facts and issues and needs the class to investigate and enlighten him/her. It is very close to being teacher and can be reassuring for a class, but also has the negativity of not changing the teacher–taught relationship enough to allow more ownership for the class.

The opposer role   This is a role that is often in authority but dangerous to and/or creating a problem for another role and, by extension, the class. Egeus is an opposer role who is against Hermia and therefore in opposition to the class role, as they take her side against his dictatorial treatment of her. This is a stimulating position for many pupils as the opposition of parents is something they have all experienced. The opposer role has to be used carefully because the response to it can be difficult to handle if it becomes too strong. We have to know what response to expect and be able to channel it productively.

The intermediate role   This is often a messenger or go-between, as the servant role used in the 'The Dream' drama. This role is then caught between opposing sides and can appeal to the empathy in the class to help them out of the predicament. In the 'The Dream' it might be a servant to Egeus who is sympathetic to Hermia but does not know what best to do as she cannot just tell her employer what she thinks he should do. So she seeks the help of the class to solve her dilemma.

The needing help role   This is a role like Hermia, who is in need of help to fight the injustice of her father's decision. This role, like the servant described above, is the best way to get empathy from a class and most raises the status of the class, putting them in a position of responsibility and thus generating interest and learning possibility because the teacher is the one who does not know what to do for once.

The ordinary person   This role is in the same position as the role given to the class. We do not have this sort of role in our 'The Dream' drama but the Steward in the 'Macbeth' drama is like this. He faces the same problem and danger as the other servants represented by the class. Even though he is in charge of them, he needs them to sort it out for him and make decisions. Therefore this is a lower status role, the teacher being 'the one who does not know', a very powerful position of ignorance that teachers cannot ordinarily occupy. It is powerful because it shifts responsibility more to the pupil roles.

The three low status roles present more possibilities for the pupils' learning because the teacher–pupil power relationship is shifted and they have a semblance of power. We say 'semblance' because the pupil power only lies within the fiction and, as always, the teacher is running the class and can come out of role at any time to assume control. 'Semblance' is not a pejorative word here. It does mean a shift of some power, but not a takeover of power. In a fiction what seems to be the truth is as powerful as if it were real.

Related to issues of power and role is the issue of power and control in the classroom. Drama has for many teachers a Health Warning attached to it: 'This substance is dangerous, handle with care!' The fear of chaos is one that puts many teachers off using drama. However, if basic rules are applied, there is no more danger of chaos than in any other lesson. Let us look at what might appear to be a potential recipe for chaos in the planning of a lesson on 'The Pied Piper' (see Toye and Prendiville, 2000, p. 225) and analyse how it is handled and chaos avoided.

The class have been told they must confront the Mayor. The angry crowd of townspeople are making their way to the Mayor's parlour:

Before we can confront the Mayor we must set out how his office looks.

You take two chairs and place them at one end of the class and place a table and a chair behind it at the other end of the class.

This is the Mayor's parlour. First you must tell me how big the doors into his parlour are.

The distance between the chairs indicates how big the class want the door to be.

Now I want you to look at the table and chair over there. This is the desk and chair in which the Mayor sits. Tell me about the desk. What is it made of? What is it covered in? Is it simple or ornate in its design? Use your 'drama eyes' and tell me what you see.

The class offer suggestions, building the image of the desk. They then do the same with the Mayor's chair. The contributions are valued and embellished. The class describe the whole room and visualise where they will work.

The townspeople are marching down to the Mayor's parlour. They are getting near enough to be heard. What are they chanting?

Suggestions are made and those that have a rhythm and meter and words that will maintain the seriousness of the event are chosen. This strategy binds the group together, makes concrete their community and an attitude they can hold as a group. The chant is rehearsed and when it feels and sounds like an angry crowd it is ready to be used.

So, we have a parlour, we have an angry crowd and a chant. When you arrive at the door who is going to be the person to knock on these great doors? How are we going to make the sound to go with the knocking on the door? Are you going to stamp your foot? We need someone to give a signal to stop the chant otherwise we won't hear the knock on the door and the conversation with the Mayor.

Someone volunteers to stop the chant like a conductor stopping the music.

Finally we need one person to be spokesperson to say to the Mayor what you all think.

A volunteer is chosen and exactly what is to be said is worked out.

OK. I am going to take the role of the Mayor and I am going wear my chain of office. When I take it off I will be your teacher again and we can talk about what has happened. Listen to the story and you will know what to do:

'The mayor sat at his desk and outside he could hear a crowd chanting getting louder and louder, nearer and nearer.'

You signal for the chant to begin, which may be something like.

> *Get rid of the mayor.*
> *Get rid of the rats.*
> *Get rid of the mayor.*
> *Get rid of the rats.*

This gets louder and louder until the signal is given to stop and there is a loud knock on the door. As Mayor you get up and move around to the front of the table, half sitting on it in an informal way.

Come in, do come in.

The townspeople come in and the spokesperson delivers his/her speech.

We're fed up of you and we're fed up of the rats. We want your resignation, you're sacked!

The mayor is acquiescent, compliant and biddable.

Yes, you are right to be so angry! Every right. It's a dreadful situation and I have let you down. I have one last hope and that is a man who is due to arrive tomorrow.

You break out of role:

OK, let's stop the drama there and look at what has happened.

This response is not expected by the class. It surprises them, defuses their anger. They expect the Mayor to argue.

The key issue in this example is the way in which a potentially chaotic event in the drama is managed by careful structuring and rehearsing before it takes place. In this way, the lesson remains under control and the learning possibilities are maintained while at the same time the class has a carefully managed experience of the confrontation.

If you consider the points, rules and suggestions we have offered, you can construct very influential roles for all sorts of teaching.

Summary of points to consider

- Why we use teacher in role – pupils listen to teachers in role
- How we expand the possibilities of story and explore story
- Operating the two worlds of drama, inside and outside the fiction
- Moving in and out of role – managing the drama and reflecting on it
- Building the teacher role with the support of the class
- What, when and how to give information for maximum influence and effect
- How to dialogue with the class – teachers learning to listen well
- How we work with the class as collaborators
- Choosing the role – the low status roles offer more learning possibilities
- Handling drama – structuring for control – imposing shape and constraint

2 How to Begin Planning Drama

In this chapter we are going to describe and analyse the main components of planning in drama. On this journey we will visit a number of key planning decisions and approaches. These are:

- How to begin a plan
- The frame of a drama – first example 'The Governor's Child'
- The frame of a drama – second example 'The Wild Thing'
- How did this drama evolve?
- The ingredients of planning
- Learning objectives
- Strong material
- Roles for the pupils
- Tension points – risks – theatre moments
- Building context and belief-building
- Challenges and decision-making

But before we begin this journey a word of warning to those who are new to this way of working: 'If I was making this journey, I wouldn't start from here!' Planning brand new dramas is complex and, while we hope to unravel some of the complexity in this chapter, the best starting point is using tried and tested dramas first. That is why we have included 14 dramas in this book. When you feel comfortable with the approach, the planning becomes more accessible.

There is even an intermediate stage in planning and that is to take parts of different dramas and remake them as new ones.

We cannot establish a simple procedure for an order of planning. Clearly the teaching/learning objective will drive the shape of the drama, but the engine that drives the drama needs fuel and that fuel is a piece of strong material, a creative idea, and that is more inspirational than an objectives-led design. This material – a book, a piece of literature, a picture or some other subject matter, fiction or non-fiction – will give us one or more of the elements of a good drama, a role or roles, an interesting context or a dilemma. In this way we may come up with an idea for a role that will provide a specific challenge for the class; we may get a mental picture of a particular situation we want the children to become involved in, or an idea for focusing a problem based on the original material. For example, when we wanted to introduce Shakespeare to a class of 10-year-olds, we wanted to use 'Macbeth' because it has a very strong story. The original idea for the drama came from thinking about how the servants in the play might feel when they bring Macbeth piece after piece of bad news towards the end of the play. That led to thinking about whether the servants in the castle were aware of what was going on and what their moral reaction was. The frame for the drama developed from that.

'The Governor's Child' arose from thinking about how to teach a sixth-form class, 17-year-olds who were studying the Brecht play *The Caucasian Chalk Circle*, the significance of the child in the play; how to underscore the girl Grusha's strong attachment to the baby, Michael Abashvili. The central idea came with thinking of how Grusha is shunned by people she seeks help from. What if a village accepted her and therefore began to shoulder the responsibility she had, to see if they could feel protective and committed to the innocent? Then the pressure point of the arrival of the Ironshirts, the soldiers looking for Michael, was the obvious key development. The drama that evolved seemed strong and suitable for adaptation to a wide range of age groups.

Then we assemble all the ideas that make up the frame for a drama. A new drama is a difficult beast and takes time to develop and grow. We must never forget that drama is an art form. As such we need to consider the way that planning drama is a creative and dynamic activity, not done by just following a set of procedures. A full drama grows over a period of time, it is organic. It is not something that can be planned and completely finished in one go. Dramas develop through their usage, like the oral tradition of storytelling; they are tried and adjusted, refined and edited. Drama for learning has to be grown slowly. With this organic nature lie the possibilities for the class to contribute to the way the drama turns out. We must plan gaps for pupils' ideas, we must be careful not to plan the pupils out of the drama. There has to be a balance of freedom within the drama for new possibilities and decisions for the children and the teacher structure that provides the constraints and necessary dynamic of the piece, the scaffolding that holds it up.

The frame of a drama

We are using the idea of a frame as a way of seeing key decisions in planning. It is originally defined by Erving Goffman (Goffman, 1975) as the way a situation develops, or in our case is constructed, to give particular viewpoints and ways of understanding the meaning of that situation.

> Goffman uses 'frame' to refer, essentially, to the viewpoint individuals will have about their circumstances and which helps them to make sense of an event or situation and to assess its likely impact upon themselves as individuals. Translated into terms of process drama as a genre of theatre, we could say that Goffman's frame constitutes a means of laying in the dramatic tension by situating the participants in relation to the unfolding action. (Bowell and Heap, 2001, p. 59)

The frame is a dynamic, interrelated and complex weaving of all the other ingredients. It has pre-text, which is derived from the stimulus material (see Figure 2.1).

In planning a drama we have to write the main frame, the scenario, in a way that indicates the relationship of the component parts and how the interactions provide tension and potential. For example, the frame of 'The Governor's Child' is shown in Figure 2.2.

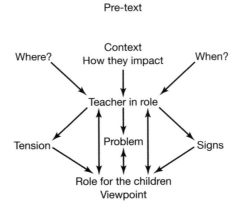

Figure 2.1 *The dynamic of a frame when planning*

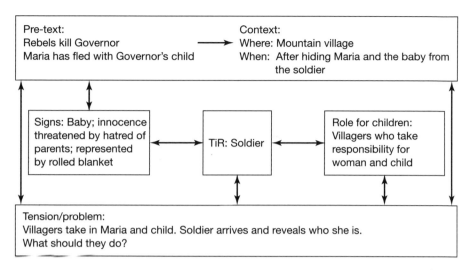

Figure 2.2 *Frame of 'The Governor's Child'*

An example of thinking through a plan

How did the 'The Wild Thing' drama evolve from initial ideas?

Looking at Maurice Sendak's book *Where the Wild Things Are* led to ideas about possible roles and situations to explore with the pupils. The book has always held a fascination because of its depiction of boys' behaviour. There is a direct link to PSHE objectives. To translate this to a drama, the first idea was: how might Max's mother feel if she went to his room and found him not there? The mother is mentioned in the book but never appears herself; there is just the meal appearing in the room at the end of the story.

Let us look at the key components of the frame here, a frame that could be outlined thus:

> Mother sends Max to bed without supper because he has been naughty. He leaves the bedroom to have an adventure. Mother finds him gone and seeks help to find him. Max returns. Where has he been? How will he behave now?

The next stage was to develop some sense of his mother, her handling of Max and her attitude to him. Learning resides in this, the parent–child relationship, something all children know about but is infinitely variable in levels of success and quality. The complexity for the drama resides in her role. We considered the mother's possible ambiguous signals, embodying ideas of softness and indulgence towards Max at the same time as being irritated by Max's wildness and wanting to control him.

Thus we are exploring ideas of why Max is like he is, an exploration that the class will experience through the drama.

Therefore the next planning decision was about who the children might be in order to encounter this experience, what viewpoint will they have to see the situation of a missing Max. Who could the mother go to for help? One answer was an agency, based on ideas of 'Mantle of the Expert' from Dorothy Heathcote's work (Heathcote and Bolton, 1995), which unites the children in a particular viewpoint with particular expertise. In this case it becomes 'Lost & Found', an agency expert in finding lost children. We then have to decide how would we build belief in that role. Then the children have to encounter the mother, desperate for help to find her son.

The frame now looks like the diagram in Figure 2.3.

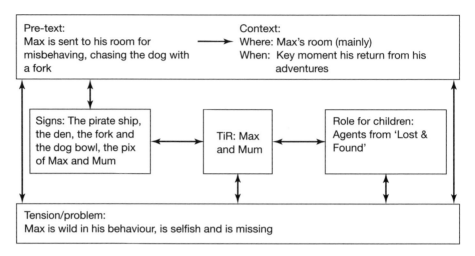

Figure 2.3 *Frame for 'The Wild Thing'*

You can see that we have begun to create ideas of what Max's room would look like, as it is the central setting. The thinking here is to use the room to allow the class to have a say in what they want and how they define Max. This will reinforce their role as agents of Lost & Found and invest more in the drama, own it more. So we can use the set up of the room to give clues as to what Max is like and what has happened to him. This will lead up to the moment where he reappears.

The technique 'defining the space' is used to establish the room. However, the basic defining of the space is further developed because the teacher inserts specific signs and symbols he or she wants as the clues. So the teacher directs the picture of Max the class forms. One of the inserts is a toy pirate ship, which is not in the book, where Max sails out in an ordinary sailing boat. But the pirate ship was chosen because it is more visual, embodies ideas of adventure and wild and violent behaviour. In the Sendak book there is a picture on the wall in the second illustration of a wild creature's face with 'Max' written underneath, clearly a drawing by Max himself. This suggested including a line drawing of Max chasing his mother with a knife. In addition we added little notes written by Max for the pupils to discover and read. They discover a rich environment to decode and from which to deduce things. The outcome of this is usually that the class, as agents of Lost & Found, suggest that Max has run away. Of course, we could have then developed a drama about finding Max, but it would be difficult to run that without descending into potentially silly non-activities for the pupils searching non-existent places. They do go to the shed his mother talks of, but there draw a blank, apart from the arrival of a figure they take to be him (raising tension), hide to surprise him, only to find it is his sister. She can provide other instances of his selfishness and wildness.

So we decided to have Max return, as he does in the book. Then he can meet the agents, and the drama is no longer about finding him. Instead they have the responsibility to confront Max and make him aware of his problem, his behaviour and the mother's attitudes.

Max's return and the confrontation with the Lost & Found agency is the central event of the drama, the moment that the previous stages have been building to and the event from which the challenges, the decisions will arise. It is the focusing, pivotal moment and all good dramas will have this. It needs to be handled dynamically to raise tension, so it is now planned in that the class are considering what they know of Max (technique – role on the wall) and thinking where they could look next, the shed having proved fruitless. They need to be gathered round the role sheet and be looking at it. The teacher then moves behind them, picks up the Max role signifier and surprises them as Max begins speaking to them: *Who are you and what are you doing here?*

The drama has now taken shape. The aim of the drama is now clearly focused, to have the children explore and consider a boy's unacceptable behaviour and look at a parent–child relationship, to give advice and solve problems. The resolution of the issues is the final stage of the drama. How will we make that happen? Usually we use forum theatre to set up the class taking over the wronged role, against the role who most needs to learn to change, to see and understand something important about themselves. In this case that is Max, who will always remain a TiR. The pupils have to show him the error of his ways and how other people, his mother, his sister, really feel about him.

Other techniques and roles are used along the way to build the class's understanding of Max so that they can best see how to help him see his responsibility to others, to change from his totally self-centred way.

The ingredients of planning

Let us take the elements of a drama we have been referring to above and look at them separately with other examples.

Creating a drama is very much like cooking. It is easy to serve up a fast food meal, which has very little quality and goodness, but it is a more detailed, careful and thorough process to create a quality meal from scratch with good ingredients. Our ingredients include the following.

Learning objectives

Learning is often focused through a key problem or issue for the children to tackle (Dorothy Heathcote's 'man in a mess'). This helps hand responsibility for learning to the pupils themselves.

The learning can be in any of five areas:

- Language Development – the medium of drama and hence the key impetus to Speaking and Listening (see 'How to Generate Quality Speaking and Listening' p. 41).
- Spiritual, Social, Moral, Cultural, Personal – there is usually this capability in any drama.
- Content – the curriculum, focused on any subject – we have highlighted possibilities in our examples for English, History, Technology, Art, Geography.
- Art Form drama – the more the class do drama the more they understand the form and the more they can manipulate and help shape the work.
- Thinking Skills – drama models the mental moves that underpin our thought processes: actions and consequences, being logical about decisions, giving reasons and arguing positions. The very reflective nature of the work, going out of role to examine the meaning of situations and events in the drama, promotes metacognition.

If you look at the sample dramas we give you, you will see a range of objectives in these areas specifically related to the material of the drama, for example, in 'Daedalus and Icarus' the following are all possible:

Objectives
Pupils will understand:
- the significance of legends as a focus for literacy work
- legend as part of historical understanding

PSHE
- consequences of actions (on taking the folder of drawings)
- father/child relationship and disobedience
- the consequences of keeping secrets

The first two could be further refined to:

- How the story of Daedalus and Icarus is related to Greek ideas about technology.
- Comparing the drama version of the story and the original myth.

Likewise, the first PSHE general objective could be focused more as the consequences of:

- taking what is not yours

and

- finding out about something that represents knowledge dangerous to yourself.

Clearly the contact points have learning areas related to them.

If we can refine an objective tightly it will help us make decisions about the structure and what it should do.

Strong material

We need a stimulus to learning, to focus the exploration. This my be a piece of writing with key learning points, that are usually unresolved by the writer of the original material. These often lie in the PSHE curriculum area. Let us again look at our drama 'The Wild Thing' from *Where the Wild Things Are*. Maurice Sendak shows us Max, a boy who is very imaginative, but whose behaviour is very wild. It also hints at him learning something important on the island, how he misses his home and his mother. The story finally shows Max returning to his room, but there is no resolution of what he will be like in the future, no exploration of his relationship with his mother, whether he continues to behave wildly in his wolf suit. In addition, no other family members appear in the story. This is a gift for drama because we have a number of PSHE issues implied through the story but not dealt with and we can add key roles to look at these issues and embody in them their attitudes to Max. For example, how does his mother deal with him? What does his sister think of him? What would a Wild Thing from the island say if it came after him? All of these are embodied in the plan we offered you in Figure 2.3.

Roles for the teacher

We dealt with this in Chapter 1, 'How to Begin with Teacher in Role'.

Roles for the pupils

The class need to be framed up as a community, where the class work together supporting each other and working for the same aims. This builds their ability to communicate with and understand each other, the best basis for all learning.

They can be an expert community, the 'Mantle of the Expert' role. We can see the use of this as the historians in 'The Victorian Street Children' (notice here, though, that they are moved on to become the street children as the drama develops) and 'The Highwayman', as archaeologists in 'The Egyptians', as journalists in 'Scrooge', as advisers to the Duke in 'The Dream', as an agency specialising in finding people, Lost & Found, in 'The Wild Thing' and as an agency again, Superhelpers, in 'The Snow Queen'.

The 'Mantle of the Expert' role gives the pupils status and an objective viewpoint to consider situations often fraught with emotions and opposing attitudes. We use this sort of communal role as they also invest the pupils with the skills and attributes that we would want them to exhibit – they have to be analytical, compassionate, communicative, thoughtful, creative, listeners.

The other sorts of communities in the outlines we give you are servants in 'Macbeth' and 'Daedalus and Icarus', mountain villagers in 'The Governor's Child', park volunteers in 'Charlie'. In all cases belief in the role is built and the learning focused through the problem they encounter.

The pupils also have opportunities to take central roles, particularly from TiR at key stages in the dramas. We see this with all the aggrieved roles in 'Scrooge', Maria in 'The Governor's Child' and with the adoption of the sister's role in 'The Wild Thing', Charles in 'Charlie', Hermia in 'The Dream', and many others.

Where they take over a role it is usually the role who needs help; the role is a victim in some way so that the takeover hands responsibility to them to resolve key issues. They take it over at a crucial moment where the chance to change things, to challenge injustice or correct a wrong is paramount. It is important though that planning does not assume success without hard work and proper arguing of a case by the class. It is important not to make solutions easy for them, a great deal of learning in drama is generated by challenging their thinking. In some cases it is enough for the issues to have been aired and that no solution happens. The learning objective must be the focus of planning.

Tension points – risks – theatre moments

Tension provides the momentum that pushes the class, demands a response, engages them. It involves taking calculated risks; for example in a recent version of a drama based on 'Snow White' the class, who were in role as people helping the dwarves at the mine, returned to the house to find Snow White, who appears to be dead. This is a very demanding moment, but one that the children, after initial hesitation, tackled with great commitment. They had to lift the poisoned handkerchief from her face and she would revive. All the times we have done the drama they have never failed to do this. There is a bit of a risk on our part because we cannot ensure they will do it, but should they not do so we plan to go out of role and discuss how they see what is happening and what they think needs to be done. They sometimes need the permission to do something they are already thinking about but unsure of taking action on.

Tension can be planned in, but needs to be seized on according to how the class react. One theatre moment happened this way. 'The Governor's Child' is planned with the possibility of searching the village and the teacher will be looking for a chance to create a moment of near discovery. The class choose how and where they hide Maria. With a class of 10-year-olds the tension was created on the spur of the moment by the teacher's use of the potential of the planned situation itself. At his second return to look for Maria and the baby, the Soldier (TiR) searched the village. At one point he stopped right next to where the pupil playing Maria was crouching 'hidden' in a shed and asked, *What's in here?*

The tension at that point was palpable with all eyes on the class member (villager) whose job it was to handle the situation. *It's hardly used*, she said. The

Soldier mimed turning the handle. *It's locked and I don't know where the key is,* said the girl. The Soldier moved on and the class sighed with relief.

The teacher playing the Soldier built the situation admirably, with never any intention of finding Maria, but the class could see the possibility. The tension rose even though, or maybe because of the theatricality of the moment. There was no shed of course and Maria was pretending to be hidden. In reality, Maria was in full view of everyone with the agreed convention of her hiding being symbolised by crouching down. This provides the fictional belief in her invisibility aided by the Soldier never looking at her. But then the Soldier is the teacher so unless the class accept the fiction nothing will work. Tension here is produced by the collective imagination, what the consequence of discovery would be.

Another example of the effect of tension occurred when another class working on the same drama were so startled by the entry of a TiR that one girl was heard to gasp, 'Scary!'

Building context

Usually having one main location helps the drama to be properly focused.

With 'The Egyptians' we did not have a single location in an early version. It started with the tomb and we planned to spend time creating it and its wall paintings as the early belief building activity. However, then the main role, Geb, was found praying at a temple separate from the tomb. Then we realised that if we had a separate temple we would have to spend time establishing belief in it as well. There was no reason that Geb's discovery should not happen in the tomb, and that gave us even more potential because he should not be there and we could raise the tension through that prohibition. The tomb could focus all the activity of the drama. That planning decision reinforced the importance of the depictions on the walls so that they can also then be used more at other stages of the drama. That consolidation of the context strengthened the integrity of the drama and helped structure it, as you will see from the full plan.

Building belief

What does this mean when related to drama? It is the need to get the class to trust in the teacher and what the teacher is creating. Why should they go along with the fiction? Only if you create the belief that there is something in it for them. How do you convince them that there is something worthwhile in it?

This is done in a variety of ways. Use of TiR can interest and build belief. The right choice of pupil roles helps that, especially if meaningful activity can be given to them to establish the roles, or the situation and place is properly realised and created for the imagination, as indicated in the previous paragraph.

All of the ingredients contribute to building belief:

- choosing worthwhile material, engaging interest, as with the dramas here;
- having the right 'hook' at the beginning, a stimulus, a picture or artefact, a role or piece of material that raises expectations, like the street children photograph which never fails to pull the class in;
- planning in times to contract and re-contract with the group, asking them to accept specific conventions, e.g. taking the cloth that becomes the baby in 'The Governor's Child' and deliberately rolling it up into the shape in front of them and asking what it is representing. We have never had a child challenge the credibility of Maria entering with the baby if contracting is done in setting up the moment;
- raising their status, genuinely, in the choice of role for them and in the way we deal with them, like the expert roles we have discussed;

- choosing the right strategies and the variety of strategies so that interest and involvement are maintained, like the thought-tracking where roles are built with their input;
- choosing the right task/activities – giving them something to do that makes sense and through which they contribute to the content and realisation of the drama, like the creation of the wall paintings in 'The Egyptians';
- planning to involve them in key decisions and the creation of the drama (see later in this chapter);
- planning to test belief and take calculated risks – and most importantly to provide tension, an unexpected moment or encounter, a role that behaves in a challenging way.

In delivering the drama we have to:

- talk to them positively … accepting answers as far as possible and looking for elements within a suggestion that might hold possibilities even when the whole idea does not. We have to remove ideas that may get in the way of the drama working (magic solutions, violence, etc.), but doing it in such a way that the pupil offering the idea genuinely does not feel rejected in the process and is willing to continue to make suggestions. It is important to upgrade by repeating answers, commenting on them, acting on good suggestions;
- go slowly, stopping and reflecting and taking the time to do that;
- isolate any problem of non-belief and dealing with it in role or out of role.

Belief in the drama comes mostly from feeling a part of the drama and that requires that the class members contribute to the way the drama develops. As such we have to plan the key moments for critical decisions for the class.

Decision-making – key developments in the drama which provide the class with challenges

In any drama there will only be one or two main decisions that have to be taken by the pupils; by main decisions we mean where the direction and outcome of the decision is crucial.

Inexperienced practitioners often think that they must give the pupils a decision at every turn, what to do next, whom to meet, where to go. This will lead to chaos, with too many possibilities to manage. There are teacher decisions and pupil decisions and we have to be clear about the timing and nature of both, why one should be the teacher's and why another should be the pupils'.

Many teacher decisions are built into the plan as givens, otherwise there will be no clear direction for the learning. As with many art forms, the constraints of the piece are critical to the quality of the product. What we embed as non-negotiable in the planning of a drama tightens the focus and ensures a concentration on the particularity of the main event. As successful dramas move from the particular to the universal this makes certain the contexts and dilemmas are not nebulous or indistinct.

The opportunity for the pupils to input and take initiative parallels the idea of Dialogic Teaching as outlined by Robin Alexander (2005) and related to drama in Chapter 3 'How to Generate Quality Speaking and Listening'. We must plan space for real dialogue, which will involve listening to and using, where possible, their ideas (see Figure 2.4).

When the plan is laid very close to expected responses, and even, in the worst case, when expected responses are laid on top of the plan, so that the plan is a predictor of the response, the correspondence of plan and responses leaves little or no room for a proper dialogue to develop. This generates a false

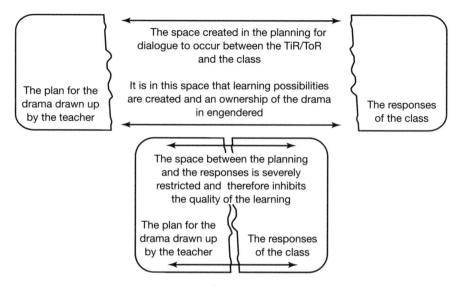

Figure 2.4 *The relationship between planning and delivery in drama – the space for dialogue*

sense of security for the teacher: 'I have my plan and it is tight and secure. The success of the lesson will be how closely the pupils follow my plan and deliver what I have planned.'

The lack of space gets in the way of quality learning and stifles commitment for many of the pupils if it is like that at all times in the drama; there are times when tight planning is necessary. It has to be recognised that in drama lessons the dynamic of teacher planning and pupil response must have fluidity. The teacher may plan for little space for pupils' decisions in some parts of the lesson and more in other parts. Highly constrained planning is often a feature of the early phases of the drama lesson where common agreements are necessary in order to build the context. In these early phases of the drama lesson the pupils do not have enough information to make key decisions. Later in the drama there can be more space and more possibilities for pupil contribution. It may be better to use a drama where tight planning is the norm throughout because the class are inexperienced and not ready to take on the responsibility of key decisions.

How does this work in practice? Here are examples of the difference between a closed access and open access approach to drama. The examples are from 'The Governor's Child' drama.

Early in the drama, when the villager comes to tell them about the woman and the baby staying in the village, there is no decision given to the class as villagers about whether to take her in: *I wanted you to know that I want my family to take her in*, said by TiR, is non-negotiable. The issue at this point is one of informing the villagers. We may get their reactions, but these viewpoints are not going to change this decision. This is because at this point we are building context, a context where Maria will be hidden by the villagers and that will provide the major challenge and decisions later. The major decision is about whether to continue to hide her after the Soldier has visited and the villagers know she represents a danger to them. Then the gap in the planning opens and access to dialogue becomes more potent. The class can have a big input here.

Planning is about creating fictions to allow children to see the possibility of change in life. The class should always have the opportunity to make choices, to see alternatives in the way we approach situations, to look at the consequences of actions, but they have to be far enough into the drama to have belief in the situation, knowledge of their position and the understanding of the roles before they can properly make decisions. These three elements are directly influenced by the constraints or givens planned into the drama by the teacher.

The drama conventions, strategies and techniques

There are many techniques for structuring the stages of a drama. Variety of activity for the class is important but each chosen technique must fit the moment and do a particular job. They may:

- create context
- build belief in the roles and therefore the drama
- focus learning
- help explore a situation and deepen understanding
- help to reflect on the meaning of the event.

For details of using the drama techniques see the table in the Introduction p. 4.

Planning as a collaborative activity

We also recommend that you plan with at least one other person. Planning for true learning is a social activity and needs to have more than one mind brought in to develop its full potential. In our team, one member may have the beginning of an idea and sketch that idea out, but usually turns to another member of the team for feedback and a planning discussion. This functions as a means to bounce ideas, to see flaws and to provide insights into the potential for learning. The complexity of drama means a multiplicity of possible learning outcomes.

For example, when planning developments to the original 'Macbeth' drama, we wanted to add the 'Witch' section. We began with the idea of facing the class with the ambiguity and teasing language that the witches in the original demonstrate. How to do this? One of us, A, had ideas about the Witch arriving at the castle door, a vagrant, carrying something. This was developed further by B with the suggestion that the bundle should contain a mirror. The symbolism of this became obvious, considering some of the imagery in the play, appearance and reality, what is truth?, etc. When searching out a mirror, A came across a cracked hand mirror and this was ideal. We can then use the mirror to get the class to look into the future for Macbeth.

Another example happened with 'The Wild Thing'. When sharing the planning so far with a group of trainee teachers and looking at the composition of Max's room, it was suggested that Max would have a den, just like he's making with a blanket hung over a rope in one of the pictures in the story. This not only parallels the storybook but also gives the teacher, as Max, a place to go and sulk when the class are trying to get him to see sense and gives a place for the Wild Thing, who comes to find Max, to hide and surprise the Lost & Found agents.

Road testing the first version

Participants in dramas offer us as the teachers insights into ways of using an established structure. Once we have the beginnings of a drama we need to try ideas out. We try out the draft plan with a good class, one we know and can rely on to be responsive, but also with the skill to offer new ways of looking at the drama, to challenge properly and be honest in response; they will help us develop the potential in the drama. When a class are responding to strong moments in a drama they not only provide ideas for future use, but also show us the sections which are weak and need replanning. Their positive responses reveal new possibilities and can often become incorporated as 'givens' when the drama is used in future. They will show you how a TiR is working.

For example, when road testing 'The Wild Thing' drama for the first time the teacher came in very aggressively as Max and growled at the class in Max's bedroom, *I am the King of the Wild Things and will eat you up if you make me angry*. The class of 7- and 8-year-olds were taken aback by this behaviour and laughed at him. He had to manage the situation carefully to avoid the drama deteriorating. It was clear that whilst that attitude in Max might recreate ideas from the book, the entry needed to be more subtle and the context of Max's adventure built more in order to work. The entry has subsequently focused more on his asking who they are, wanting to share his adventures with them if they are careful in how they handle him.

Another example of the class offering new ideas as to what to do and the form to use when you run the drama occurred in a run of 'Daedalus and Icarus'. At the point where the servants have to decide whether or not to tell King Minos what they have found out about Daedalus's plan, we were out of role discussing the pros and cons and putting forward powerful arguments on both sides when one pupil said, *I'd like to see two of the servants discussing what to do*. This was a gift, so the teacher set up a forum, asking for two pupils who had strong arguments on each side to take the chairs, gathering the others around and having them offer to take over the seats as they wanted to add different points. The discussion was thus more potent as they argued the choices in role. This method of moving forward can then be taken as the planned possibility for exploring the issue in future use of the drama.

The group even took the drama further themselves. Finally, when the arguments became circular, they were asked to stand behind the chair representing the choice they now most favoured and we got a clear outcome, not to tell. They moved immediately to spontaneously suggesting ideas as to how to avoid telling the truth of Daedalus's plans – evolving a substitution of a decoy set of plans and drawings instead of the ones for flight. Even the minority who had opted to tell Minos began to contribute ideas to the decoy approach and we had the next stage of the drama, a group to produce the decoy drawings and two groups to work on building the wings for Daedalus and Icarus.

The quality of the drama develops in these ways. You can choose to incorporate them in future versions of the drama.

You will see other added ideas from work with classes highlighted in the dramas in Part Two, where the plans are outlined.

Types of drama

There are two main types of this sort of classroom drama that have evolved: 'living through drama', where the pupils face the events at a sort of life rate in the here and now, and 'episodic drama', or strategy-based drama, where the class are led by the teacher in creating situations and events through specific techniques or strategies and where chronology is more broken. Of course, most dramas have a mixture of the styles, but the younger or more inexperienced a class, the more 'living through' will dominate to create the tensions and challenges more directly. The more sophisticated the group, the more they will look in a more abstract, artistic and less realistic way. For example, 'The Egyptians' has a more living through feel, but 'The Dog in the Night-Time' is more episodic. Sometimes a drama will start in a living through way and the resolutions and final explorations will be more episodic, as with 'The Governor's Child' or 'Macbeth'.

The more you plan the more you will sense the needs of the group and the style that suits.

What about endings to dramas?

The most difficult thing can be resolving a drama satisfactorily in the time and to the satisfaction of the class. This is to some extent in the planning but mostly in the handling of the drama.

The class must always go away feeling they have achieved something. They need to have solved the problem. If a final resolution is possible, for example, as a result of the forum, Max realises he must think of other people, then let them win, but the class must have worked hard for it in putting the case across to him. You, in role as Max, will feel the pressure if they apply it well and can begin to signal that you do see you might be wrong always to think of yourself, that you are listening for the first time. We look to the class tackling the problem, the issue, the difficult role, the wrong attitude. However, the ending is not always a happy ending where all people become friends and the problem goes away. If the issue is not easy to solve in reality then pupils will see through it if you give them too easy a change in the problem role and too soft a landing. When one group of trainees were doing a drama with a class, a difficult role melted into compliance with such suddenness that one boy commented to a role, *Look, you say sorry and she will give in and we can all live happily ever after!* We were convinced by his tone that he had said it ironically and was showing how unbelievable this transformation was.

Avoid that easy ending. We must be satisfied ourselves with the feel of the drama at all times; it must feel authentic. It is better for the class to have struggled with the issues and to see possible futures without the problem role necessarily changing or the dangers being completely avoided.

In one outing of 'The Governor's Child' the class could in fact see a greater dramatic satisfaction in partial success. The three teachers who were observing one of us teach this drama had discussed between the sessions what they thought the class would choose to do in the second session. Two thought they would resolve in a happy ending, the third saw them choosing complete disaster as the outcome for that sense of destruction children can seek at times. In the final analysis, the class did neither; they opted for Maria, the baby's nurse, to give herself up to the Soldier, a sacrifice to save the baby's life, and that was what they set up as the ending.

The feeling was strong as the Soldier led Maria away; the comments of the villagers as she left were thoughtful and convincing. They then set up a very telling memorial to Maria with lines for the epitaph contributed by different group members:

> *Always remembered,*
> *The stranger who entered this village.*
> *She was the most loving, caring person.*
> *Born, not of this world.*
> *She changed all our lives from bad to good.*
> *She wasn't what we thought she was.*

There is also the possibility of alternative endings, visions of the future that may be different and even contradictory. These enable individuals to share their understanding and open up further debate without being locked into one solution that they may not adhere to; it is almost the 'minority report' of a drama.

Finally – the key decisions

With all plans you need to ensure that a tension moment comes early to spur the interest of the group and that a TiR features early to model the commitment and seriousness of the drama.

Summary of points to consider

- How to begin a plan – facing the problems of starting from scratch
- The frame – the way the elements link together to provide viewpoint for the class
- The elements of planning including: learning objectives, a stimulus to learning, roles for the teacher and for the children, how to create tension points, building context and belief in the drama, the decision-making for the class, the choice of strategies and techniques
- Planning with someone else
- Road testing the first version

Appendix: Drama starters

Here are some beginnings of ideas for dramas that can be used to provide short TiR events or can be developed more fully as dramas by taking the approaches suggested in this chapter. In each case we have supplied a 'learning intention', a starter role and the situation to be set up. The 'key moment later' shows potential for further development.

1. An idea from 'Romeo and Juliet'

Learning intention   Parental control over children.

Contact role   A teenage boy discovered writing a letter.

Context   The pupils are all in role as workers on a rich family's estate. They have been ordered to patrol the estate and gardens for their employers, in advance of the important forthcoming wedding of the daughter to a cousin of the Prince's. Their job is to ensure that all the area inside the estate walls is secure, all the gates locked and that there are no strangers around.

They question the boy about what he is doing and why he is here. He initially refuses to speak, but asks them to take the letter secretly to the daughter of the family.

Key moment later   Depending on what the pupils decide to do, the daughter of the family approaches them either to attack them for siding with her father or to thank them for the letter and seek their help to escape that night.

2. An idea from 'Macbeth'

Learning intention   Confidentiality and dealing with a crime.

Contact role   A maidservant to the Queen.

Context   The pupils are in role as physicians to the King. The maidservant approaches them with a request for a confidential conversation. She reveals, *I have found my mistress to be sleepwalking regularly, talking in her sleep about matters that disturb her.* She refuses to say any more but asks them to come and observe that night.

Key moment later   The King calls the physicians to report on his wife's condition.

3. An idea from 'Danny Champion of the World' by Roald Dahl

Learning intention   Responsibility and children.

Contact role   Danny is discovered upset on the steps of his gypsy caravan.

Context   The pupils are in role as estate workers on Lord Victor Hazell's estate. They discover Danny but he is reluctant to speak. He doesn't know where his Dad is, but he doesn't want to get him into trouble. He knows his 'special bag' is missing.

Key moment later   Danny's Dad returns – cannot say where he has been or what he was doing. He pleads with them not to tell Lord Victor Hazell.

4. An idea from 'The Hobbit'

Learning intention   About riddles and dealing with a tricky opponent, who is a bully.

Contact role   Bilbo Baggins

Context   The pupils are all in role as map-makers for Gandalf the Wizard. Bilbo has got lost and a creature called Gollum has promised to give him a map if he can invent a riddle that Gollum cannot answer. He has already solved one that Gollum gave him:

> At night I come without being fetched
> At dawn I disappear without being stolen
> You can see me even when I have gone
> And I am a sailor's guide
> What am I?

Can the map-makers solve the riddle, but more importantly can they help Bilbo make up one to fool Gollum?

Will the pupils take the rhyme to Gollum and save Bilbo from being upset again?

The map-makers meet Gollum (TiR) and try out their riddle. Gollum struggles and eventually, reluctantly, gives them the map.

They give the map to Bilbo, who leaves in haste.

Key moment later   The map-makers get a panicky message. Bilbo has got lost again. They find him still underground. He is very scared and stuck. He's not very good at reading the map and Gollum told him the Dragon's Lair is the best way out. Bilbo reads the word as 'Dragoon' and the word 'Lair' he thinks is a type of gate. Gollum is in fact directing him to the dragon Smaug's lair. When Bilbo finds out he has been cheated he asks the class what he should do? Other travellers are going to be sent to their death. How can they help others get out?

3 How to Generate Quality Speaking and Listening

Authentic dialogue – teacher and pupil talk with a difference

What is speaking and listening ?

Speaking and listening is the most important communication form that human beings use. Really effective oracy, developmental speaking and listening, will help pupils build their language, their understanding, their ability to handle their own world, making sense of it and who they are in it.

It has to be an interaction with others where both sides are contributing. When a pupil is speaking and listening properly, he or she is able to see how each contribution arises from what has already been said.

Reading and writing come later in language learning and should not come until the child's head is full of the words that reading and writing will demand.

True speaking and listening for learning is effective 'talk', not two separate activities, as the phrase 'speaking and listening' suggests; it is an oral language interaction, which, at its best, is complex, demanding and truly creative. Learning is a social activity and thus talk is its real source. Writing is a solo activity, which allows the individual to distil ideas already learned; it comes later.

Teachers are encouraged to generate this sort of work:

> We're convinced that excellent teaching of speaking and listening enhances pupils' learning and raises standards further. Giving a higher status to talk in the classroom offers motivating and purposeful ways of learning to many pupils, and enables them and their teachers to make more appropriate choices between the uses of spoken and written language. (QCA, 2003, p. 4)

We believe that to develop the most productive talk, we need to think about it as dialogue.

Dialogic teaching

This is one of the most interesting, potentially powerful and new concepts being promoted in educational circles in the UK. It is the result of extensive work by Robin Alexander and others (Alexander, 2000, Alexander, 2005). This approach to oracy in the classroom raises the profile of talk, speaking and listening, from the poor relation of English in the National Curriculum, to become the central focus, the pivot of learning across the curriculum.

Alexander's work is a prompt for the greater awareness, for the growing importance of talk in the classroom. However, it is clear from his research that many classrooms in England lack the authentic dialogue to promote true learning, where talk lacks the status it has elsewhere in Europe.

> We registered a clear difference .... mainly in England and Michigan, in which there was much informal conversation, a great deal of reading and writing, but relatively little structured talk. (Alexander, 2000, p. 427)

Alexander goes on to suggest that the ethos of many classrooms does not promote proper dialogue:

> as extrapolated from observation in English classrooms, the research emphasised pupils' strategies for providing the 'right' answer and for avoiding being singled out if they did not know it. English pupils, in this characterisation at least, are individuals struggling to survive in the crowd. The context within which mistakes are admissible, as in the Russian classrooms, greatly reduces this element of gamesmanship. Here communicative competence is defined as answering well as much as answering correctly. This explains the apparent paradox of why, although the climate of Russian classrooms tends to be viewed by Western observers as authoritarian, even oppressive, Russian pupils are eager to answer questions while in the supposedly more democratic climate of English classrooms they may be reluctant to do so. (Alexander, 2000, pp. 457–8)

From his own and others' research, he summarises the picture of classrooms' negative aspects of speaking and listening, particularly primary, as follows:

> the low level of cognitive demand in many classroom questions; the continuing prevalence of questions which remain closed despite our claims to be interested in fostering more open forms of enquiry; the habitual and perhaps unthinking use of bland all purpose praise rather than feedback of the kind which diagnoses and informs; the seeming paradox of pupils working everywhere in groups but rarely as groups; the rarity of autonomous pupil-led discussion and problem-solving; and the tendency of classrooms to be places of risk and ambiguity rather than security and clarity, in which pupils devise strategies to cope and get by rather than engage. (Alexander, 2005, p. 14)

In schools too often speaking and listening is seen as question and answer, usually the teacher questioning and the pupils answering. What we see in classrooms is very often the IRF approach, where the teacher initiates, a child responds and a teacher gives feedback. Here's one teacher describing how this limited exchange works: 'A colleague, observing me, pointed out that I have a technique, which I was not aware of, where, if I ask a question and I do not get the right answer, I rephrase the question, making it simpler and can repeat that simplification until they do get it,' describing this as if it were good practice.

This approach limits the pupil's speaking and listening engagement with the teacher, as well as preventing engaging with, and listening to, other pupils. We need to see pupils initiating the talk much more with pupils asking questions rather than the teacher.

Too often talk is this 'recitation' (Alexander, 2005, p. 34) where teacher speaks most and pupils listen or only answer questions. The resulting classroom games include:

- guessing what is in the teacher's head – pupils avoiding having to answer the question
- linguistic tennis – where it is about getting rid of the ball quickly not about developing an exchange of ideas
- point scoring – getting the answers right or getting them wrong and feeling a failure.

Speaking does involve risk but pupils should be encouraged to take that risk knowing that making a mistake is not a problem but part of the learning process; classrooms must be supportive communities where pupils risk opening up and do not have the fear that shuts them down. We need to encourage a culture of 'failing safely', where not 'getting it right' first time is recognised as part of the process.

This lack of proper talk is all the more serious as it is clear that the primary school years are critical in the development of the brain:

It is now recognised that the period between 3/4 and 10/11 – the primary phase of schooling, more or less – is one in which the brain in effect restructures itself, building cells, making new connections, developing a capacity for learning, memory, emotional response and language, all on a scale which decreases markedly thereafter. (Alexander, 2005, p. 12)

Talk, being central to the development of the brain, must be a priority for teachers. Alexander promotes dialogic teaching as the most powerful form of talk in the classroom. He identifies its key elements as:

- Collective: teachers and pupils address learning tasks together, as a group or as a class;
- Reciprocal: teachers and pupils listen to each other, share ideas and consider alternative viewpoints;
- Supportive: pupils articulate their ideas freely, without fear of embarrassment over 'wrong' answers; and they help each other to reach common understandings;
- Cumulative: teachers and pupils build on their own and each other's ideas and chain them into coherent lines of thinking and inquiry;
- Purposeful: teachers plan and steer classroom talk with specific educational goals.

(Alexander, 2005, pp. 26–7)

Drama shares the elements listed above, and it promotes pupils' thinking because of the quality, dynamics and content of talk that can develop.

Why is drama so powerful in promoting good talk? It is about pupils having the desire to speak rather than being required to speak.

Alexander, in examining current research in the use of dialogical teaching, highlights three areas that are essential for the achievement of authentic dialogue but which are very demanding and more difficult for teachers to achieve in ordinary classroom settings. They are:

- Learning talk and teaching talk – the achievement of understanding what the child says matters at least as much as what the teacher says.
- Is extended talk dialogical teaching? – pupils' answers and other contributions are becoming longer, but do these necessarily add up to a dialogue?
- Form and content – how can we best ensure that classroom talk is cumulative and purposeful as well as collective, reciprocal and supportive?

(Alexander, 2005, p. 44)

As for the first, within a drama pupils are often given the status they do not have in a normal classroom by the role they adopt; in addition, the teacher's role is often inferior to the pupils'. For example, in the drama 'The Wild Thing' the main teacher role is the little boy Max, where the pupils are the experts from

Lost & Found, the missing persons agency. In one run of the drama pupils used their role to point out the error of Max's ways, asserting, *You are only 7 and must listen more to your mother*, at the same time making clear that they saw their role as adults and the teacher's role as only a little boy. This gives pupils confidence in speaking and they see that their contributions matter a great deal. In this way we structure into a drama the very possibility of pupils' talk mattering.

The second concern, the question of whether 'extended talk is dialogical teaching' is important to reflect upon in drama because poorly managed dramas can lack direction as much as any discussion. However, if the drama is properly planned and focused, if the learning objective is clear, then we have the capacity for the dialogue to be at its most purposeful.

'Form and content' are central to the planning of drama. The drama itself provides a form which ensures that the pupils are part of a context with roles that always have direction, often a problem to solve, a person to help, and with strategies and structure that ensure a framework for the language. Thus they have a very definite purpose.

As the drama develops the pupils develop as a community on the basis of the shared experience. That in itself provides a cumulative language world which is very rich and where the pupils, if the drama engages properly, care in a way that promotes collective, reciprocal and supportive talk. So drama is a more coherent approach to teaching talk.

We would maintain that drama is more effective in developing pupils' ways of thinking, ways of understanding, than ordinary classroom discussion because the language of drama, as the language of all artistic creation, is a heightened version of the language of everyday talk. The reason for this is that drama utilises a new context, a fictional world which is parallel to reality, but in which the uses of language can be as rich and varied as we want. Its usefulness to speaking and listening, and thus language development, is that we create together a shared experience which frames the language and makes us, the pupils and the teacher, communicate more effectively than mere discussion ever can. That shared experience is more effective because, when we discuss in any other form, we can only talk to each other from our separate realities. Most discussions begin with a stimulus of some sort. This can be a picture, a story, a topic. The limits are that each person sees the stimulus from their own reality; their experiences colour the way they see it. No one person has the same experience of that stimulus and consequently we are limited in how we understand it because of the baggage we bring with us. This is particularly true for older primary pupils, ages 7–11, who can bring more separate experiences than younger pupils and are often starting their discussion with greater gaps between them, preventing their chances of shared understandings.

Very often in discussion pupils are not really listening to each other because they are more concerned about what they want to say than what they can learn from other pupils. In discussion it can be seen as a very valuable thing to share personal experiences, but how valuable are those experiences to other members of the group, who do not know anything about that experience except what the person relating it tells them? In contrast, communication within the drama is based on the shared world that we are creating together. All of the pupils still bring ideas and opinions from their separate experiences, but they are all remade by the creation of a new context.

Drama produces greater motivation for the pupils, motivation because of their interest in the problem-solving of the drama. They become more confident. They are often feeling so motivated to speak that they find new voice.

At the time that this chapter was being written the sort of excitement and interest that drama generates could be seen in a group of training teachers preparing roles for drama. They were very much taken with the creation of the roles, with the new possibilities, motivated by the creative act, such that, although they were being assessed on the preparation of these roles, their enjoyment and motivation, focus and concentration were high-level.

Drama gives the pupils plenty of opportunities to think through speaking and listening. It promotes speech from the pupils because they want to speak, not because they are being asked to speak. Drama sets up more fluid situations with more possibilities. Mistakes can be made and looked at because any particular stage of the drama can be reworked to make it work better for us. In fact the making of mistakes is seen as part of the learning, a major part of helping to negotiate the meaning and to create the drama itself.

What does dialogic teaching demand of the teacher?

It demands changes – in the handling of classroom space and time; in the balance of talk, reading and writing; in the relationship between speaker and listeners; and in the content and dynamics of talk itself. (Alexander, 2004)

Drama certainly demands these as well. One of the key changes that drama brings is a different position for the teacher. When the teacher uses role herself she is able to dialogue in a very different way with the pupils; she leaves teacher talk behind. If the teacher is the young boy, Daedalus, who has taken his father's secret project design, without his permission, and the pupils are the family servants, then they have important decisions to make about what they do with this knowledge. They will talk to Daedalus in a way that they can never talk to a teacher.

The teacher working through drama is intervening as teacher but also as other roles within the drama, roles that are models and anti-models to promote the pupils' language in ways that teacher language cannot. In his or her roles the teacher will model, through positive roles, all of the positive aspects for the pupils and can also portray, through negative roles, many negative aspects of behaviour and language; roles can be aggressive, thoughtless, self-centred, silly, anti-social, etc. The pupils will not adopt these because the context tells them that the negative aspects are not what they want to see or hear; in fact the drama requires that they have to oppose these behaviours and deal with them. They are framed within the drama context to oppose or sort out this behaviour, all the more motivated by the fact it is their teacher behaving in this way through the use of role. This happens when they tackle Macbeth or Max in 'The Wild Thing'.

So the teacher is able to talk and interact with the pupils in many ways and with many purposes. The teacher engages with the class and their contributions help build the fictional world. The magical world of the fiction and the parallel real-world that we exist in can help each other, so that the language the pupils use in the drama can be looked at from the real world when we stop the drama. This 'metaxis' (awareness of two worlds at once, Bolton, 1984, p. 142) makes the language possibilities far richer than mere discussion can.

When dropping out of role, the teacher promotes a different form of language, reflecting on what has just happened, examining it and defining what it means before planning what to do further. All of this ensures that the pupils are thinking about what they are part of, looking at actions and consequences and considering options, looking at what to do and why. This reflective mode is special to drama. Together we create a fictional experience and then the possibility of reflecting on it.

> Experience in itself is neither productive nor unproductive; it is how you reflect on it that makes it significant or not. (Bolton, 1979, p. 126)

It is possible to reflect in ordinary discussion but not as fully. It would be odd to stop a discussion and say, *Let's look at ourselves and what we said, how we were standing, what it meant.* In drama we do that routinely and the learning from the elements of the drama becomes even more potent. Pupils become more reflective generally as a result; they are learning a new skill. This is particularly relevant to 7–11-year-olds, whose self-awareness is growing.

In the dual world of drama, pupils find that they have to engage in a language where they are: responding, initiating, sharing, encouraging, questioning, speculating, probing, challenging, exploring, creating, arguing, examining viewpoints, enquiring, evaluating, interrogating.

How is listening of high quality taught through drama?

Drama is the creation of meanings in action and pupils have to struggle all the time to make sense of what is going on around them so that they can engage with it. They have to make sense of the fictional situation as it develops. Unless pupils listen they do not know what is going on. The teacher can provide surprises, challenges, interesting people to meet in the forms of teachers in role; pupils can provide models of language use for each other because lead pupils begin to take initiative and provide input.

In drama we can get new levels of listening because of the pupils' interest in the problem-solving of the drama itself. The focus of the problem or dilemma that the pupils face embodies the nature of the language. In order to carry out all of these speaking activities they are, of course, inevitably developing their listening and we see this in all its powerful and active modes, listening that is: open, sensitive, reflective, receptive, supportive, attentive, collective, creative. This is because each pupil has to make sense of what the teacher and the rest of the pupils are gradually building up around them.

Pupils feel valued in drama and consequently have more confidence in what they want to say and show more respect to what other contributors to the drama say.

In order for drama to work the teacher has to listen very closely as well, to see where the pupils are, to pick up what the pupils are offering and use it within the drama.

Let's look at a class showing these skills as they engage in a dialogue in 'Daedalus and Icarus'. This is the sort of dialogue that can be generated by a drama. We will take an actual extract from a lesson and consider what is being achieved.

We will consider this in the light of dialogic teaching (DT) and the Speaking and Listening requirements of the English National Curriculum (EN1 S&L levels, National Curriculum, DfES, London).

Transcript from a session on Daedalus and Icarus

This comes from the third hour-long session of this drama with a class of mixed 8- and 9-year-olds. The teacher is taking the role of Daedalus and another adult the role of Icarus at the beginning of this. The class are enrolled as the servants of Minos the King. (See the outline of the drama in Part Two of this book for details.)

ToR: *The inventor was looking for Icarus. Do you remember?*
  [DT – teacher and pupils address the task together]
  [After a recap of the work from last time the teacher moves to stand outside the group]

TiR as Daedalus: *Icarus! Icarus!*

Adult as Icarus: *What shall I do?*

Pupils: *Hide! Hide!*

  (The tension at this point is high even though it is picking up from the previous session. Tension is a strong promoter of listening.)

Daedalus: *I must speak to you. I can't see where you are. There are too many rooms and passageways.*

Icarus: *I'm here. I'm here.*

Daedalus: *Can you come to me please? I don't have a lot of time. I have things to get on with.*

Icarus: *I'm here.*

Daedalus: *Yes, but I want to see you.*

  [Icarus comes out of hiding]

Daedalus: *What have you been doing?*

Icarus: *Just playing.*

Daedalus: *With the servants?*

Icarus: *Yes.*

Daedalus [to the servants]: *What's he been doing?*

  (Notice how the teacher uses the role to challenge the commitment of the servants to siding with Icarus.)

Servants: *Playing. Catch.*

Daedalus: *Playing catch with you?*

Servants: *Yes.* (S&L levels 2/3 – listening carefully and responding with increasing appropriateness/shows an understanding of the main points.)

Daedalus [to Icarus]: *I want to talk to you very seriously, Icarus. Something has gone missing from my room and you were in there earlier today. And I want to find out about it.*

ToR: *Can we just stop the story a minute?*
  [Moves OoR to manage the drama by setting up the forum theatre where Icarus and Daedalus sit facing each other with the class gathered on either side]

Pupil: *Say it's in the bin.*

Icarus: *It might be in the dustbin.*

Daedalus: *But that will be the fault of the servants. They would have tidied up. I'll have to have words with the servants if it's got in the dustbin.*

Pupils: *Tell him the truth.* (S&L level 4 – making contributions.)

ToR: *Let's stop a minute.*
  [Moves OoR to let the class discuss the approach Icarus should adopt, as there is a split within the class in their advice to the person playing the role. This is the chance for reflection on the activity, important metacognition. DT – teacher and pupils share ideas and consider alternative viewpoints]

ToR: *Several people are saying 'Tell him the truth' and what then? Bring back the folder?*

Pupils: *No ... Yes ...*

ToR: *Why not, Brian?*

Brian: *I think you should keep it to yourselves – not tell the truth.* [DT – pupils articulate their ideas freely, without fear of embarrassment over 'wrong' answers]

ToR: *Why do some people think that Icarus should tell the truth at this point? Helen?*

Helen: *Because it could be very important to tell him the truth. It was wrong and it could be very, very important that he told.*

ToR: *That he'd been honest to his father? Anne, what do you think?*

Anne: *Well, it might get found out in the end.* (S&L level 4 – develops ideas thoughtfully, conveying opinions clearly.)

Other pupils: *Yeah! ... Yeah!*

ToR: *And he could be in trouble then you mean? It would be better that it comes out now. Is there another reason why it might be important for the father to get the file back now?* [DT – cumulative – teacher builds on pupils' ideas]

Lucy: *To get away from the King, because he doesn't want to live with him any longer.* [DT – pupil builds on own and others' ideas]

ToR: *Right, if he hasn't got his invention, how can they get away from the island?*

Lucy: *Well, they can't.*

ToR: *Is there anything else? Some people say he should tell the truth. Is there anything else they can do now? Sally?*

Sally: *He can say, 'I'll have a look for you.' Icarus might go and he might pick them* [the folder and drawings] *up and say, 'I have found them' and say they were in the dustbin.*

ToR: *So you could say 'I'll have a look around' and find them, pretend that he's found them, when he knew where they were.*

Some pupils: [spontaneously] *No!*

Other pupils: [spontaneously] *Yes!*

ToR: *It's lying or telling the truth, is that what it's about?*

Lucy: *I think you should tell the truth because if you ... We've been telling lots of lies in the story and if it all comes out, we'll get into deep trouble for telling all these lies.* (S&L level 6/8 – takes an active part in discussion, showing understanding of ideas and sensitivity to others/shows that he/she has listened perceptively and is sensitive to the development of the discussion.)

ToR: *All right, because lies can get you into trouble.*

Version 1: telling a lie

ToR: *We'll do both of them and then we can see what happens in both cases. Is that OK?*

[DT – teacher steers the talk with specific educational goals]

[From this point pupils one at a time take over the role of Icarus from the adult. They sit in Icarus's chair. Sally tries her 'lie' first]

(Here one aspect of drama that reaches beyond ordinary discussion is vital, the non-verbal communication. Sally keeps her face serious, stares clearly and unblinkingly back at TiR, 'her father'. She adopts the role perfectly and there are no official attainment levels to record the drama skills, taking role effectively, for example.)

TiR as Daedalus: *Do you know anything about this folder?*

Sally as Icarus: *No, I haven't seen it.*

Daedalus: *Well, I need it very, very ... much. It's for both of us, because we've got to get away from the Palace and the folder helps with that. If I haven't got it, I have lost all the work that I have spent weeks and weeks on.*

Icarus: *I'll have a look for you.*

Daedalus: *If you can, but I've looked everywhere ... you're not lying to me, are you?*

Icarus: *No.*

Daedalus: *You wouldn't lie to your father?*

Icarus: *No. (The tension in the group is palpable here.)*

Daedalus: *You'd better go and have a look then and if you find anything bring it to me.*

[Sally goes to get the folder from where the pupils previously hid the folder when Daedalus first called to Icarus]

Daedalus: *That was very quick. Where was it?*

Icarus: *In the dustbin. I thought it would be.*

Daedalus: *I'm going to have to have words with those servants.*

Pupils: *Shrieks* [as they realise the implications].

Version 2

[Sally leaves the chair and Mary volunteers to take over and illustrate telling the truth]

TiR as Daedalus: *Now, that folder is very important to me, Icarus. It's very important to us. Do you know anything about it?*

Mary as Icarus: [nods and mouths] *Yes.* (S&L level – How do we assess this? Mary is a very quiet girl in the group and just to take the chair is a major step for her. She tackles the task shyly but determinedly and appropriately – the descriptors do not seem fit to cover this adequately.)

Daedalus: *I thought you did. Well tell me then?*

Icarus: *It's behind the piano.*

Daedalus: *Why? What's it doing there?*

Icarus: *We were hiding it.*

Daedalus: *Why did you do that? And why did you have it anyway?*

Icarus: *We were having a look at it.*

Daedalus: *That was very ... naughty. Those are my private papers. I hadn't given you ... Why didn't you ask me?*

Icarus: [no response]

ToR: *Just a minute. To help her, what should she say?*

Pupils: [make some suggestions to Mary]

ToR: *Hang on. Liam, why don't you swap with Mary. We'll give you a chance. Well done, Mary.* [Liam swaps into the seat to take over Icarus]

Daedalus: *Why didn't you ask me?*

Liam as Icarus: *I wanted to see what we were doing because if we picked a bit that was ... a little too heavy and I didn't know that, then we wouldn't be able to get off the island so quick.*

(Liam adds a dimension to the truth of the confession but subtly. Here he hints at knowing what the folder of documents concerns – that it is about making a flying machine.)

Daedalus: *So you know what it's about, you mean?*

Icarus: *Not exactly, no.*

(He baulks at fully owning up. The dialogue is complex at this point and Liam shows he believes in the delicacy of the negotiation with the father, is afraid of what he might do, senses the danger of the situation. Again there is no descriptor in the S&L levels to cover this; the language he uses is not of level 8 – 'structures what is said carefully, using apt vocabulary' – but is it possible the emotional content is at that level – 'is sensitive to the development of the discussion'?)

Pupils: [*laugh* as they realise the implications of what he has done]

Daedalus: *How did you know I wanted to get off the island with it?*

Icarus :   [speechless as he realises what he has revealed – other pupils laugh]

ToR: *Sarah, swap with Liam. Anybody can have a go. If you get an idea for something you want to say, you swap. Listen carefully to what other people are saying and then I'll give other people a chance.*

Daedalus: *Now, Icarus, you knew about this did you? You worked out what it means?*

Icarus: *No.*

Daedalus: *Well, you said about getting off the island ... Do you know how I'm intending to get off the island?*

Icarus: *Yes, we do know.*

Daedalus: *What did you know about it?*

Pupils: *Oh! Oh!* [as they all want to have a turn]

ToR: *Shush ... now I'm not going to choose anyone who interrupts.*

Icarus: *Flight frames.*

Daedalus: *So you worked out what the pictures meant did you? Because there is no writing. I thought you were very clever.*

ToR: *Lucy, just swap. Well done, Sarah.*

(Lucy decides to go for the full confession, knowing that this is what this version was set up to try out. She is clearly operating at least at level 7 – confident in matching talk to the demand of different contexts – or level 8 – shows that she has listened perceptively and is sensitive to the development of the discussion – the word discussion as used in the attainment target is also inadequate to cover the nature of this fictional dialogue.)

Lucy as Icarus: *Well, we weren't playing catch.*

Daedalus: *You weren't?*

Icarus: *No.*

Daedalus: *What were you doing?*

Icarus: *We were looking at the folder. The servants and I ...*

Daedalus: *'We'! You mean you've shown the servants?*

Pupils: [Laugh at the tension and the sense that the truth is coming out with all these implications for them in their role as servants]

Daedalus: *That's very serious. Don't you realise they might tell?*

Icarus: *I told them not to tell.*

Daedalus: *Did they promise?*

Icarus: *Yes.*

Daedalus: *I must have a word with them. You must bring them to me straight away.*

Pupils: [Shrieks of excitement about what they will have to face as the servants!]

Lucy OoR: *Either way gets the servants into trouble* (i.e. whether Icarus lies about the stealing of the folder of drawings or tells the truth).

Conclusions

Lucy, one of the brightest members of the class, who saw the implications of lying from the beginning, very shrewdly sees how the teacher is making the pupils face the consequences of Icarus's taking of the folder. So we are exploring the meaning of the situation and the complex and demanding issues of truth or lies. Centrally, the idea of actions and consequences is brought into very sharp relief, the teacher and the class together exploring the consequences of taking the folder in the first place.

We have the subtle language of Sally's lie as Icarus to 'her father', with its clear brief denials accompanied by non-verbal commitment to the role. Then come the frank and bold statements of Lucy deciding to be honest and owning up to not only having taken the folder, but having shared it with her friends, the servants, servants of the King, Daedalus's jailor and enemy.

So the consequences for the father and son could be catastrophic as the plan to escape may be in jeopardy. Lucy has taken the drama on and helped the teacher explore this important area. The class have paid very close attention, listening not only to the teacher but also their peers, their representatives in the hot-seat. This forum theatre piece lasted all of 40 minutes and there was never any hint of a lack of concentration. Their feeling of involvement shows clearly by the way they shriek when Daedalus talks of having to speak to the servants about either the throwing away of the folder, or in version 2, their knowledge of the plan. Obviously the teacher stopped to talk this through with them after Lucy's final pronouncement but they did not need the implications interpreting at the moment of revelation in the drama. All of them knew.

Summary of points to consider

- The importance of speaking and listening in the teaching/learning process
- How to dialogue with a class so that it is collective, reciprocal, supportive, cumulative, purposeful
- The teacher intervening as teacher, but also as other roles within the drama
- How drama produces ilistening of high quality
- Do the Speaking and Listening levels in the National Curriculum do justice to the levels of talk pupils can achieve here?

4 How to Use Drama for Inclusion and Citizenship

This chapter is concerned with the relationship between inclusion and drama as a pedagogical approach. We look at the expectations for schools to be inclusive and the demands made upon them to fulfil these expectations. We look at how drama, through its idiosyncratic approach, facilitates inclusion. We then make the link to the Citizenship curriculum and how drama's approach to inclusion is an intrinsic part of this area.

We will begin by defining what we mean by inclusion. We will then present a model of how drama relates to inclusion and describe a particular drama session which aims to 'promote tolerance and understanding in a diverse society' (Ofsted, 2006, p. 7).

Drama's inclusion is embedded, first, in its dialogical approach to teaching and learning. This is reflected in two contracts that form part of its rubric. These are:

1 Everyone will take part, including the teacher both in and out of role.
2 We will treat members of the group with respect by listening to them and allowing them to express their views without fear of derision or humiliation.

Secondly, the subject content of dramas can have specific learning potential to give a voice to groups whose ideas may not be heard easily in the real world. More of this later. So inclusion will always be found in drama's approach to learning and it may also be part of its subject content.

Let us begin with defining what we mean by inclusion. We have taken the United Kingdom's inspection training manual as a source for this definition. (In the United Kingdom the Office for Standards in Education (Ofsted) trains all inspectors in making judgements about inclusion in pre-school, primary and secondary schools.) Educational inclusion has a broad scope. It is essentially about equal opportunities for all pupils, regardless of age, gender, ethnicity, background and attainment, including special needs or disability. A school that is inclusive will provide racial harmony; it will prepare pupils for living in a diverse and increasingly inter-dependent society. The inclusive school will have, within its policies and curriculum, strategies to 'address racism and promote racial harmony where all pupils know they are valued and important to the school' (Ofsted, 2006, p. 30).

Inclusion pays particular attention to the provisions for different groups of pupils. Provision in the primary school will apply to all of the following groups:

Girls and boys
Minority ethnic and faith groups
Traveller, asylum seeker and refugee children
Pupils who need support to learn English as an additional language (EAL)
Pupils with special educational needs
Gifted and talented pupils
Children looked after by the local authority
Other children, such as sick children, young carers, those children from families under stress
Any children who are at risk of disaffection and exclusion.
(DfEE, 1999, p. 12)

Of course, the drama lesson is not the only place in the life of a school where inclusion can be promoted; pupil mentoring, links with parents, links with the wider community, promoting good race relations, promoting good standards of behaviour and attendance, pastoral care and study support are venues of inclusivity. We would argue that drama has, by its nature, a distinctive role and it is this role we wish to explore further.

What can drama offer in terms of inclusion?

- Drama offers 'new opportunities to pupils who may have experienced previous difficulties' (Ofsted, 2006, p. 7).
- Drama takes account of pupils' varied life experiences and needs by using fictional contexts and roles which enable pupils to explore the underlying issues safely.
- For some pupils drama may offer experiences that are different to those they experience in the real world, for example taking the role of the outsider or the role of the one in charge.

In drama we are dealing with the 'as if' world. In this fictional world we can behave 'as if' events are taking place and 'as if' we are there. It is a world that the teacher and the class create and fill with people and events that do not exist but are analogous to the real world.

We need to be very careful about the efficacy of drama. Just as any teacher and learning resource has an ethical dimension, drama and the creation of fictional contexts, roles and the use of symbols needs to be thought through from the possible negative and counter-productive effect of their creation and use. Well-intentioned planning can produce unintended and counter-productive dramas unless particular safeguards in that planning are adhered to.

The concept of drama and keeping pupils safe

There is a perception of drama dealing with issues in a safe way because it uses fictional contexts. It is almost as if by shifting to the fictional, a safe emotional distance is automatically created. But what do we mean by keeping pupils 'safe', safe from what, and is this automatically achieved when we use drama to teach?

It would be simplistic to believe that just because we work within fictional contexts, using fictional roles and events, that the experience for pupils is therefore immediately safe from the negative and destructive emotions of real life experiences. In teaching, whether working inside or outside fiction, we need to be constantly aware of the need to treat pupils in ways that demonstrate respect for persons and awareness of their particular social and emotional circumstances in that learning situation.

We must remember that pupils have no choice about attending school; they are required to attend, whether they want to or not and there are consequences for pupils and parents if they do not do so. This puts them in a particular power position when they attend a lesson because they may well be there reluctantly. It becomes critical for the teacher from an ethical (and survival) point of view to negotiate how *we as a class can make it work for us*. On one level, the teacher must make the content interesting and appropriate for the pupils, that is, it should be related to their needs and structured in such a way as to grab and hold their attention. The social environment should be one conducive to productive learning. If making mistakes, or the possibility of making mistakes, is a necessary component of learning, then the teacher must make sure there is an atmosphere in which pupils can fail safely, that is, make mistakes without the risk of humiliation from others. Teachers recognise it is part of their role to behave in a supportive manner to the learner by protecting them from the dangers of being devalued or criticised by their peers. The risk of criticism and humiliation by pupils has to be removed or at least made clear as an unacceptable way to behave. This can be done by the teacher modelling how to behave when they make a mistake. Teachers need to demonstrate how to deal with mistakes made by pupils and by protecting and defending them if they are subjected to negative response by classmates.

The risk of making mistakes does not automatically vanish because we are using role-play. In fact, it could be argued, the risk increases because the opportunity to behave as someone else may be perceived as giving licence to anti-social behaviour. The opportunity to act in ways that are not our usual selves can be extremely valuable because it allows pupils to adopt other attitudes than their own, to test out viewpoints, but the teacher has to structure this in such a way that it does not, under the licence of fiction, leave pupils vulnerable and emotionally damaged or hurt. The principle of protecting pupils from humiliation and embarrassment remains inside and outside the fictional world of drama, in fact, it underpins good teaching and helps raise the social health of the class by modelling positive ways of treating each other.

Gavin Bolton makes an important distinction when writing about pupils and emotion in drama:

> I cannot stress enough how important it is for teachers to realise that because drama is such a powerful tool for helping people change, as teachers we need to be very sensitive to the emotional demands we make on our students. The notion of 'protection' is not necessarily concerned with protecting participants *from* emotion, for unless there is some kind of emotional engagement nothing can be learned, but rather to protect them *into* emotion. This requires a careful grading of structures toward an effective equilibrium so that self-esteem, personal dignity, personal defences and group security are never over-challenged. (Bolton, 1984, p. 128; emphasis in the original)

This does not mean we do not take risks or put pupils in situations that feel risky but these risks are perceived rather than actual. Like a fairground ride the participant feels the excitement of the ride without the danger of an actual accident, or as with the trapeze artist in the circus, the safety net allows the chance to take risks and look at the consequences and yet not break any bones.

Gavin Bolton suggests:

> to handle [subjects] *directly*, that is, to open up the central issue that arouses the pain, sensationalism or the controversy, is not necessarily the best way of protecting pupils into emotion. (Bolton, 1984, p. 129; emphasis in the orginal)

He suggests three ways to deal with a topic *indirectly*:

1 Enter the topic at an oblique angle to the main issue.
2 Put the pupils in a role that only obliquely connects them with the topic.
3 Use analogy for content.

The drama teacher plans dramas with these devices in order to shift and adjust the emotional proximity of the class in relation to the social event they are examining. These planned structural mechanisms create a safe place to learn and make sense of the issues being looked at while at the same time providing the opportunity to work at a feeling level.

We can illustrate this by looking at a drama without structured protection by the teacher and then comparing this with the same drama with devices planned into it. For an insensitive and blundering version of our 'Workhouse' drama, you could begin by telling the class that they are going to be inmates of a workhouse and that the teacher is going to take the role of the Workhouse Master or Mistress. You hold a stick or truncheon and the class sits on benches. You go into role as the workhouse boss and aggressively tell them to stand when you enter the room. You then berate them for their idleness and tell them a new inmate called Martha is about to arrive and they are to witness her induction to remind them of the rules of the institution. One of the class has a rolled up cardigan to represent her baby and takes the role of Martha. The class witness her humiliation, they see her baby being taken off her and given to an older woman who is too ill to work and therefore has to look after the babies. This living-through style of confrontational drama with its raw emotion can be received with derision and light-heartedness by pupils. Their involvement is too direct; they are not protected into the emotion. They avoid the discomfort of the way they are being treated by not treating it seriously, attempting to destroy it or feeling humiliated by it. It will get a response but one that has little to do with learning.

Later in the drama one child is asked to stand upon a chair with the label 'infamous liar' around her neck. The rest of the class again have to witness her verbal humiliation by TiR as the workhouse boss.

This approach is familiar in play or film form, where the actor acts out the appalling events that took place in workhouses, and from the safety of the stalls of the theatre or cinema, they can be powerful performance moments. They are totally inappropriate as ways of structuring a drama lesson. We have no right to subject pupils to this kind of treatment because it is under the cloak of drama and fiction. Our first concern is to take the class to looking at the disturbing reality of the nineteenth-century workhouse and to do that we must find a role for the pupils which gives them power. It is from a position of power and authority that they can view the circumstances of the inmates and learn about the nature of these institutions.

As the drama progresses and trust in the teacher and the medium is built then the pupils can move closer to the role of the inmates. The stopping and starting of the drama helps defuse the raw emotion and allows pupils to reflect, negotiate and manipulate the fiction to clarify their own understanding. The role of the teacher as workhouse master/mistress is too near angry teacher, parent or adult to be used in such a confrontational way. For it to be used successfully it has to be distanced and managed in such a way as to allow pupils who have had negative experiences with angry adults to look at the role more rationally.

It is important to remember that when dealing with issues that are close to the real world of pupils we need initially to create a distance that enables them to view the events more dispassionately. That does not mean we cannot move closer to these issues as the drama develops, but it does mean we need to find a way into the drama that will not generate counter-productive learning, behaviour that will seek to undermine or destroy the drama.

Let us draw an analogy with the social ritual of the funeral services in Western society. There is a convention in the church or crematorium that relates to how near the coffin you sit. Usually the closer to the coffin or front of the service you sit, the closer your relationship to the deceased, with family and close friends in the pews at the front, more distant friends and relations further away. This proximity often, but not always, replicates the emotional distress of the experience. Those further away from the front may see the experience more rationally and pragmatically. If in drama we are dealing with a potentially emotionally charged topic or one where the cultural taboos of our society are to be examined, we need to take the class there very carefully. We need to build their trust in the fictional world we create through the roles we put them in and the strategies we use. It is this that makes it safe for the participants, for as long as we, as teacher and manager of the fictional world, intervene and reflect upon it, we can facilitate learning and protect the vulnerable.

The dramas we include in this book cover some challenging ideas. We need to disturb the class productively. For example, in the Christopher Boone drama (based upon *The Curious Incident of the Dog in the Night-Time* by Mark Haddon), the first meeting tableau of Christopher and the dead dog can be seen as disturbing, especially the albeit mistaken idea that he might have killed it, that it is 'still warm'. However, the use of the art form, the way the class is accessed to the event with signs and labels round the TiR, distance it and make it a managed moment. The gradual making of meaning out of this moment unites the class and fully allows for a variety of levels and activity in response so that it is truly inclusive. Of course, the giving of a voice to an autistic child also produces inclusion in the subject matter too. When doing this drama in school we were not surprised when a child with autism asked Christopher's Mum (TiR) whether she thought he might be autistic?

With the protection of the class role – people who can help worried parents (The Worried Parents Organisation, the WPO – 'Are you worried about your child? We can help you') – he was able to distance himself from the drama being about him, using the given role of someone who can help parents of pupils with autism. In fact he could bring considerable knowledge, understanding and expertise to that role. In preparation for this drama there were consultations with his parents, his key worker and the head teacher, all of whom were supportive of him taking part. Inclusion has to be a transparent process in which there is discussion of the measures being taken to support the pupil's learning.

Another example of a powerful and demanding moment occurs in the 'Macbeth' drama when the servants are meeting to discuss what to do. Unexpectedly, TiR as Macbeth shouts for them to report to him. This is a shock and can cause anxiety to the members of the class in role as servants. The feeling generated at this moment is an enjoyable fear; the sort that drama engenders is similar to the excited surprise and fear hide and seek games produce. It is prevented from becoming too threatening for them because:

- The angry Macbeth is fictionally in a different room so the oppression is distanced and they can think what to do.
- The servants know they have knowledge about him at this point which gives them power, unlike the powerless inmates of the Workhouse.

This challenge from Macbeth is welcomed by the class, especially when, as usually happens, a class member comes forward with an excuse for the servants' absence, like *We thought the banquet was so successful last night, your majesty, that we were looking to plan another*, as one inventive pupil said to one of us as Macbeth. The feeling of relief in the class was audible as Macbeth (TiR) relaxed a bit and said, *That is admirable loyalty and yet you must not all be absent when I need you.*

In both of these cases the class are protected by the fiction and if necessary the teacher can go OoR to negotiate what to do, so that the class is never in any danger from the moment of anxiety. In fact, dealing with the challenge off the cuff can unite and include everyone in a way that is confidence-building for all.

Having a voice in society

If we return to the central idea in drama of creating an 'as if' world we see that it is a world that is, at least in part, created by the participants through their ideas. As we have seen in the planning section, good planning creates gaps and spaces for pupils to input their ideas.

If we plan for pupils' ideas to be part of the drama lesson and we are creating a safe environment for this to happen, we are in effect giving them a voice to express their understandings and perspective on the world in which they live.

Figure 4.1 describes the pupils who have the confidence to express an opinion in the drama lesson. There is a congruence between what we think, what we say and what we do and these factors have to be seen against the background of the society in which the pupil lives and the events of their lives; they bring these dimensions into the drama lesson. Their self-esteem will also be an important factor; the more confident pupil with a highly developed sense of self will be more willing to express their viewpoint.

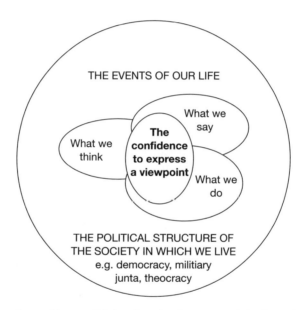

Figure 4.1 *What the confident pupil brings into the classroom and the drama lesson*

Having no voice in society

In the following diagram (Figure 4.2) we see the pupil whose voice is not heard. What these pupils think, say and do often bears no relation to each other. They come into the drama lesson wary of saying what they think and reluctant to express a view or make suggestions that may be challenged by the majority or dominant group.

We cannot leave our real-world selves outside the door of the classroom and consequently there is a dynamic relationship between how we think and behave in the fictional world of the drama and how we think and behave in the real world.

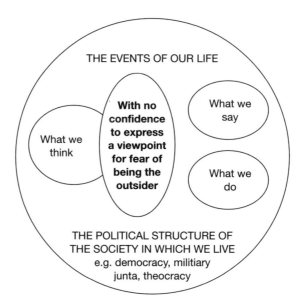

Figure 4.2 *What the pupil with little confidence brings into the classroom and the drama lesson*

Let us examine this more closely. In the drama lesson the individual's responses have three components:

- What we think (thoughts)
- What we say (utterances)
- What we do (actions)

There will be a relative congruence or not in the relationship between these components. Whether what I think is close to what I say, whether what I say bears any relationship to what I do will shift in relation to the social circumstances of the moment. In the classroom we hope there is a congruence between these three factors. If there is we can assess the learning and needs of the pupil more easily. One can imagine that more secure pupils whose self-worth is high will present a more congruent view of these three factors. The less confident may reveal less of what they really think and take actions that do not reflect what they say or what they really think. This may be because of the risks involved in disclosing those feelings and beliefs, there may be issues of status or conformity which prevent saying what they feel and acting how they see fit. In fact, if we relate this model to individuals or groups who may feel they are indeed outsiders their reluctance to disclose their true feelings and remain silent may be the safest option. If they do not, they may feel the wrath of others in the group, not necessarily during the lesson but afterwards. They may, by expressing how they really feel, end up feeling more isolated that they were before; in other words, they do not have a voice. In these circumstances silence or tacit agreement with the dominant view, one that is not their own, is the safest place to be.

If the concept of 'giving pupils a voice' means enabling pupils to express their feelings, their ideas and their suggestions for action, then drama holds the possibility of being a truly inclusive experience. It can do this by shifting pupils into a fictional world where they are no longer speaking as themselves but through the fictional context the teacher has structured for them and the class. The safe distance enables them to say and do the things they may not say or do in the real world. The dialectic that exists between the real world and the drama fictitious

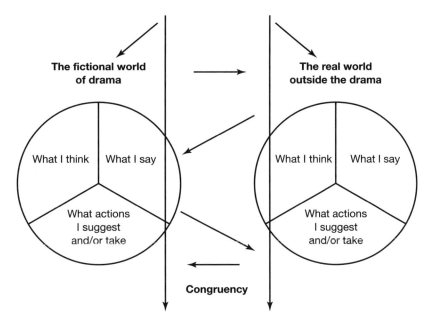

Figure 4.3 *The secure pupil inside the drama lesson*

world means real experiences, thoughts and feelings can be shared without the danger of the real consequences. It is this 'no penalty zone' that provides a means to inclusivity for pupils in drama (Johnson and O'Neill, 1984, p. 104).

The relationship between inclusion and citizenship

If drama by its very operational values is an inclusive way of working and if the contents of some dramas are in themselves examining the nature of the outsider, then Citizenship and PSHE are an integral part of the drama experience.

The QCA booklet on Citizenship for the primary age groups defines the area as follows:

> The PSHE and Citizenship framework comprises four interrelated strands which support children's personal and social development. The strands are:
>
> - developing confidence and responsibility and making the most of their abilities;
> - preparing to play an active role as citizens;
> - developing a healthy, safer lifestyle; and
> - developing good relationships and respecting the differences between people.

(QCA, 2002, p. 4)

How to approach Citizenship and PSHE through drama: practising being part of a society

This seems a big task and very amorphous as described. It is important for us to help pupils to understand and participate in the world around them by giving them particular and specific experiences to build up the qualities listed above.

There are limited opportunities for pupils in the primary school, even the older pupils, to directly participate in the world. They can of course be involved in the school itself and learn about responsibility by taking part in school activities and institutions like the school council.

To a limited extent they can have experience in the community as part of their school experience. They can make trips out or relevant visitors can be brought in to make pupils aware of the important structures and ideas that community involves. However, running a project like these, having trips out and visitors to school cannot happen every day. Indeed, if children get very committed to a real-world project there is a dilemma for the school. How can they enable the children to develop a real project very far? The curriculum restricts how far any project can go and if the political implications become too great the school would have to stop the work. For instance, what if some 11-year-old children become concerned that the home for senior citizens that they visit regularly is under threat because of economic pressures and want to take action on that issue? Would the school support and allow them to mount such action, especially if this led to confrontation with councillors or officials? There are dilemmas for the school in such a situation when the children are demonstrating the very citizen commitment that the project sought to awaken.

The classroom-based drama world that we create can happen much more frequently and in a more focused manner. It is less problematic and costly to organise and to supervise, and with much less immediate risk.

The opportunity to explore situations, to consider attitudes, values and other points of view is exactly where we can see drama working for children in the age group we are considering. Drama's relationship to citizenship works on two levels, as a methodology that demonstrates aspects of citizenship in action and when the content is specifically focused upon issues of citizenship.

When we consider that drama can link citizenship with personal and social education, and spiritual, moral, social and cultural education, then we can begin to understand the importance of drama as a teaching method.

Drama as citizenship in action

How does the drama method promote this learning? The process of drama itself is democratic in nature. The underlying rules of drama embody key democratic values. These are:

- that the class work as a whole group, dividing into sub-groups for some tasks, but experiencing their class as a democratic community;
- that every member of the group may speak and contribute to the development of the drama;
- that all members of the group must respect the other members – their opinions and viewpoints;
- that we stop the drama at any point to consider and discuss what is happening and what it means so that everyone may clarify their understanding and therefore have a greater chance to make a contribution;
- that when group decisions are to be made, debate may happen, but it is the majority view of the group that will be taken;
- that we reflect together on the meanings we are forging and that together we are stronger in that creative act.

So any whole class drama carried out in the methodology represented in this book is strong on the model of democracy, corporate learning, responsibility and tolerance.

A drama for teaching about citizenship

If we want the pupils to experience a particular political idea or social situation, the fictional world of drama can provide that situation efficiently and with an immediacy that reality cannot provide. Whilst the fiction also protects the pupils into learning at the same time and allows all avenues to be explored without the real consequences that we indicated above.

As one example let us consider the use of 'The Governor's Child' drama (see Part 2 for the full drama) as a vehicle for uniting these areas. The drama builds the pupils' roles as citizens of a mountain village and places them in the situation where the community is under threat. They have taken in a refugee woman with a baby who is being sought by revolutionaries. As citizens the pupils have to take on the responsibility of hiding the woman and baby, thus endangering themselves. The drama opens up the issues of justice and revenge as sought by a revolutionary soldier, the idea of what you undertake when you give someone hospitality and ultimately the question of the worth of the single life against the community. The soldier has suffered under a dictator and now represents a new regime.

One class working on this drama had the unique experience of seeing how closely fiction and real life relate. They heard a story from one of their number whose grandmother had related it to her on hearing her account of the drama. The grandmother had been involved in a similar real life situation in her country of origin, where an old man had sought refuge from soldiers of the opposing faction in her country village. The villagers had taken him in and saved him.

We can see from a summary of the drama that a number of citizenship issues are immediately contextualised and presented to the children. Drama ensures that they have to explore them and get involved in them, to challenge and seek solutions in a number of ways. How much of the Citizenship curriculum does the drama open up? The Framework for PSHE and Citizenship outlines the areas covered as:

> At key stages 1 and 2, the Framework emphasizes the development of social and moral responsibility, community involvement and some of the basic aspects of political literacy, for example, knowing what democracy is and about the basic institutions that support it locally and nationally, as essential preconditions of citizenship as well as PSHE. (QCA, 2000, p. 7)

The group, when they have taken in the woman and child and have been visited by the soldier searching for her, have to decide collectively whether they will continue to protect her, given that she lied to them originally about her and the baby's identity. They have to come to a democratic decision by which they all have to abide, or the village will fall apart anyway.

One group spent a while outlining the pros and cons and then declared where their allegiance lay, the minority being against the woman. The minority had felt strongly that they were risking more lives, their own lives, as against just the woman and the baby, but when they saw the majority result they seemed to accept it as they began wholeheartedly to enter the discussion as to how to outwit the soldier and save the lives of everyone. Hence the ideas of 'social and moral responsibility', 'community involvement', 'democracy' and its consequences were clearly to the fore.

Here is a list of the issues and ideas that were identified as present in this drama by a group of teacher trainees when they examined it:

Giving the children something they can relate to.
They have their say – they have ownership of the key decisions in the drama.

The villagers as:
Negotiation – w
Moral and citize
- Caring
- Trusting
- Respect for p:
- Acceptance o
- Putting yours
- Judging othei
- Lies – excusec
- Protection of

Empathy – the v   tion of:

- The feeling of   l them the truth
  when she can
- That is set aga   tect the child
- Dealing with

(See the followin   – often misrep-
resented in dram

We can see th   the Citizenship curriculum. In addition, the content of a specific drama can be planned to high-light key Citizenship areas. If we examine the thinking behind the planning of the stages of 'The Governor's Child', we can see how by the nature of the tasks, techniques and content, it promotes elements of the Citizenship curriculum.

A key element of the approach is again the use of the teacher to provoke, to challenge, to guide and to model. Use of role-play is always a key strategy for Citizenship, but for us it must involve the teacher role-playing too.

We have given examples from 'The Governor's Child' so that you can see how abstracts like fairness, democracy, identity, community, belonging, respon-sibility, can be made concrete through the process of drama. The process makes them more of a community that can work together to the benefit of each indi-vidual's understanding. In the end we can only provide a framework for learning how to be a member of society. If we give a sense of how it is benefi-cial to the individual to participate and interrelate rather than be selfish and anti-social then right thinking has a chance. If we model how the future can be, it has a chance of being better.

Summary of points to consider

- Drama is an inclusive way of working because it is structured on the principle of 'respect for persons'
- It makes demands upon the teacher to adopt a teaching and learning style that generates positive social health in the group
- The teacher models an attitude that protects pupils from humiliation and derision
- Dramas themselves may examine the concept of the outsider and the inclusive solutions to problems
- Drama protects pupils through the roles they are given, the roles teachers take and its analogous way of working
- Drama is a method of delivering the Citizenship curriculum that embodies an inclusive approach

5 How to Generate Empathy in a Drama

What is empathy?

In this chapter we would like to examine the relationship between drama in education and the concept of empathy. Drama is often promoted as a teaching and learning methodology that generates empathy in pupils, yet there is little debate about exactly what is meant by this idea. The word empathy is sprinkled liberally throughout education documentation and literature. For example, the Social and Emotional Aspects of Learning (SEAL) documents that are, at the time of writing, being trialled in the UK make reference to empathy (SEAL, 2006). For our age group (7–11), under the theme heading of New Beginnings, they outline the following overview:

> This theme focuses on developing children's knowledge, understanding and skills in four key aspects of social and emotional learning: *empathy*, self-awareness, social skills and motivation. (DfES 2005, p. 3; emphasis added)

And later describe these learning outcomes for 7- and 8-year-olds:

> They will continue to build on their capacity for empathy and on their awareness and management of feelings, particularly fearfulness in relation to meeting new challenges (both work-related and social). They will have the opportunity to consider and put into practice ways to support people experiencing these feelings. (DfES, 2005, p. 2)

These attitudes and feelings are key to children developing the right social skills, to be able to relate to others. Drama makes one of its greatest contributions in modelling and generating this sort of learning. For drama to operate most effectively we need to understand what is happening and how we most effectively create the conditions for empathy to thrive.

Therefore, before we start we need to liberate the word from its woolly and misleading usage. What do we actually mean by the word, what do we mean by an empathetic response and what is drama's relationship to this concept?

A phrase commonly linked with empathy is 'standing in someone else's shoes', the idea of, at least for a short time, seeing the world from someone else's perspective, as if you were standing in their shoes. An even more extreme version of this idea is this definition from the 1972 edition of the Chambers dictionary:

> the power of entering into another's personality and imaginatively experiencing his experiences. (p. 424)

The temporal idea behind standing in someone else's shoes is in this definition extended to entering into someone else's personality! Let us return to the less extreme idea of 'standing in someone else's shoes'. Is it really possible to do and what does that mean? The inference is that in some way we can see the world through someone else's eyes, we can think and feel as they would and in some way put ourselves in their position. However, even the most superficial engagement with this idea uncovers deep-seated problems with it in practice.

Let us take for example a drama/history lesson where we wish to get the pupils to empathise with the plight of London's street children of the 1870s (see Chapter 6, How to Link History and Drama). Do we really want our class of 10- and 11-year-olds to 'stand in the shoes' of the desperately poor and under-nourished of urban Victorian life? The Nike-shod twenty-first-century pupil is as far removed from the barefooted 'street urchin' in dress as in life experience. In fact 'entering into another's personality and imaginatively experiencing' is probably the last thing we would want them to do. The mental and physical discomfort of such an experience is hardly what they contracted into when they came into the history lesson. We want them to look at, engage with and reflect upon the lives of children of that time. We want to work in a way that grabs pupils' interest, maintains their attention and beguiles them to look at Victorian life for poor children and understand it in relation to their own.

To do this we make a shift into a fictional world, where time and place can be reallocated and we can behave 'as if' it were happening now, where it is possible to dialogue with fictional ideas of people who no longer exist and where we have an understanding of the empathetic process that engages emotionally without the cruel consequences of the real Victorian world for children.

Of course, we could argue that when we are 'stepping into someone else's shoes' we are sharing universal aspects of human existence, for example, love, loss and generosity. These universal aspects of the human condition exist throughout time and are what we can connect with through empathising. But empathising does not take place at this generalised level, these emotions are too big, too broad for us to empathise with and they need to be framed in particular moments of time and space, events, people and contexts.

To do this we need to move from the general to the particular. Empathy, like drama, is framed in the particular and so we need to move from broad-brush emotions to their demonstrable particularity. Drama works by focusing upon the particular and moving from the particular to the general. To understand drama's relationship with empathy we need to deconstruct the process of empathetic behaviour and see how this is replicated in drama.

A working definition of empathy

Let us begin with a less metaphorical definition of empathy than 'standing in someone else's shoes' and therefore one that is more behaviour-specific. We need a definition that not only belongs to the real world but can be replicated inside the drama lesson. Pupils will then be able to empathise without having to bear witness to or have the actual life experiences of those to whom they are directing their empathy. In this way we protect pupils from actual real life experiences and yet generate the opportunity to empathise with those caught up in these experiences.

Professor Simon Baron-Cohen, the director of the Autism Research Centre at Cambridge, suggests that 'empathizing is the drive to identify another person's emotions and thoughts, and to respond to them with an appropriate emotion' (2003, p. 2). Here we see a behaviour-specific definition that divides the process into two distinct phases: identification and response.

> Empathizing does not entail just the cold calculation of what someone else thinks and feels ... Empathizing occurs when we feel an appropriate emotional reaction, an emotion triggered by the other person's emotion, and it is done in order to understand another person, to predict their behaviour, and to connect or resonate with them emotionally. (Baron-Cohen, 2003, p. 2)

This human attribute is critical to our making sense of the world around us. In 'recognizing and responding to any emotion or state of mind' we are able to manage and ameliorate problems we are confronted with or we perceive others to be faced with: 'Empathy arises out of a natural desire to *care* about others' (Baron-Cohen, 2003, p. 2; emphasis in the original)

It is in this statement that we can make the connection between empathy, learning and drama, for if we can through the acting out of imagined realities generate empathetic behaviour in pupils, they can not only learn from each other but also examine and refine their empathetic skills. And all this is taking place within the safety of pretend worlds without the consequences of the real world. In the game of drama 'the pain of life can be recaptured, encountered and safely switched off as required ... a game and all other forms of playing including the arts, are deliberately created second order experiences, removed from the rawness of living' (Bolton, 1984, p. 105).

The components of empathy

The idea of a 'cognitive' stage and an 'affective' stage in the empathetic process is taken from the writings of Alan Leslie in his work at London University, as summarised by Simon Baron-Cohen (2003, pp. 29–30).

Component One – the cognitive component

Baron-Cohen suggests that there are 'two major elements to empathy' and the first of these is the 'cognitive component: understanding the other's feelings and the ability to take their perspective' (2003, p. 28). He goes on to say: 'Jean Piaget called this aspect of empathy "responding non-egocentrically" as it entails the "setting aside of your own current perspective" and "attributing a mental state (sometimes called an attitude) to the other person . . ."' (2003, p. 28). This is sometimes referred to as 'theory of mind' or the ability to read someone else's mind (Baron-Cohen, 2003): 'The cognitive component also allows you to predict the other person's behaviour or mental state' (Davis, 1994 and Wellman, 1990 in Baron-Cohen, 2003, p. 28).

Component Two – the affective component

'The second element to empathy is the affective component. This is an observer's appropriate emotional response to another person's emotional state' (Baron-Cohen, 2003, p. 28). Having recognised the emotional state of the person, the observer is moved to 'alleviate their distress' (p. 28). There is here a desire to do something, to take action, and therefore empathy is not just about recognising the emotional state of someone but also doing something about it.

An example of structuring drama for empathetic response

Let us use these ideas to analyse how empathy might be generated using as an example 'The Workhouse' drama. The class have been enrolled as government commissioners. Their task is to visit and report upon workhouses.

Building the cognitive component

Out of role, the class have studied a photograph of the workhouse and now move into a fictional context, that is, standing outside the workhouse and 'using their drama eyes' in describing it. One of them knocks upon the great oak door and TiR as Crimmins, the Workhouse Master's assistant, opens the door: *Who are you? What do you want? We want no charity here! The Master's very busy. Go and do good somewhere else!*

ToR then talks to the pupils about what has happened: *Who do you think this man is? What was his attitude? His demeanour?* They then question him further and tell him who they are. It is agreed that they wish to see the Workhouse Master and they intend to inspect the workhouse.

TiR as Crimmins: *I am most humbly sorry. I thought you were the charity people poking their noses in. I didn't realise, what with ladies being in your party. Do come in. Perhaps a glass of something, some supper after your journey from London? I will get the Master.*

ToR discusses why his attitude has changed: *Why would he be confused by the presence of women in the party? Who did he think they were? What was his attitude to 'charitable visitors'?*

In the next part of the drama the pupils are told that a new inmate is expected and that they are to witness her induction to the workhouse. First, they look at the Workhouse Master (TiR) as he watches the girl walking towards the gates. They tell the teacher how they want him to stand and how they want him to look. He holds a stick. One of the girls in the class is enrolled as Martha, the new inmate. She carries a rolled up cardigan to signify she is carrying a baby.

She stands at one end of the room holding her baby and TiR as the Workhouse Master stands at the other, tapping his stick into his hand. The class form a corridor between the two roles for her to walk along. The class listen as TiR voices what the Master is thinking as he watches her approach: *Another waster. Another scraggy baby to feed. I hope she's a good worker. She and that baby better not be ill. Don't want her bringing her disease in here. I'll take that baby off her straight away. Maybe wait till this lot have gone. Must impress the inspector do-gooders while they're here. Can get back to normal when they've gone.*

ToR discusses these comments and how the class feel about the Workhouse Master. They also discuss why Martha might be going to such a dreadful place. What might have happened to her? We don't know but we can guess and talk to her later.

Framing the affective component – thought-tracking and dealing with the Workhouse Master

We return to the drama. The pupils voice the thoughts of Martha as she passes. They don't have to speak but they must listen to each other and speak as if they were Martha as she approaches the workhouse and the Workhouse Master. This strategy of conscience alley will enable the class to sympathise with Martha's circumstances.

Pupil 1: *I'm frightened.*
Pupil 2: *My baby will die if I don't go here.*
Pupil 3: *Must look like I can work hard.*
Pupil 4: *I don't want them to take my baby.*

The cognitive stage

The first stage of structuring for empathising is the **cognitive** stage. In the example given it has three components:

1 The role – Martha represented by a pupil walking down the conscience alley.
2 The attitude of Martha as negotiated and agreed with by the class and teacher.
3 Martha's purpose – to enter the workhouse and save the baby.

This representation of the cognitive stage of empathising has been contracted with the class before the strategy is enacted. Its success is generated by the constraints imposed on the roles, the context and the events leading up to Martha's approach to the doors of the workhouse, in other words, the pre-text.

The roles   First, empathy is generated by Martha and this is reflected by the pupils as the voices of Martha's thoughts. Empathy here is a response to the attitudes of the roles they have met. Crimmins – uncaring, deceitful – and the Workhouse Master – cruel, untrustworthy, manipulative – and finally the low status role of Martha, vulnerable and limited in the choices she can make on her own.

The context   If we then put these roles in the context of a workhouse – dangerous, forbidding and the last resort of the poor – while at the same time requiring the class to make judgements and a report about the workhouse, we are giving them power to take action.

Events leading up to her approaching the workhouse   The pre-text to Martha approaching the doors of the workhouse involves her poverty, vulnerability, the symbol of a baby giving her little choice but to go the workhouse. When the class meet roles with cruel and negative attitudes, i.e. Crimmins and the Workhouse Master, roles who are clearly willing to deceive the Commission, they are set up to empathise with the role of Martha. However, this is not truly empathising until they are given the opportunity to voice those concerns and to ameliorate her situation.

The affective stage

The second stage of structuring for empathising is the **affective** stage. The three components this time are the pupils' role, the context in which they find themselves and their witnessing of Martha's treatment by Mards, the Workhouse Master.

The roles   First the pupils' role as commissioners is high status, fair-minded, responsible, not easily fooled and trying to make the world a better place.

The context   If we then put these roles in the context of a fact-finding commission with the power to change practices, we give them the opportunity to take action.

Events leading up to their debrief of the Workhouse Master   The pupils share the experience of witnessing the induction of a new inmate.

While the class's attitude to Martha represents the **cognitive** state, the second stage of the empathetic process is the **affective** state. After the class have had the opportunity to speak the thoughts of Martha as she approaches, they are able to confront the Workhouse Master and comment upon his treatment of Martha. They are in a position to criticise him and to make recommendations as to the procedures of the induction process. They may even ask for the process to be re-run with their recommendations enacted upon.

Of course, this situation is manipulated by the teacher structuring the roles and events in a particular way – the initial meeting with those who run the workhouse, listening to their attitudes and witnessing their deceitful behaviour. All these planned events build towards the opportunity for empathetic behaviour to take place. In doing this we are not certain every pupil will respond empathetically. Part of the function of teaching and learning is to create opportunities for assessment. Of course the nature of the response may vary from mere sympathy with Martha's predicament to a more dynamic response to help the person by initiating action to help.

What distinguishes empathy as a response is its appropriateness to the person's circumstances. 'Feelings of pleasure, smugness, or hate' would not be empathetic responses (Baron-Cohen, 2003, p. 28). What the structuring of an empathetic response does is enable you to diagnose an aspect of social health within the class, or within groups in the class, for example, boys and girls. Those pupils who find it difficult to empathise will have the opportunity to see the skills modelled and the positive consequences played out.

Can we plan for generating empathy?

We can generate empathy through structuring roles and creating a drama frame where it is likely to happen. There are three parts to this process: the role of the teacher, the role of the pupils and the frame in which they are placed.

The role of the pupils

While placing the pupils in a positive, problem-solving and high status role (government commissioners) gives them the power to make judgements about people's circumstances from a positive point of view, it is also possible to generate empathy for the dispossessed. Later in the workhouse drama the pupils shift their role to inmates, demonstrating life in the workhouse through tableaux based upon the workhouse rules. One rule, 'the rule of the infamous liar', entails an inmate having to stand on a stool in the dining room with a label around their neck declaring them 'an infamous liar'. The inmates form a sociogram that describes their feelings towards the accused by how close or far away from her they stand. They are then thought-tracked. Despite their low status roles empathy is still generated as they confront the fact 'that could be me'.

The role of the teacher

Like the role of the pupils, the role of the teacher is also important in the generation of empathy; the relationship is co-dependent. The role of the pupils needs in the first place to be a community one so that they see the situation from one point of view and are not divided in their attitude. Just as the role of the pupils gives them a perspective from which they can empathise, the role(s) you plan for the teacher is also part of structuring for an empathetic response. The Workhouse Master generates an empathetic response towards Martha from the pupils by his lack of humanity. The modelling by the teacher of roles who are unable to empathise enables the pupils to witness their shortcomings and therefore have a sense of how disabled they are without these skills. All this sounds very manipulative and it is! We are deliberately structuring drama to engage with issues of empathy and our learning objective is that in this process pupils will 'learn ways to identify and label these feelings ... they will have opportunities to develop empathy and work out what others are feeling' (DfES, 2005, p. 2).

Summary of points to consider

- Empathy is often misconstrued
- The components of empathy
    Component One – the cognitive component
    Component Two – the affective component
- How to structure drama for empathetic response
    Building the cognitive component
    Framing the affective component
- Planning the role of the teacher and of the pupils for generating empathy

6 How to Link History and Drama

A problematic alliance

For drama there is a fatal attraction with history as a source for its content. Drama as a medium with which to engage with the past is established in theatre, film, literature, radio and television. In fact one of the Key Elements in the History National Curriculum is the interpretation of history,

> People represent and interpret the past in many different ways, including: in pictures, plays, films, reconstructions, museum displays, and fictional and nonfiction accounts. Interpretations reflect the circumstances in which they are made, the available evidence, and the intentions of those who make them (for example, writers, archaeologists, historians, filmmakers). (QCA/DfES, 2000)

So it is not surprising that the teacher using drama should engage the class through the use of roles, contexts and symbols from the past.

We are not historians, and in writing this chapter we shared our approach to using drama to teach history with Professor Hilary Cooper at St Martins College. Professor Cooper's vast experience in the world of education and history teaching illuminated and clarified issues that exist between a pedagogical approach firmly rooted in the creation of fictional worlds and a subject striving to find truth and authenticity in views of the past.

In using the arts pupils are creating their own interpretation or account, based upon sources. In Professor Cooper's words: 'This helps them to understand how historians and others create accounts of the past and why accounts may be equally valid, but different.' (The ideas that we discussed are embodied in *History 3–11: a Guide for Teachers*, by Hilary Cooper, published by Fulton, 2006.)

In view of the fact that the use of drama to teach history is not straightforward it is important for the teacher that a conceptual framework be adopted that balances the tensions between the medium and the content, between fiction and fact.

> I argue that historians make suppositions based on sources and on what is known and that the more reasonable suppositions they can make the more likely they are to be able to understand possible thoughts and feelings of people in the past. Validity depends on whether inference is reasonable and what else is known. (Professor Hilary Cooper)

We have a responsibility to the historian to make clear the dangers and risks in a dramatic approach.

As was discussed in Chapter 5, the phrase 'to stand in someone else's shoes' is one often used to describe the concept of empathising and it is never more liberally tossed about than in the History and Drama curriculum. We have already indicated that teachers should be wary of using it. If we believe that 'standing in someone's shoes' is adopting their perceptions, feelings and understandings of the world then we are forgetting the social and psychological distance between us now and those who have lived in the past. To expect a child to 'step into the shoes' of a 10-year-old evacuee or a servant in the household of a wealthy family in the nineteenth century, is ignoring the impossibility of this shift for pupils with twenty-first-century minds.

Dressing up to go back in time

One popular method of 'empathising' in the teaching of history takes the form of dressing up in costumes from the past. Schools across the country plan days of 'visiting the past' by dressing up and sometimes actually going to historic sites in their costumes. Alternatively, schools will suspend the usual timetable and devote lessons and other activities to a particular period in time. Teachers may even be locked into roles from the past (one could almost say trapped in roles from the past), thinking, misguidedly in our view, this will generate 'empathy' in the pupils with people from history. If we do a simulation of evacuees by standing with pupils on a railway platform, with cardboard boxes hanging from their necks and singing 'Run, Rabbit, Run', are we taking them any nearer the actual event? Will merely donning a costume and shifting location take us emotionally closer to those children who experienced this situation? Do we want this even if it were possible? To structure the learning so they may experience the distress that many suffered who went through this event could never be the function of this exercise and if this is not the purpose what is it? If I dress up in a *circa* 1968 Bobby Charlton replica kit and kick a ball about (even if I go to Old Trafford) will I start to think like him, let alone play like him? While dressing up in costumes is a very popular history/drama experience, we must be guarded about what we think children may learn by the experience.

Using drama to make meaning of the past

Let us begin by looking at three elements of historical enquiry:

- A concern with **facts**
- A concern with **reasons**
- A concern with **meanings**

Historians are interested in making deductions and inferences about sources and then selecting and combining sources to create accounts of the past. Historical imagination is filling the gaps when sources are incomplete. In drama we are particularly interested in the last element. It is here that drama synthesises story and past events.

As a teacher planning a history-related drama this does not mean abandoning facts and reasons. In striving to accommodate the potentially un-reconcilable dimensions of fact and fiction, we need to balance imagined realities with authenticated realities. In other words, we need to research our history and bring the fruits of that research to the lesson. If we are to take on roles, and some of these roles are people who actually existed in the past, then we must research these roles. If we are asking pupils to take on roles of people from the past we need to frame this task in such a way as to respect the need for authenticity and to give them roles that will enable them to look at the past in a way that respects the work of the historian. Of course, the research is not just a task for the teacher but one that can be shared with the pupils in lessons introducing the topic and before the drama work takes place. The drama then has an assessment function, as knowledge gained in the research activities will be exposed during the drama.

Balancing the tensions – stories and history

Much of drama in education operates from creating fictions and telling stories. Of course this is not necessarily in conflict with history as we can approach individuals' viewpoints in history as their stories of the past. Essentially history is story; it began as oral history and is a shared story of society. Many people's view of Victorian England is coloured by the work of Charles Dickens and particularly spin-offs such as films, TV serialisations and musicals. Just as painters or novelists will present a view of the past in their work, the pupil in the drama will use it to create their understanding of history, and the challenge for the teacher is to plan the lesson conscious of the tensions between the imagination and the need for authenticity. The first rule must be complete honesty with the class about what we know, what we think we know and what we need to find out. We need to be clear about our learning objectives, about what we are trying to teach.

We are going to use a drama about Victorian street children to illustrate how drama and history can be structured to work in harmony. In using drama we are using a dense form of teaching, because the currency of drama is language, listening and speaking, and we have a cross-curricular approach that will touch upon learning objectives from several areas of the curriculum. Let's begin with the English and the History National Curriculum learning objectives.

Learning objectives: History
Victorian Britain:

> A study of the impact of significant individuals, events and changes in work and transport on the lives of men, women and children from different sections of society. (QCA/DfES, 2000)

Learning objectives: English, Speaking and Listening
In English pupils have the opportunity:

> To present a spoken argument, sequencing points logically, defending views with evidence and making use of persuasive language
> To understand different ways to take the lead and support others in groups
> (Year 5)
> To use a range of oral techniques to present persuasive argument
> To understand and use a variety of ways to criticise constructively and respond to criticism
> (Year 6)
>
> (QCA, 2003, pp. 10, 11)

We cannot separate the values of past societies from the events that took place. In this way drama confronts pupils with the ideas, beliefs and values of people from the past. The juxtaposition of values and beliefs from the past with pupils' own values and gives them the opportunity to 'use techniques of dialogic talk to explore ideas, topics or issues' (QCA, 2003, p. 11) through the prism of history and the safety of fictional contexts.

So how does this work in practice? Where are we making up the past and where are we demanding authenticity? The 'Victorian Street Children' drama (see Part Two for the full drama) illustrates how the tensions between history and drama can be managed. While this drama illustrates how drama and history can work together it must be remembered that the drama lesson should not be seen in isolation from history lessons that precede or follow it. It is part of a series of lessons and issues raised in the drama can be dealt with in other more appropriate teaching and learning settings. The starting point for this drama is a photograph (see the photograph in the 'Victorian Street Children' drama in Part Two). This is the same starting point used by Cecily O'Neill and Alan Lambert in their book *Drama Structures* (1982), although we have used it to develop a different drama.

The photograph immediately nails the first important rule of drama and history, the importance and value of historical authenticity. Photographs and artefacts are a key approach because they can grab the attention of the pupils. They can also generate a context, a time and a place, roles and even a possible dilemma, all ingredients of drama. We need to take the class to the drama. The initial viewpoint is that of the outsider, the historian. The subject matter is delicate, the plight of the poor, and more poignantly, poor children. This needs to be handled carefully and each lens or frame we look at this subject through will initially, at least, be there to create distance. We are making a conscious decision to move into the fiction of the drama using the authenticity of a primary source, a photograph. We are taking the pupils to the harsh reality of the past by distancing them through the collective role of historians. We start from now and move with the class back in time. The subject matter requires this because of the sadness within it. We manage this through their role, as historians, we give them high status, the Mantle of Expert. These are people who will approach this task seriously. They are presented with a photograph, a primary source; this will capture their attention. In this way we generate and manage the commitment of the class by 'beguiling them' (Fines, 1997, p. 106) into a fictional world of the poor at this time in history. A photograph enables us to begin to interpret the past and acts as a means to 'find out about aspects of the past' (QCA/DfES, 2000). We can examine how the past is represented and this begins the process of enquiry into the past that is central to the function of the historian. We need to go to other sources in our teacher research, and a chapter by Blake Morrison in *Too True* provides us with another source to validate our understanding. In 'Barnardo before and after' he uses his literary skills to describe the circumstances of the taking of the same photograph:

> A rimy morning in 1874. Thomas Barnes, photographer, leans against a wall and coughs. He has had a bad cold for months. These damp mornings do it, the yellow Stepney fog and hanging rain. He hopes the brick will warm his back. Across from him, at the edge of the yard, the Doctor fusses with the urchins, knowing what he wants, unable to get it yet: will they stand like this, can the boy on the end come in closer, would they straighten up and keep their eyes fixed right ahead? (Morrison, 1998, p. 41)

He also so provides some further information from his own research, the place in which the photograph was taken, information relating to Edward Fitzgerald, the man in the photograph and the photographer, Thomas Barnes. These snippets of information provide hooks for the teacher in role to hang information upon. This information mixed with the attitudes expressed by the teacher roles will connect the pupils with the particularity of the photograph and at the same time some of the values in the period being studied.

This in turn juxtaposes pupils' own attitudes with those adopted by the roles. In confronting the attitudes of the roles, for example, the acceptability of the physical chastisement of children, pupils are looking at issues of continuity and change. Analysing the photographic process in the 1870s compared to digital photography today would be an example of pupils dealing with similarity and difference. Continuity and change, similarity and difference are key concepts in the teaching of history and through drama these are made concrete experiences. So we have two types of similarity and difference, those related to technological change and those related to social values.

We cannot separate the second set of differences from the economic and social problems of the time, the problems of industrialisation, the growth of big cities, the lack of state intervention to support the poor, etc.

Setting up a historian's frame

The drama begins as a history lesson, with the idea of taking on roles in the lesson introduced from the beginning. The pupils' first role is of high status and expertise:

> *In the drama you will have several roles, one of them will be historians and at other times you will be the people we are concerned with in this drama – that is, the poor street children of the 1870s in London.*
>
> *Let's start with your role as historians. Before we do, you need to tell me:*
>   *What is a historian?*
>   *What do historians do?*
>   *What skills do they need?*

In order to help the class to look at the photograph sensitively we give them a role that carries both power and professional distance. The discussion of the role of the historian is a preparation for this. This imposition of high status and expertise is designed to engage the class with a sense of responsibility for the task ahead and leads into the introduction of the first piece of historical evidence, the photograph.

The photograph on its own is not enough, however. We need to frame the class's thinking in such a way that they are constrained to think like a historian. To do this, we ask three questions about the photograph:

What do we know?	What do we think we know?	What do we want to ask?

This approach replicates Facts – Hypothesis – Research.

The facts are those statements that the whole class can agree are indisputable, for example, 'there are five boys and one man in the photograph'. The 'think we know' section opens up the possibilities for the class, for example, an observation such as *the boys are poor* will present a possibility based on the evidence of their dress and demeanour. This category will enable a high level of success in terms of acceptable responses because the constraint of 'indisputable fact' has been lifted. Contradictions and disputes can live side by side because it is not until will have put into action the last section that the hypotheses can be resolved, and not all hypotheses may be resolved. For example, we may have theories about why the photograph has only boys in it. This may generate further research and it may not be resolved. However, it may also draw the pupils' attention to the fact that girls did live on the streets and were taken into Barnardo's homes. This in turn raises the opportunities for further research outside the drama lesson.

To focus the work further we start by describing the 'givens' in the task. By this we mean the statements under the Facts ('What do we know?') column that are given and cannot be contradicted. These are as follows:

- This is a genuine photograph taken in 1874.
- There are five boys and one man in the photograph.
- The name of the man in the photograph is Edward Fitzgerald.
- Edward Fitzgerald is holding a lamp.
- The photograph was taken outside some derelict buildings in London.

This approach allows us to focus the pupils' attention upon the interpretation of the photograph and how this might be structured. It also underlines the need for research questions and exposes how little we can be certain of at this early stage of the enquiry.

Meetings with teacher in role

Having collated some evidence, hypotheses and research questions we can use drama as a means to test out some of their observations. The role of Edward Fitzgerald, the man holding the lamp in the picture, is a good starting point as it opens up the possibilities drama offers as a way to access history and what it means to the class:

If you could talk to the man in the picture holding the lamp what would you like to ask him? What could you ask to check out some of your ideas about the photograph?

ROLE RESEARCH

Preparation for role

- The man holding the lamp is Edward Fitzgerald.
- He worked for Dr Barnardo; he was a beadle.
- He would find children who were homeless and needed help.
- When photographed with the children he would carry a lamp to symbolise his role in finding 'lost' children and leading them 'out of the darkness'.

It is important to find out what the class will ask you; by doing it this way you can get a sense of what they are interested in and at the same time feel prepared for the initial couple of questions. Questioning Edward Fitzgerald serves several purposes, first, to shift the dialogue into the present tense and in this way take the class into the attitudes and values of the past. In the role of Edward Fitzgerald you are able to answer questions about your job, why you are carrying a lamp, who the boys are, etc. It is important to clarify some of these issues but at the same time not to tell the whole story and in this way maintain the interest of the class. Here are some typical questions from pupils interviewing Edward Fitzgerald along with the responses from the teacher in role, the key to this being the withholding of some information and the hints at the underlying values of the man being questioned.

Pupil: *What's your job, Mr Fitzgerald?*
TiR: *I work for the Good Doctor.*
ToR: *What does he mean 'the Good Doctor?'*

This question is there to gauge the pupils' knowledge at this early stage of the lesson. Doctor Barnardo has not been mentioned so far and this will diagnose whether they are to discover that this photograph is connected to him or whether it is to be discussed at this point.

Pupil: *So, what do you do?*
TiR: *Well I go round and persuade these street children to get shelter at the home.*
Pupil: *What home?*
TiR: *Why, the home the Good Doctor has set up, of course. More and more good people like yourselves are finding out about the fine work he is doing. Doing it in Our Lord's name.*

Already there are hints at the evangelical nature of Barnardo's exploits and these can be further examined out of role. If reference is made to why the photograph was taken this can be deferred by saying: *You can ask that one to Tom Barnes; he's the man for the photograph questions.*

The class will then meet TiR as Thomas Barnes, the photographer, who will open up issues about the behaviour of the boys: *I leave that to Fitzgerald, he can handle them. They're rough, this lot. They need a firm hand.* He will also describe how the photographs were used to raise money, how he took 'before' and 'after' shots. 'Before' they were given a warm bath and fresh clothes set alongside an 'after' photograph to show the immediate and dramatic change Barnardo's home had made to them. These photographs were put into booklets of twenty and sold to the charitable middle classes and rich. He will open up the issues related to the technology of the photography, how the children would have to stay still for up to half a minute. How the photographs were posed.

All these issues stimulate a dialogue about the underlying attitudes in the roles responses: the ethics of this way of raising funds, the attitudes to children, to the 'chastisement' of children, the concept of the 'deserving poor'.

History lessons using TiR confront the learners with attitudes and perceptions that may not belong to now but are being presented 'as if' they were now and, even more challenging, as if they are acceptable now. It is this juxtaposition of then and now that grabs the attention of the pupils.

Having drawn the class into the photograph through their interviews with Fitzgerald and Barnes, they can begin to learn about the boys in the photograph and interview them. For this you need five volunteers from the class to take on the roles. Not all pupils will feel comfortable in taking on the role of the children in the photograph at this point, so a process of selection and contracting the demands inherent in adopting these roles is critical to the success of the next part of the drama. Let us now look at how to set up this up and the necessary steps for its success.

Meeting the boys in the photograph

Modelling the roles

Part of the process of setting this up is the modelling of roles by the teacher *before* asking pupils to take on this responsibility. They will have seen you taking the work seriously and you need to make clear the demands that will be made upon those who decide to do it.

We're going to move the drama on now and meet the boys in the photograph we have been looking at. I am going to need five volunteers to do this, but before you decide whether you want to be one of them I want to explain what you will have to do.

You must be good at keeping a serious look on your face because, as you can see, the boys in the photograph are going through unhappy times. They are poor, hungry and desperate for help.

Secondly, you are going to have a chance to work with me away from the rest of the class to decide on your histories, where you are from, how you ended up on the streets, etc. So when you meet the historians you will be able to answer their questions.

Thirdly, I will stop and start the drama so we have a chance to talk about what is happening; this means you are not trapped in role and unable to come out of it.

Finally, I will be with you as Edward Fitzgerald and so you won't feel left on your own to do this.

The rest of the class will be wealthy ladies and gentlemen who are keen to support Dr Barnardo and have requested to speak to some of the children he cares for. Their task is to decide upon the questions they wish to put to Fitzgerald and the boys.

That is the initial contract and by making those elements explicit the pupils can decide whether they want to volunteer. The role of the majority of the class has two facets. First is the caring and interested investigator. This role mirrors Henry Mayhew, the nineteenth-century author of articles in *The Morning Chronicle*, which formed a survey of the London poor. This role requires a sympathetic disposition; the questions to the boys have to be presented in a caring and compassionate fashion. The other facet is one of power and class. The role will put them in a powerful position in relation to Edward Fitzgerald. While the boys may be in fear of the beadle the questioners will not, as their class and superior education puts them in a position of power. Should they wish to talk to the boys on their own, without the inhibiting presence of Fitzgerald, they may request to do so and this will be acceded to, albeit reluctantly by TiR as Fitzgerald.

Setting up the boys

Away from the rest of the class (you might do this at a break time or lunchtime), those who have decided to be the boys meet with you. They must decide upon the following things:

- *What are your names?* Discuss Victorian boys' names – royal names and Old Testament biblical names were common. Avoid any names of pupils in the class.
- *Are any of you related?* In the photo some of the boys do look like brothers, others do not. Why might they be together then? Issues of safety in numbers, older ones looking after younger ones. In Saõ Paulo gangs of street children go round together and refer to each other as 'uncle', hinting at a family-like grouping.
- *How did you end up living on the streets?* Possibilities – too many mouths to feed, violent fathers, death and disease amongst those caring for them or avoiding the dreaded workhouse could all be discussed.
- *Are any of you ill? Are you doing this to survive but don't intend to stay?*
- *Which one of you is the leader?*

Having answered these questions and built up a history, there are four 'givens'. Without the agreement of the group on these the next part of the drama will not work.

1 *We must agree that you are afraid of Fitzgerald. In those days you would have experienced physical violence from adults and in your eyes he will present that threat. If the drama is to work you must agree that you are afraid of him. Is that OK?* This generates tension in the interview and it will be interesting to see if the class pick up on this. It also works in another way; the TiR as Fitzgerald must not be seen as an opportunity for the pupils to say whatever they like to him, just because he is in role. In order to maintain the tension this fear needs to be signalled to the rest of the class. They can hesitate and look at Fitzgerald before answering; this will be seen by the class and may even lead to them asking Fitzgerald to leave the interview, which he will do while mut-

tering under his breath to the boys, *Remember what I said … and call them Sir or Madam, understand?*

2 They must agree that they want to go into the home. This may be a short term agreement but it is one they have made.

3 During the interview one of them will cough and indicate they are not well. This needs to be done subtly – low key but enough to hint that one of the group is not well.

4 Initially in the interview they do not look at each other or their classmates, they just find a spot on the floor or ceiling to look at. This will help them not to smile and to look serious, as this is crucial to the authenticity of the interview.

This very carefully engineered setting up of the boys is essential for the success of the task. Whatever happens as teacher you will be moving in and out of role, managing the teaching and learning process, checking understanding, negotiating the next question, the next move and using the as-if-it-is-happening-now to engage the pupils attention. They are the scriptwriters, but they are constrained by the 'givens', the non-negotiables of frame through which they are exploring how they make sense of this part of history.

In a session with some students, those taking the role of the interested wealthy benefactors asked Fitzgerald to leave, which he did, warning the boys to be *best behaved* as he left. Realising this presented an opportunity to say things that could not be said in his presence, a student as one of the boys leaned towards his questioners and whispered, *Have you got any food for us? Give us a penny, will you? He won't know.* This was a marvellous opportunity to discuss the implications of his request. Should they give money and food now? What are the implications of this?

From that moment we can incorporate it into the drama. We can tell the pupils in their planning of the boys that if Fitzgerald leaves they can ask for food and money. They can beg and see what response they get. This is a good example of how ideas from students and pupils can become embedded in the planning for the future.

Whole class participation – a sculpture of children living on the streets

In this drama each frame takes the class closer to the children who are the subject of our historical investigations. The next task is to engage the whole class as a sculpture of the children living on the streets. The use of still image is important here because it constrains the action and forces the class into a holding moment which, like a painting or a photograph, allows us to examine the detail and what it means for us. The whole class need to consider where they are in the sculpture. If the dying embers of a fire (represented by a chair turned upside down) are the centre of the picture, where are they? Questions of status, pecking order and rank are immediately raised and discussed:

Who would be furthest away from the fire on this freezing night, December 24th 1874? Who would be nearest and why? Would anybody be standing? Would there be a look out? What would they be looking out for?

As these questions are answered a picture is built up, identities are adopted:

When you find your place in the picture decide are you with others? Think about your hands and feet, concentrate on them, how would they look? Find a position you can hold still for at least a minute. Do not look at anyone else, just concentrate on yourself and find a spot to look at that will help you concentrate.

This careful building of the image is important because it helps the class create the sculpture by giving them guidance on how to achieve the necessary stillness for its success. When it is complete let them hold it still for a few moments. To share this image we can divide the class in half, with one half standing back to look at the other. To do this we need to create a physical distance for the participants. The distance is achieved by one half of the class sustaining their representation of the street children through the sculpture and the other half framed by the idea of visitors to a museum set in the future. For those sustaining the still image, the distance will enable them to hold onto the stillness and seriousness of the picture, and for those observing, the distance will help them stand back to view the image from a watcher's perspective. The frame of visitors to a museum set in the future can be set up through TiR as the curator of the museum.

Welcome to our new exhibit on the theme of children in the nineteenth century. In the next room we have an interactive exhibit, a sculpture of children who were known as street children. What is exciting about this exhibit is that not only can you view it, but you can, through the wonders of modern technology, hear what the children represented in the piece are thinking. They are programmed to say what they are thinking at this moment in history. They may not all speak. Some of them are too cold.

As half the class watch, the teacher touches each of the pupils on the shoulder and they voice their thoughts. Of course, not all pupils will speak and some will repeat what others say, but this is not a problem because the overall effect is to create a sound collage of their thoughts in this situation while at the same time not putting unnecessary pressure on those who cannot think of anything to say and would prefer to listen. Then the other half of the class do the same so that the class is able to share the work and also be part of it.

This slowing down of the drama and looking in detail at a particular moment is important and a feature of how drama in education works. Unlike performance and product-orientated drama, the purpose here is to negotiate meanings and consider implications of particular issues. The pupils have been moved frame by frame to make sense of the world of the street children by a gradual edging towards their perspective.

Whole class improvisation

We can use the sculpture and thought-tracking work as a starting point for a whole class improvisation or 'living through' part of the drama. The class remake the sculpture and this time TiR enters into the work which now takes on a 'living through' mode of working. What is important here is the manner in which this is achieved; all the time as teacher you are enabling the participation of the pupils in a way that is non-threatening and accesses them to speak when they feel comfortable to do so. The fear of humiliation by making a mistake or getting it wrong, fears that are sadly part of the culture of too many classrooms, are eroded. If we listen to the teacher setting up this part of the drama we can hear the contracting, the instructions and constraints that help the task to work for both teacher and pupils:

We are going to remake our whole class sculpture only this time I am going to join you. I am going to take the role of a wealthy gentleman who comes across these street children on a bitterly cold night. Go back to the sculpture you made before and listen to the story and you will know what to do.

The teacher begins to narrate:

It was a bitterly cold night on December 24th 1874. A wealthy gentleman was making his way home. He had been unable to get a carriage home and so he decided to take a short cut through the back streets to his mansion. It was as he was on this journey that he met a sight that appalled his eyes. Dozens of children huddled together desperately trying to keep warm in front of the dying embers of a fire. He immediately organised his servants to bring soup, bowls and bread to the children and as they greedily ate bread and soup he sat with them.

The teacher continues – this time OoR:
I want you to pick up your bowls. Now just imagine the bowls … Cup your hands … Imagine you have a bowl … Concentrate on your own bowl … Don't think about anybody else's … The soup in the bowl is the one thing you need … You've forgotten about everyone around you … You have a nice hunk of bread … I want you to mime dipping your bread … concentrating on your own bread … your own soup … slowly, try to make it last … eating the bread and the soup.

Teacher as narrator:
And as the children ate their soup the gentleman began to question them.

The next section is a transcript of some 10- and 11-year-olds at this point in the drama.

TiR as a wealthy gentleman: *What are you doing here? Why are you not in your homes?* [No response] *Why? It's Christmas Eve, you should be home opening your presents!* [No response] *Can none of you tell me? What are you doing out here?*

1st pupil (girl): *Our parents didn't want us. They beat us!*

TiR: *Your parents didn't want you? If they beat you then you must have done something wrong! What did you do that was so wrong that they beat you?*

2nd pupil (boy): *Why don't you ask them!*

1st pupil: *We didn't get enough money for them, so they beat us and pushed us out.*

TiR: *They pushed you out onto the street!*

The teacher realises the class is too far away and that only the children close to him are responding verbally to him, although they are all engaged with what is going on.

TiR: *Come in closer. I want to speak to you all. I've never heard such things.* [The class move into a tighter group around the TiR] *Is this true for others of you? That you were beaten and ended up on the streets? Why didn't you go and stay with your aunties and uncles?*

3rd pupil (girl): *I haven't got anyone.*

4th pupil (girl): *I've never met them*

TiR: *But how do you survive out here? … This isn't a house, it's a derelict building.*

5th pupil (girl): *We do our best.*

TiR: *You shouldn't be here.*

6th pupil (boy): *We've nowhere else to go.*

TiR: *Look, I could take you somewhere. Somewhere you will have food and shelter. I'm a governor on the board of a workhouse. Now in the workhouse you will be looked after. You will have work.* [The class show little enthusiasm for this] *So how do you eat? How do you survive? Where do you get your food?*

7th pupil (boy): *We steal.*

TiR: [with indignation] *You steal! Do you not know your Bible? THOU SHALLT NOT STEAL. Do you not know this?*

7th pupil (girl): *I never heard of it.*

TiR: *You've never heard of it?*

The class have taken a position that exposes the ignorance and patronising attitude of the wealthy gentleman. They offer their contributions safely in the knowledge that there is no requirement to act or perform, that they need only make a contribution when they feel it is safe to do so. The lesson has been structured to ensure their inclusion and their responses are spontaneous and offered genuinely from the viewpoint of the roles they are representing. They connect with the plight of the street children by recognising the lack of understanding of their position embodied in the teacher roles. They are confronted through the teacher roles by viewpoints that are flawed:

> there was a good deal in the orthodox Victorian outlook which was a positive hindrance. If you insisted on seeing most problems in moral terms and if, on the whole, you believed that virtue was rewarded and vice punished, then it was easy to blame the poor for their own misfortunes, which they could put right by sobriety, industry and devotion to their masters' interests. Hence the misdirection of much well-meant effort into charity of the 'deserving poor'. (Reader, 1974, p. 98)

Drama teaches about history by creating carefully researched historical contexts and roles. These roles will generate the need to do something about a particular issue, however this debate about the particular is really a means to make sense of larger more general themes. The drama approach must be seen as a particular pedagogical approach to the subject. Its particularity lies in the use of TiR as a means to generate other kinds of dialogue beyond the usual teacher–pupil one. It should be supported by the more traditional approaches to history teaching which are effective in ways that drama is not, for example, the searching and retrieval of information. Drama needs to be recognised for what it does best, which is to negotiate meanings through engagement with imagined realities.

History as a metaphor for now – the global dimension

It is important that we make the connections between issues in history where they remain issues for us over time. The issue of street children is an example of one of these. In *Life on the Streets: Children's Stories* the BBC published stories of homeless or underprivileged children from St Petersburg, La Paz and Delhi. Their stories echo the issues that are raised in the history drama – exclusion, poverty and survival. Here is an extract from one of them:

> I came to Delhi with my mother and her second husband. I was seven then. I am thirteen now. My mother abandoned me at the bus terminal while I was fast asleep and I have not seen her since. Suddenly, I was an orphan. I met some boys who used to beg at the station and I joined them in begging to feed myself. I did not have a name, so friends started calling me Rajan, which means the king. I started wiping cars when they stopped at a red light. After a while we moved to Connaught Place, the main shopping area in the capital, where we started picking rag. I also worked in a roadside eatery for a while.
>
> While working there I met people working for a charity that help destitute children, called Jamghat. I work for them now.
>
> I am quite happy here. Even if I find out where my mother is I will not return to her.
>
> I am studying. I am also learning sewing, not neatly but now I can write letters to some extent. I like cricket. I went to Pakistan recently to play. It was an event called Cricket for Peace.

Police have beaten me several times. They beat me once while I was sleeping. I do mime for the Jamghat in which I portray what the police do.

Whenever I feel like rambling I go to my old hangouts. I still see my old friends. I take a bus but do not pay the fare.

I have seen the whole capital without paying any fare. I have travelled to many cities without a ticket. I have been to Mumbai, Haridwar and Dehradun.

I am living with kids like myself and I am very happy. I think I will study well and then help children like myself. (BBC, 2004, online)

We can see from this that the 'Street Children' drama acts as a metaphor for now and enables us to open up issues that may be hindered by prejudice in a way that uses history as a prism through which to view global issues.

Summary of points to consider

- There are tensions between history and drama but they can be resolved by adopting a conceptual framework that is clear about the learning intentions
- Research is a key element in planning roles from history
- Using a variety of sources helps to support the validity of the work
- It is important to be clear about what you mean when you use the word empathy in relation to drama and history teaching
- Using signifiers, not full costume, when taking on a role allows you to come in and out of role
- Reference to modern day parallels allows you to make the connections between then and now

7 How to Begin Using Assessment of Speaking and Listening (and Other English Skills) through Drama

We went through a very interesting and useful process in beginning this chapter. The two of us were initially unclear as to what exactly a chapter on drama and assessment would contain. We have in our work used many approaches and many ideas for the philosophy and practice of assessment.

To help our thinking and planning for the chapter we decided to bring in another perspective and met with a colleague, Tony Martin, from English teaching, a very respected and published practitioner, nationally and internationally. Before we met we gave him a draft of Chapter 3 on generating speaking and listening so he had some context.

The result of the hour-long discussion, much of it focused through looking at drama work with pupils on video, was that we had the powerful sort of dialogue, exchange of ideas, challenge of assumptions, that we are putting forward in this book. The conversation confirmed to us the centrality of speaking and listening for developing learning for all of us. It was a model in itself of why talking through ideas, understanding our thoughts through discussion, is so valuable.

As a result, we had a much clearer idea of how we see assessment, and the chapter reflects that thinking.

What is assessment?

> The primary aim of assessment is to provide information about the development and achievement of those involved in the teaching and learning situation. Assessment records evidence related to students' abilities, both actual and potential, and charts their progression. The intended audience of assessment feedback should always include the students themselves. (Clark and Goode, 1999, p. 15)

We are looking at how best to obtain the information on the students' abilities in Speaking and Listening.

Drama is not just about speaking and listening, but the creation of a fiction, where the art form of drama is essential and the success of that enterprise depends on valuable interaction between all participants. However, we must stress we are primarily looking at assessing speaking and listening, the focus of this book, and we are *not* providing in this chapter a framework for the assessment of theatre skills, the art form of drama, for personal and social development, nor other learning areas that drama can address.

The currency of drama is speaking and listening and in its nature it is swift, fleeting and ephemeral. When trying to assess it we do not get a piece of tangible evidence in our hands. So how can we assess this process?

Some teachers say we should not be assessing speaking and listening at all because it is too complex a process. In addition, teachers often do not know the speaking and listening programmes of study and particularly the Speaking and Listening attainment levels of the English National Curriculum in any significant way. Where speaking and listening is assessed, there is a tendency to assess it not as an interactive situation, but as a very narrow construct, something that is not actually speaking and listening at all – the class talk. A talk by one pupil to the rest of the class does not usually involve dialogue, except, perhaps, at the end when there might be questions. In what sense is a talk like this speaking and listening? It is easier to assess, of course, because it is an isolated target, one person delivering a set structure in front of the teacher and class, a performance. This is not what we want to assess; we are interested in the fluid and often powerful exchanges that a drama brings.

Whatever the difficulties, we must consider assessing speaking and listening for very good reasons:

- How do we promote better speaking and listening unless we assess and reflect on the changes in pupils' handling of the medium?
- Are we being fair to those pupils who demonstrate ability in this area if we do not honour their abilities, especially if they lack success in other areas?

These considerations have driven our own use of assessment of drama and speaking and listening for many years.

What do you look for?

Jim Clark and Tony Goode identify key ways that drama promotes speaking and listening:

Drama as a context for speaking and listening

- Negotiating and co-operating with others in the creation of drama work and the roles within it
- Expressing imaginative ideas when contributing to the drama work development
- Taking and using effectively the opportunities within the drama that require oral and aural communication
- Modifying, selecting and relating language and vocabulary to the changing roles, moods and situations in the drama work
- Controlling effectively oral and aural communication particularly in challenging sequences of drama work, e.g. questioning, dilemmas, unfair or emotional situations
- Responding with enjoyment and enthusiasm to the exploration of speech, gesture and sound
- Contributing effectively to critical evaluation of their own work and that of others

(Clark and Goode, 1999, p. 22)

We would add to that:

- Reflecting on the meaning of the fiction both within and outside the drama.

If we believe that drama offers all these opportunities to promote speaking and listening, we cannot neglect its assessment.

What is the purpose of the assessment?

To:

- give feedback to the pupil
- report to another teacher
- report to a parent

As we have indicated, the first is vital. Pupils need to know what they are doing, how they can improve and to be encouraged in speaking and listening, after all it is the primary communication skill.

Formative assessment – honouring what children can do

Since the inception of the National Curriculum, assessment of Speaking and Listening has been formative and informal. We would not change that approach. Our approach is not to produce league tables, but to give a snapshot of pupils' communication skills in order to recognise achievement and to chart possible development. The prime requirement on teachers when doing assessments is to listen to the pupils and to look carefully at the activity.

In the formative role of assessment we need to be feeding back to the pupils during and after the drama. We might stop a drama and say to everyone, *Can you see what Nafisa's question made the Soldier say? That is very important here. Let's see what the outcome is.* Then we are building esteem and boosting achievement.

How do we collect data more formally?

It is not easy and not necessarily useful to assess with reference to fixed lists of criteria. The approach has to be more than ticking a set of boxes, because if we do that we are often going to miss the point. The power of the language exchange is contextual. (See the example we look at later in this chapter, p. 87.)

A simple starting point might be to grasp the level of comprehension of a passage read to the class. One way of doing this is to go into role as a character from the book and take questions from the class. You will get a better understanding of what the class have understood than if you ask them questions about the passage. You can note afterwards key exchanges and contributions by members of the class.

Assessment in this context is the detailed study of episodes of speaking and listening. We need to describe what we see and teachers need to operate as researchers of the dialogue in their classrooms. Educational research is becoming more encouraging of detailed description of events, particularly when looking at classrooms in the action research method we are advocating.

We must gather and record the critical incidents and chart whatever we notice. Teachers can work in pairs and observe each other's lessons to record what they see. Some Preparation, Planning and Assessment (PPA) time, which teachers in England are entitled to, could be used for this purpose. To set this up properly, the senior management team need to become involved in planning a whole school strategy for the assessment and development of speaking and listening.

One teacher can be freed to observe a partner. The pair target a particular time in the year and work for each other. With A as a critical friend, a lesson or lessons can be carried out by B and the events are logged by the observer A, as well as noted afterwards by B. Then they reverse roles for the other class.

How do we manage the thick data that we collect? The observer will tell the story of the lesson and what it shows. The participant teacher of the lesson can also note what he or she saw and understood. From the evidence, judgements need to be made of the speaking and listening and pupil profiles built up based on the thinking and the empathy demonstrated during a drama. Further evidence is collected by the class teacher from other contexts to check out whether what has been observed in the drama is unique to that context or a general tendency and ability.

For the development of speaking and listening, we need to regard the class as colleagues. The class is creating the work with us and they will only develop their skills if they are provided with rich environments in the dramas by the teacher, especially working in role. If you consider the example later in this chapter, the teacher's responses and management of the language opportunities are key in generating good quality contributions from the class.

Other issues to consider

How do we judge whether a pupil is demonstrating the ability to listen? We often only allow that a pupil is demonstrating engagement in talk when they contribute and demonstrate they have listened. There are other signs of listening. We must learn to read body language, including facial expressions during the drama. If a pupil only speaks once we must look at that single contribution and at other evidence drawn or written after the event to see what they know from the drama. That will show how they have listened.

We have to manage the exchanges in a drama so that the naturally dominant voices in the classroom learn to listen and we allow others space to talk. However, there is an unhelpful myth about speaking and listening that speaking is the major partner, with the accompanying vain aim for classroom talk that all must contribute equally. It is important to remember that not all class members are ever going to contribute in the same way; some members will listen more and make one key observation that needs to be noted for what it shows. Such pupils may distil ideas in a way that frequent contributors fail to do because they do not listen as well. Other class members are naturally quiet and we will not change people's personalities so we should not expect them to be as vociferous.

Capturing the samples of speaking and listening

There is readily available technology that can record work and allow us to consider it at greater length after the event, particularly video recording. This is an approach we have been taking for a long time now; it provides evidence that we use to assess our own performance as teachers working in drama. Again, if teachers are paired to do the assessment, one can handle the camera while the other teaches.

Some teachers object to the use of video recording on the grounds that it distorts the drama process. Our experience is contrary to that. If it is used frequently and if it is negotiated with the class, they soon forget the camera and the work continues in its spontaneity. In fact, if anything, we find that it helps raise the status of the work and aids concentration levels.

Analysing video recordings of drama we need to look at issues relating to:

• the language used
• the non-verbal communication

- proximity to the teacher – who are the invisible pupils, the outsiders of the drama who do not seem in any way engaged?
- the empathetic and affective tendencies of pupils, their speech and their actions as they intervene.

We will now look at a transcript from a video recording of a drama lesson at a key moment and consider the way it can be assessed. This is from a session using 'The Highwayman' drama with a class of mixed 8- and 9-year-olds; it occurs after first meeting Tim the Ostler, in the inn. It is the end of some discussion out of role about what Tim is like and what is happening. Previously, when asked his name, TiR as Tim has answered, *Tim, but I wish it wasn't*. The class are sitting on chairs facing Tim's chair. At this point teacher OoR is standing up talking to the class.

ToR: *Do you want to ask him any other questions?* [pause] *What did he say to you when you spoke to him about the stables and so on? Did he say anything a bit odd?* [pause] *What's he looking like anyway? How is he looking?*

Rosie: *Upset.*

Chloe: *Under the weather.*

ToR: *He's certainly described as being.* [that is, in the poem, of which they have read the first part before starting the drama]. *He doesn't look as though he's very well at all.*

Neil: *You know the lights changed. Did that mean they were going back in time?*

ToR: *It does, yes.*

Charlie: *He couldn't see the time fly by.*

Teacher: *So they're back in his time. So it is the stables at the back. So what do you want to ask him?* [pause] *He's not very happy. He's been muttering about the horses. What do you want to ask him? Because you, as historians, can find a lot about the legend.*

Alan: *Why don't you like your name?*

ToR: *Do you want to start again? You ask him that and then if you've got any other questions ...*

TiR as Tim: *Yes?*

Alan: *Why don't you like your name?*

TiR as Tim: *I wish I wasn't me at the moment. Something terrible's happened. Oh, I don't know what to do.*

Neil: *Is the Highwayman still around?*

TiR as Tim: *What do you mean? What do you know about him? What do you mean? I don't know no Highwayman. I've never seen him. I've heard about him. I've never seen him.*

Ruth: *What's bothering you?*

TiR as Tim: [drops voice] *It's the soldiers. We need to keep very quiet. There's a lot of soldiers arrived here.*

Charlie: *We think we know why. As the Highwayman's ...*

TiR as Tim: *Shush! Shush! Shush! The soldiers are here. Don't ... Keep quiet. They're out the back having a meeting apparently.*

Charlie: [whispers and leans forward towards Tim conspiratorially, mirrored by other children in the class] *They're here because they're trying to get the Highwayman. The Highwayman stole some gold for the landlord's daughter to get the keys.*

The following analysis is written by the teacher who was leading this session.

There are a number of critical moments to assess here. As the teacher I was looking for a way of raising the tension and you can see I am out of role outlining certain key atmosphere setting points about Tim: *He's not very happy. He's been muttering about the horses. What do you want to ask him? Because you, as historians, can find a lot about the legend.* My intention is to engage them more fully with Tim and then with his dilemma about whether to tell on the Highwayman to the soldiers, which is the central focus of the drama at this point.

Alan's contribution is worth assessing for its value. He seems to have been thinking about what Tim said before we stopped and out of the blue says he wants to raise the issue with Tim. He is not responding to what I have immediately said, but is taking us back to the previous conversations with Tim and may be picking up on what the two girls have observed about how Tim is, *Upset. Under the weather.* It is a gift for me running the drama as I can use his focus on what Tim is complaining about to connect to the issues I want to emerge in the drama so I go straight back into role and take his question.

Alan is not the most vocal member of the group so for him to volunteer to lead in on the next part is good; he is also not the most able academically so this is a significant contribution from him. He is interpreting what Tim said and showing possible level 4 attributes on the Speaking & Listening Levels – 'talk adapted to purpose: developing ideas thoughtfully'. He has 'listened carefully' as I dropped in the *I wish I wasn't* as a throw-away line, almost inaudibly. In answering him in role I can expand on why Tim is wishing himself away, *something terrible's happened*, hinting at but not telling what is happening. Other members of the group are then able to interpret what this means and are keen to introduce the Highwayman themselves. Neil introduces the subject and at once the tension of the situation can be raised. Charlie is creative in developing ideas of what he thinks the soldiers and Highwayman are doing, *They're here because they're trying to get the Highwayman. The Highwayman stole some gold for the landlord's daughter to get the keys.*

The level of engagement in the drama for him is very high. He is introducing storyline ideas that are original to him and can be used by me in developing the drama later if the class agree to take on the ideas. He is operating within the parameters of the drama as I am setting them: he lowers his voice as Tim indicates the danger of open discussion with the soldiers there and is modelling for all of the class. The nature of the situation changes as these historians from the twenty-first century are drawn into the mesh of Tim's difficult situation. Alan's contribution can be seen to have opened this up and he can be rewarded for empathising with Tim from the previous exchange.

Pictures and captions

There are other models of recording what is created, using the current technology to freeze moments of the drama.

We can take digital photographs and project these onto a white board, where children can annotate what it means, showing their ideas by adding captions or notes of the speech by their roles, bubbles with the thoughts their roles might have at the moment, etc. If we go lower tech, drama techniques can be used to help the class themselves assess what is important. The class can look back over a drama and key moments can be recreated as tableaux. These can be added to with captions summing up what the picture means. This can help self-assessment by the children or peer assessment, when reflecting on their contributions to the drama work, because they are critically analysing what is important about what they have done.

Teachers should talk to children after drama sessions in order to elicit their understanding. Children need to reflect separately and together on the process. Then they will understand more about their own achievements in speaking and listening. Such discussions will provide yet more evidence of what has been going on, particularly the listening.

Talk for writing – the wholeness of communication

In a school with a strong policy on speaking and listening there will be major gains in other areas. We can get clear evidence for assessment of the effectiveness of speaking and listening, particularly the latter, from other forms of communication like writing or art work. In addition the writing itself can benefit.

It is important that the current re-write of the National Literacy Strategy for England locates Speaking and Listening central to the proper development of literacy skills, where the original version neglected to include them at all. All modes of language learning are influenced by the language we use every day and all the time in talk with others. There is clear research evidence that the spoken and written relate closely, the latter being dependent on the former for depth and detail.

Drama and its attendant speaking and listening has been shown to improve the writing of underachieving boys in a study in three local authorities in the UK:

Key findings

- The project has impacted not only on standards of boys' achievements in writing, but on teachers'/practitioners' professional development and capacity.
- The planning and teaching model with the integration of drama and/or visual approaches was successful in promoting marked and rapid improvements in standards of boys writing.

(UKLA, 2004, p. 2)

The project cited here was set up to do concentrated Literacy work involving more visual stimuli and drama.

Effects on speaking and listening:
The project emphasised the importance of speaking and listening as part of the writing process and, of course, used drama and role play as central themes in developing writing. (UKLA, 2004, p. 18)

Here are some outcomes observed by the teachers:

One teacher observed, 'the children have become more involved in the texts that we read' ...
'it was clear that those who use drama as part of their integrated planning were beginning to choose specific drama conventions suited to the overall learning intention.' (UKLA, 2004, p. 35)

'my planning now incorporates more drama – I've adapted it into the main part of the lessons as opposed to separate from Literacy lessons' ...
'I want to allow ideas to be worked out through drama: explored, refined, spoken through, and I'm going to use drama as a means to scaffold writing more frequently.' (UKLA, 2004, p. 36)

And the project report summarises:

> The expectation of many was that drama would become a regular – at least weekly – feature of Literacy and that in particular more work needed to be planned to prompt adults to model drama in order to support the children. (UKLA, 2004, p. 36)

Here are two examples from 10-year-old pupils of persuasive writing that were produced between two sessions on 'The Governor's Child'. The task set was to record the arguments in favour of or against helping Maria and the child, who are pursued by the soldiers.

Example One – An argument in favour of helping her:

Firstly, if anything happens to Maria it is our responsibility to take care of both of them.

Secondly, what if Maria is telling the truth and the soldier is lying? What would you do?

Furthermore would you like it if you and your baby's life was in danger?

If her life is in danger our life is in danger.

So you should tell the soldier to leave her and the baby.

If you spoil the baby's life now the baby's future will be spoilt.

We strongly believe that Maria and the baby are innocent and we will always support her. What would you do if you were in her state?

Example Two – A argument from the opposite viewpoint:

Why we should not keep Maria.

Do you want our whole village to give up all of their lives just because of that one Maria?

Whatever happens we won't let Maria stay in this village.

Lying does not happen in this village.

Why should we suffer just because of her?

How can we trust her when she lied to us?

She is not a member of this family so how can we trust her?

She has broken our family into pieces. She shouldn't stay here else she will make us extra trouble. She's proved she's a true liar.

If Maria doesn't give the baby to his mother she will feel guilty by ruining an innocent baby's life.

We can see from this work that the two 10-year-old children are very focused by the arguments that were rehearsed orally within the drama as the villagers discussed the decision as to what to do with Maria. They are able to record the ideas they were involved with and the pieces are informed by the passion that was displayed in role by the villagers. The writing has become a way of formalising the argument. In the first example the pupil has picked up the persuasive argument template: 'firstly, secondly, furthermore'. The second is more discursive but strong in its feeling.

This material can be used as further evidence if we were tracing how well members of a class have listened to the dialogue. In addition, they have been motivated to write by the drama and produced creditable pieces.

In conclusion, we know that assessing and recording speaking and listening is a demanding task, but we would contend that is no more demanding than other assessment if it is approached in the right way. Furthermore, we would maintain that the absence of evidence of pupils' speaking and listening in a school limits their progress in all areas of literacy and is depriving them of a key entitlement.

Summary of points to consider

- The nature of assessment of Speaking and Listening
- Taking account of the context and the interactions
- The purpose of the assessment
- Formative assessment – feeding back to the pupils
- Recording and analysing what we see
- Talk as the basis for writing

Part Two:

The Dramas

Introduction

These dramas are set up to develop Speaking and Listening for 7–11-year-olds. We have indicated the target ages, but some of the dramas, with some adjustment, have been used across the full age range we are catering for here. 'The Snow Queen' was even adapted for children of ages 5 and 6.

To show you the sort of work we think we are generating, we illustrate some of the areas of Speaking and Listening and the language demands made on participants during the dramas in this book:

Drama	Ages	Language areas
'The Wild Thing'– based on *Where the Wild Things Are* by Maurice Sendak	7–9	What is good and acceptable behaviour and what harms others Relationships between humans and with others Deductive language Interpreting evidence Avoiding anger and confrontation Comparing the drama to the picture book
'Daedalus and Icarus' – based on the Greek legend	7–9	Language of ancient technology Language of ancient architecture Language of parents and children Language of morality – secrets and/or lies
'The Snow Queen' – based on the story by Hans Christian Andersen	7–9	Poetic language Poetry reading Oral structure of poems, rhythm metre Power and language Geography/mapping
'Charlie' – based on *Voices in the Park* by Anthony Browne	7–9	Language of compliance Appropriate language to break down inappropriate compliance Class and language and culture Exploring children's private language Prejudice and challenging it
'The Maasai Boy'	7–10	Geographical language of various sorts of maps and places, of animals and people of another country, of artefacts and ways of life, of here and there About responsibility About ownership About gender and prejudice About difference and similarity About adults and children

Drama	Ages	Language areas
'The Governor's Child' – based on the *Caucasian Chalk Circle* by Bertolt Brecht	8–11	Language of community – and community under threat – the outsider Language relating to the power of a child – in relationships, i.e. mother or family or community Protection and lying Love and loyalty
'The Highwayman' – based on the poem by Alfred Noyes	9–11	Using evidence from poem Look into and understand – listen to … Persuasive language Appropriate language for handling a difficult/aggressive situation Comparing the characters and themes of the drama and the poem
'The Victorian Street Children' 'The Workhouse'	9–11 9–11	Use of archaic language To explore and identify moral standpoints Using the technical language of historians Usage of analytical language – to interpret and develop ideas from a primary source Use of empathetic language
'The Egyptians'	9–11	Language of archaeology Language of privilege and exclusion Religious language – ritual and ceremony Loyalty to family against faith
'Macbeth' based on the play by William Shakespeare	10–11	Playing with Shakespeare's language Use of language relating to power and powerlessness Language relating to trades and tasks – in an Elizabethan culture Symbolic language associated with witchcraft and 'murder'
'Ebenezer Scrooge' – based on *A Christmas Carol* by Charles Dickens	10–11	Language of journalism Language of epitaphs and eulogies Language of youth and testament and obituary Language and viewpoint Persuasion and supposition defence

Drama	Ages	Language areas
'Christopher Boone' based on *The Curious Incident of the Dog in the Night-Time* by Mark Haddon	10–11	Prejudice and challenging it Persuasive language Appropriate language for handling a difficult/aggressive situation Language as an indicator of personality traits Language of reconciliation
'The Dream' based on *A Midsummer Night's Dream* by William Shakespeare	10–11	An introduction to Shakespeare's language Dealing with a difficult and prejudiced person Using language diplomatically Dealing with a headstrong girl The language of relationships

The dramas are developed from materials related to three other areas: Literacy, the wider curriculum and PSHE and Citizenship. In the following table the bold type refers to the emphasis we have put in the example dramas. However, the other elements are also there and teachers may if they wish highlight those areas instead.

Drama	Relates to Literacy	Relates to PSHE and Citizenship	Relates to other curriculum areas (especially History)
'Wild Thing'– based on *Where the Wild Things Are* by Maurice Sendak	Themes and characters arising in the story can be compared to the drama	**The issue of class prejudice**	Geography – special layouts and journeys
'Daedalus and Icarus' – based on the Greek legend	Greek legend	**The consequences of being inquisitive Telling the truth to parents**	Technology in an historical context Leonardo Da Vinci's inventions Art and History
'The Snow Queen' – based on the story by Hans Christian Andersen	**Creating poetry with narrative Purpose of poems Poetic form**	Sibling relationships – loyalty, courage and jealousy	Geography – maps and climate.
'Charlie' – based on *Voices in the Park* by Anthony Browne	**Book as script/ differences in register**	Family, class and language	Art – illustration and reading pictures

Drama	Relates to Literacy	Relates to PSHE and Citizenship	Relates to other curriculum areas (especially History)
'The Maasai Boy'	Researching in non-fiction books and on the Internet Recording and reporting information	A child being punished for a mistake Ownership of cultural objects	**Geography – the study of distant place. Kenya and a particular place**
'The Governor's Child' – based on *The Caucasian Chalk Circle* by Bertolt Brecht	Text as a basis for drama	The power of a child in society	**Isolated communities – social implications of the outsider**
'The Highwayman' – based on the poem by Alfred Noyes	**Themes of Romantic Love and 'The Hero' Author's viewpoint Expressive/ descriptive language**	Choices in personal relationships	Poetry within an historical context (changing values/ mores)
'The Victorian Street Children'	Non-fiction texts and history, source material to understand and use words, fact and opinion	Children, poverty and society	**The historian as a researcher, sorting evidence, asking questions**
'The Workhouse'	Study of the rules and the language	Oppression of the weak	**History – can be local history based if you have material from the local workhouse – rules, names, etc.**
'The Egyptians'	Graphology and iconography	Personal choices and family/peer pressure	**Social stratification beliefs and ritual in Ancient Egypt**
'Macbeth' – based on the play by William Shakespeare	**A way of making accessible complex text in KS2 Shakespeare's language**	Issues of the consequences of actions	Using a painting to stimulate a shift back in time and create historical context.
'Ebenezer Scrooge' – based on *A Christmas Carol* by Charles Dickens	**Using pre-text to generate text How characters are presented**	Personality and character formation	Class and social attitudes in the nineteenth century

'Christopher Boone' – based on *The Curious Incident of the Dog in the Night-Time* by Mark Haddon	Exploration of from the book Compare extracts	**Presenting the view of the autistic child Inclusion**	ICT and plans of rooms Pictorial representation and re-enactment in Art
'The Dream' based on *A Midsummer Night's Dream* by William Shakespeare	**Introduction to the play, the language and the characters**	Parental power versus child's demand for independence	The Elizabethan context of the play Laws related to the history of the period

Timing the dramas

All of the dramas are designed to take at least two sessions. Most are written without defining those breaks because it depends how you want to split them up. Some teachers might want to run three 45-minute sessions. It also depends on how quickly you run the various activities. The rule is always to slow drama down, to look at what is happening, to encourage participants to be reflective. Some of the dramas here indicate where the useful divisions occur.

Learning objectives

We have not related learning objectives directly to National Curriculum, or National Literacy, or Primary National Strategy documents because that will not apply to all readers and those documents have changed and are changing as we write. We have raised some elements of QCA material. We indicate how we see the foci and allow you to choose how you see that relating to the National requirements. It is clear to us that drama fulfils many of them, especially with the current emphasis on encouraging more speaking and listening, and creative and cross-curricular approaches.

Contracting into dramas

All dramas begin with a contracting of the drama. Its nature depends on the experience of the participants.

When we indicate the need to 'negotiate doing drama' then a contract like this is envisaged:

I am going to introduce the drama we are going to do today. I am in it and you are in it. I will have a number of roles within the story.

I know how it begins but I don't know how it ends and your in-put will affect that.

Ask if there are any questions. We will stop the drama at various points to discuss what is happening and you can always ask to stop if you want to raise any points.

Is that OK? I am going to take my first role in the drama now and you will work out who you are in the drama from what I say.

What do you think are the rules that help make drama work properly?

Possible responses to the last point are: cooperation, listening to each other, respecting each other's views, contributing effectively and appropriately, asking when unsure of anything.

Gender of roles

The genders of teacher roles can be fluid in some cases and can fit the gender of the teacher taking the role. For example, in 'The Wild Thing' Max's sibling could be male or female. In 'The Victorian Street Children' the children could meet a gentleman or a lady. In other cases the role must be of a specific gender whatever that of the teacher. Max in 'The Wild Thing' betrays generally male behaviours and the drama was evolved to help boys look at that. His parent could be male or female, however. Macbeth is fixed, as is the Snow Queen and the genders in 'The Dream'.

This does not mean, however, that you need to have a teacher of that gender to play a fixed gender role. All that is needed in our experience is to negotiate that you are playing an opposite gender from the start and that in the fiction that will work because the group can help you by just accepting it. No voices are changed, no effort is made to be male or female in movement or stance. It is all in the attitude of the role. Otherwise, we play roles as ourselves.

Happy dramas!

'The Wild Thing'

A drama based on *Where the Wild Things Are* by Maurice Sendak

Learning objectives

Pupils will understand:

PSHE N.C. KS2

- 1a. how to talk and write about their opinions, and explain their views, on issues that affect themselves and society
- 2e. how to reflect on spiritual, moral, social and cultural issues, using imagination to understand other people's experiences

Refined to:

- respecting differences between people
- learning how their behaviour affects their parents

Research and preparation

?Lost & Found?

- Create a logo for the Lost & Found Agency similar to this
- Source the objects you need. See point 7.

Roles

	Role	Signifier
Teacher	Organiser of Lost & Found Max Mother Sister/Brother Creature	Clip board Cap and toy creature A bag containing something of Max's Big coat Toy creature
Pupils	Lost & Found agents	N/A

Structure

1. Negotiate doing drama

Contract

I am going to introduce the drama we are going to do today. I am in it and you are in it. I know how it begins but I don't know how it ends and your input will affect that.

Is that OK? I am going to take my first role in the drama now and you will work out who you are in the drama from what I say.

2. TiR as Organiser of Lost & Found

TiR sets context

(Lost & Found logo on the wall and clipboard)

I am impressed with the performance of our teams yesterday. I want to congratulate you on helping that 6-year-old who was lost yesterday in the supermarket and also for tracing the 3-year-old who had wondered off from her house.

OoR: *What is happening? Where are we in the drama and who are you?*

How did the Lost Child centre find the parents for the boy and find the girl who wandered off?

What sort of skills do you have? What makes someone good at finding people?

Building belief in pupil role

Go on to elaborate on what had happened and how the Lost & Found personnel had used their skills. The class can create the scenarios, verbally or in still image.

3. Set up roles and activities in the office

4. TiR as Organiser of Lost & Found

I have to go to an important meeting with the Council about some more money to help us so you'll need to look after any issues that come up for this morning, but you can contact me on the mobile.

They get on with their work.

5. TiR as Mother (Mrs Jackson)

Enters in a panic muttering to herself ands plonks herself on a chair.

He has run away. I know it. What am I going to do? [muttering to herself]

TiR raises expectation and builds context

OoR – [if they do not speak to her]: *What has happened? What do you need to do?*

Mother is interviewed and tells what Max has done.

ROLE BRIEF

Mother

She is reluctant to tell to start with because she knows she shouldn't let him get away with what he does. They have to be canny to get to the truth. She sent him to his room without tea and when she went to take his tea up later there was no one there.

Her attitude to the naughtiness is excusing him:
He is just a boy, full of fun and likes playing a lot.

I blame his sister who always nags him and tries to stop him doing things.

She wants them to come round to see his room where he was last night when he disappeared.

6. Narration

The team immediately took Max's Mother back to her house.

Mother leads them in and then leaves.

7. At the room

Use 'define the space' to get the class to define the basics in the room, but add the givens as the clues to what Max is like and what has happened:

A pirate ship, pictures of the jungle, piece of fur, broken toy, a teddy hung up by arm, upside-down dog bowl with toasting fork.

Drawings and notes by Max.

A den made with a blanket draped over two chairs.

Notes from Max including the three shown here. The first is lying with the pictures of tropical islands; the second is folded up and put on the pirate ship where it can just be seen; the third is poking out from the den.

Where shall I go?	I wish I could go sailing on my pirate ship and then I would be able to do wicked things and make people do what I say	I hate my Mum

OoR discuss how investigators would approach this.

8. Making sense of the evidence

They look at the evidence and interpret what it shows.

They make some speculations and plan what to do next.

9. Hot-seating Mother (Mrs Jackson)

They can ask to see Mother and ask her any questions.

(*Optional* strategy at this point: Thought-track Mother when she sees the 'hate' letter.)

If the pupils offer anything, like *Does he have a secret place?*, TiR as Mother must pick up on it. If not, Mother must offer that he has talked about an empty shed somewhere and she is not sure where. She must see if they create some sort of idea of a place they think he might be from the evidence

Margin labels: Define the space + set problem; Use of written input

in the room, like the park, a zoo. Then she says, *Oh yes, I remember he did mention water nearby* OR *He said the trees were massive*, etc. and ask if they can go down and have look to see if there is a shed, adding *But be careful he does not run away if he hears you coming.*

10. Role on the wall 1: Max

Role on the the Wall

After interview collect their judgements, views and perceptions of Max.

11. Narration

The investigators quickly and quietly made their way to the ??? [insert the relevant place *park, zoo* that they suggest] *where they see a shed which was in some very tangled brambles and overhung by trees.*

Mark out the shape of the shed. The class 'hide' all round it.

Do the creeping up on the place like a game of 'keeper of the keys'.

One of them is about to open the door when …

OoR: *I am going to be someone who comes along to the shed at this moment while you are hiding. I want you to watch and listen to this person then we will talk about who it is.*

12. TiR as brother/sister

Raise the tension

Narrate: *They hear a noise and know that someone is coming – they hide in their places to wait and see who comes.*

A figure huddled in a big coat comes in. (The role can be either gender depending on the teacher. We will write it from here on as a girl.) She is talking to herself.

Sister: *My brother – Disappeared! Huh! What is she like, letting him run away? I bet he's hiding in here. She lets him get away with everything. And he gets more than I do.*

The Lost & Found agents approach and surround the figure to make sure whoever it is cannot get away.

It turns out to be Susie (or Tony), Max's sister (brother).

ROLE BRIEF

Sibling role

Susie is very much against Max and how he behaves, bullying her, getting her into trouble, damaging things. She is against the Wolf suit, etc.

She shows them photos of what he was doing yesterday – pictures from the book of Max chasing the dog and hammering a nail in the wall.

She assumes they have come to sort him out and make her life better. How she responds depends on how the class treat her.

They finally get out of her that he had muttered something about a boat, but he was always fantasising anyway and he only has the toy pirate ship, which he won't allow anyone else to play with.

She'll wait here and let them know if he comes here: *You go and tell Mum.*

13. Narration

The investigators return to Max's room where they tell Mother.

She is upset he is not found and exits.

TiR main role- Opposer

14. Role on the wall 2.

Add further ideas to Max's role outline in the light of what has happened.

15. TiR as Max (main role)

Make sure the class are gathered round the piece of paper looking at the Role on the Wall. As they discuss, Max arrives in the room behind them.

What are you all doing in my room? How dare you come in here without my permission? I am the King of the Wild Things and I am VERY powerful.

Main tension point

I have come back to get a fork to chase the Wild Things.

I will have such fun and they will shout when I stick it in them.

But you get out of here, out of my room.

OoR: *Who is this and what is he like? What are you going to say to him? What do you need to do now?*

If the investigators don't go, Max must shout for his mother and be expecting her to get rid of them. When she does not come he starts towards the door.

TiR: *I must get back to the island.*

I am going away again now and need my fork.

He says he hasn't got time for them and is just going to go to the kitchen to pack some food for the journey back. Exits.

16. Max on the island

Create moving pictures

In order to understand more about Max the Lost & Found agents create the story of Max on the island in groups by creating moving pictures (tableaux with one movement and one line for each role depicted) of what Max did as a King with the Wild Things.

Go OoR to discuss what the agents should do. Their job now is to try to make sure he stays, to stop him leaving and to argue the case that he must stay to talk to his mother.

17. Extra challenge

TiR extra challenge (optional)

Narrate: *As they decide how to deal with Max they hear a sneeze from the den.*

Negotiate becoming another role. Hide in the den.

This is a creature, Yagmur, from the Wild Things land.

> ### *Yagmur*
>
> This role has *come to fetch the King back to his loyal servants who are so sad since he left.* The creature is full of energy and excitement at having found where the King lives, when the Lost & Found agents reveal he is here.

As they persuade the creature to come out Yagmur appears from the den.

TiR as Yagmur: *Have you seen the King? I have to see him now if his Majesty will grant me an audience.*

As the Lost & Found agents interview the creature they discover:

He was so good to us. He could dance and sing and howl and was so bossy.

We miss him so much. He must come back as all the creatures are very down.

OoR: *What does this show us about Max?*

What do you do? Do you tell the creature he is here? Should he go back?

The Lost & Found agents must resolve the situation and get rid of the creature so that Max can stay here and learn to live properly with his family.

How do they get rid of the creature?

18. Giving advice – tackling Max and Mother

After getting rid of the creature … they set up the room for the meeting between the two.

Set up two chairs for the two roles in the room.

Forum
Theatre
The
resolution

Put the signifiers for each on the chairs and talk to the Lost & Found agents that *the time has come to give your advice to each of these two.*

(*Optional*: this can be done with the class speaking to Mother at least part of the time as sister. Set it up by saying: *The agents bring in her daughter, Susie, to give evidence of what she sees happening between her mother and Max.*

The same goes for the arguments to Max:

Susie wanted the chance to put her views to Max and the agents gave her the opportunity.

Advice to Mother

They talk to Mother (TiR) first and tell her of Max's return plus give advice on how she should handle him.

She will ask for details about where he's been, etc. She does not believe where he has been. Mum is upset and wants them to sort him out, to make sure he stays and behaves himself. She will do her part,

I'll tell him, 'If you don't go I'll make sure you don't regret it. I'll buy you a big present, whatever you want.'

She must begin to listen to their advice if they are clear about how she indulges him on the one hand and then is hard on him at other times and is inconsistent.

They must get Mother to see how she should handle him.

Advice to Max

Max (TiR) wants to have a big row with his mother about her *letting these people into my room without my permission.*

He thinks he can do what he likes: *The dog enjoys being chased. I was only playing.*

The Lost & Found investigators have to calm him down and try to get him to see what he is doing and that his mother missed him, etc. They must get him to learn how to behave and has to treat his toys and pets. They must get him to understand he has to be responsible and give up his Wolf suit and ways.

(*Optional:* Have the class sculpt how he should be with the dog, toys, his mother).

He begins to listen a bit if they show him the effects he is having on his mother and sister. He is not going to be easy to persuade and it might be they have to leave the situation uncertain of how it will be in the future.

Structured summary

1 **Negotiate doing drama.**

2 **TiR as organiser of Lost & Found.**

   I want to congratulate you on helping that 6-year-old and the 3-year-old ...

   OoR: *What is happening? Where are we in the drama and who are you? What sort of skills do you have? What makes someone good at finding people?*

   Go on to elaborate on what had happened.

3 **Set up roles and activities in the office.**

4 **TiR as Organiser of Lost & Found.**

   You'll need to look after any issues that come up for this morning.

5 **TiR as Mother.**

   Enters in a panic muttering to herself and plonks herself on a chair.

   OoR [if they do not speak to her]: *What has happened? What do you need to do?*

   Mother is interviewed and tells what Max has done.

6 **Narration.**

   The team immediately took Max's Mother back to her house.

7 **At the room.**

   Use 'define the space' and add the given objects.

   OoR discuss how investigators would approach this.

8 **Making sense of the evidence.**

They look at the evidence and interpret what it shows. They plan what to do next.

9 **Hot-seating Mother.**

They can ask to see Mother and ask her any questions.

(*Optional* strategy at this point: Thought-track Mother when she sees the 'hate' letter.)

10 **Role on the wall 1: Max.**

11 **Narration.**

The investigators quickly and quietly made their way to the ??? [insert the relevant place *park, zoo* that they suggest].

Mark out the shape of the shed. The class 'hide' all round it.

Do the creeping up on the place like a game of 'keeper of the keys'.

One of them is about to open the door when …

12 **TiR as brother/sister.**

[They hear a noise and know that someone is coming.]

A figure huddled in a big coat comes in. The Lost & Found agents approach and surround the figure to make sure whoever it is cannot get away. It is Susie/Tony, Max's sister/ brother.

She'll wait here and let them know if he comes here: *You go and tell Mum.*

13 **Narration.**

The investigators return to Max's room where they tell Mother.

14 **Add further ideas to Max's role on the wall.**

15 **TiR as Max.**

Make sure they are gathered round the piece of paper – Max arrives.

What are you all doing in my room? How dare you come in here without my permission?

If the investigators don't go, Max must shout for his mother and ask her to get rid of them and then to disappear herself.

He says he hasn't got time and is just going to go to the kitchen to pack some food for the journey back. Exits.

16 **Max on the island.**

In order to understand more about Max the Lost & Found agents create the story of Max on the island in groups by creating moving pictures of what Max did as a King.

Go OoR to discuss what the agents should do. The class need to stop him leaving and argue he must stay to talk to his mother.

17 **Extra challenge** (*optional*)

As they decide how to deal with Max they hear a sneeze from the den ...

This is a creature, Yagmur, from the Wild Things land.

How do they get rid of the creature?

18 **Giving advice – tackling Max and Mother.**

Set up two chairs for the two roles in the room.

Advice to Mother.

Advice to Max.

(*Optional*: Have the class sculpt how Max should be with the dog, toys, Mother.)

Additional material for other drama starters based on *Where the Wild Things Are*

1. Children as experts on Wild Things

Learning objectives

- Science – about researching and studying animals
- English – non-fiction writing
- PSHE – treating animals with respect

Contact role

Person who has seen a new species of wild creature

Context

(1) Create a Wild Thing Experts' office

Researchers

Telephonists

The experts plan a book on Wild Things – experts on different aspects of monsters

Each group takes a section

- How to catch

- How to tame

- How to groom

Each group decides and teaches the other groups how to do the skills.

'Wanted' posters designed about specific dangerous monsters

OR

(2) Setting up an expedition to study Wild Things in their habitat

Each group responsible for a different aspect of the expedition

- Maps routes and navigation
- Equipment for studies
- Safety

Play at

- Preparing equipment
- Choosing transport
- Planning route
- Planning studies

Key moment later

Max returns from the land of the Wild Things.

He goes to see the experts, to tell them he knows where new Wild Things to study live. He wants to go with them to see the Wild Things captured. He wants to make fun of them, to humiliate them.

The experts' job is to take him and show him the error of his ways.

2. The Boat Builders

Learning objectives

As for the full drama.

Contact role

Max.

Context – A boatyard

Building a boat:

- Working at tasks
- Designers
- Carpenters
- Sail makers
- Painters

Max approaches the Boat Builders for a boat to travel to a far-off land.

He gives them a contract to sign with a secrecy clause in it: *Don't tell anyone I came here.*

They work on the boat and give him a big send-off.

Key moment later

His mother visits the Boat Builders to find out if Max has been there.

He has taken money from her special savings box.

Do they lie to Mother? What about the contract?

Following Max to the Island to get him back.

They find a very sad boy sitting on the shore, but who pretends he is very happy on the Island when they approach.

'Daedalus and Icarus'

A drama based on the Greek legend

Learning objectives
Pupils will understand:

- the significance of legends as a focus for Literacy work
- legends as part of historical understanding

PSHE

- consequences of actions (on taking the folder of drawings)
- father/child relationship and disobedience
- the consequences of keeping secrets

Research and preparation

- The legend of Daedalus and Icarus
- Pictures of the Palace of King Minos at Knossos
- Leonardo da Vinci drawings of flight and flying machines to make up a folder on flight for the inventor Daedalus
- Greek alphabet to transliterate the title 'FLIGHT' and the phrase 'The Palace of King Minos at Knossos'

(See bibliography and possible sources at the end of this chapter.)

Roles

	Role	Signifier
Teacher	Minos Daedalus Icarus	Sceptre Metre rule Small ball
Pupils	Servants of Minos	N/A

Structure

Contract

1. **Negotiate doing drama**

Stimulus

2. **Pictures of the Palace of King Minos at Knossos**

   Show and discuss these. *Our drama begins here.*

   Get them to puzzle out the Greek lettered phrase.

   This palace is the home of King Minos.

   When do you think he ruled?

   In the drama you are his servants ... What do you think you do as his servants?

3. Set up the Palace and routines

Possible jobs – cleaning, cooking, wine-making, gardening, looking after clothes, guarding.

4. TiR as Minos

> ## *King Minos*
>
> His concern is to preserve the secrets of the Minotaur which Daedalus knows about (the myth does not feature in this drama except as pre-text. It might be useful to read that story as the drama develops).
> Thus he is anxious to keep him and Icarus prisoner and sets up his servants to watch them.
> He is played as a clear authority figure but trusting his servants and expecting them to be loyal to him.
> He interacts with the servants as they work and stresses how important it is that they look after his guests well. Play it as strict but fair.

OoR: . . . *tell me about this man.*

5. Observed event

OoR: *Here is some other evidence of how King Minos is at this time ...*

They witness TiR as Minos talking to himself in his sleep. Lie on the floor and then wake up as out of a nightmare.

What if he tells? I must keep an eye on him.

OoR discuss what they have witnessed and what it might mean.

6. Minos has a plan

King Minos addresses his servants:

You are my most trusted servants and I have summoned you to tell you of a special job I have for you.

You know I have the famous inventor Daedalus working for me. He is working on a special invention for my guests, but I think he is also doing something else, secretly. I want you to keep an eye on him and see what he is doing. You can do that easily as you are in all parts of the Palace at all times. And make sure that he and his son, Icarus, don't get off the island ... What do you need to do? Report back to me in a week's time.

7. TiR as Icarus

TiR setting
key
dilemma

The servants also have another job. They have to help look after Icarus and they play ball with him.

Set up role as Icarus. Play a game with the servants and then sit down with them.

I've got a secret. Can I trust you?

Shows his father's folder on flight which he does not understand. The servants have to interpret the pictures. (You need the folder of pictures of the drawings by Leonardo da Vinci of his flying machines and drawings of wings, etc.)

8. TiR as Daedalus

TiR raises
the tension

They are interrupted by Daedalus looking for Icarus and his folder. Do this by putting down the ball Icarus has and saying:

OoR, *The servants are all with Icarus in the room looking at the folder when this happens.*

Then pick up the Daedalus role signifier, a metre rule, and walk away from the group. Bang the stick and say:

TiR: *Icarus, where are you? I need to talk with you. This place is a maze of corridors. I know you are here somewhere, but I can't find you.*

OoR: *What does Icarus do? He cannot get out of here without passing where his father is. How should he answer and what should he say to his father?*

9.

Forum
theatre –
ownership
for pupils

Set up a forum theatre – two chairs facing each other at a short distance and the class seated either side of the gap. They will have the chance to sit on the Icarus seat and try ways of dealing with it. The key issue is whether he should lie or tell the truth about taking the folder of drawings.

How does Icarus handle this?

Possible directions

- How does Icarus get the folder back to Daedalus?
- Does Daedalus find out that Icarus has told the servants the secret?

10. Facing Daedalus

Servants are called to Daedalus. Are they accused of knowing what is in the file if Icarus owns up? What happened to the file?

11. Facing Minos

Servants are called to Minos to report what they have found out. Do they tell?

Possible subsequent directions and teacher inputs to raise tension

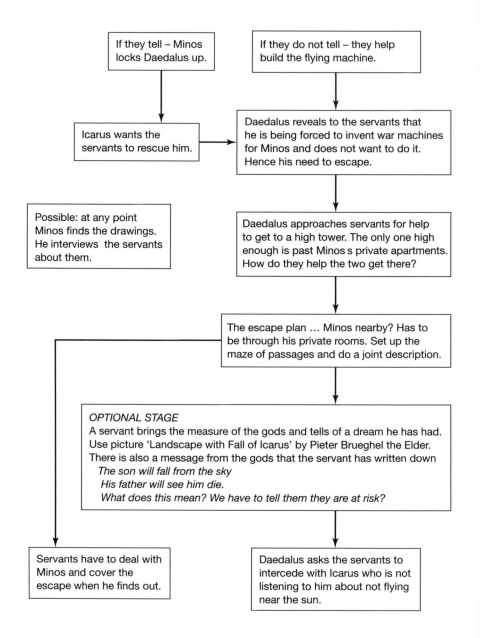

12. Final stage (especially if you do not have time for the above)

Tableaux
possible
outcomes

Class groups show how they think it would end – two tableaux, one showing success and one failure for Daedalus and Icarus.

Structure summary

1 Negotiate doing drama.

2 Pictures of the Palace of King Minos at Knossos.
Show and discuss these.

3 Set up the Palace and routines.
Discuss possible jobs.

4 Introduce TiR as Minos.
He interacts with the servants as they work.
OoR: ... tell me about this man.

5 Observed event.
They witness Minos talking to himself in his sleep.
OoR: ... discuss what they have witnessed and what it might mean.

6 Minos has a plan.
The servants will spy on Daedalus.

7 TiR as Icarus.
The servants also have another job, to help look after Icarus, and then Icarus shows them his father's folder on flight.

8 TiR as Daedalus.
They are interrupted by Daedalus looking for Icarus and his folder.
OoR: What does Icarus do?

9 Set up a forum theatre of Icarus and his father.

10 Facing Daedalus.
Servants are called to Daedalus. Are they accused of knowing what is in the file if Icarus owns up? What happened to the file?

11 Facing Minos.
Servants are called to Minos to report what they have found out. Do they tell?

12 Final stage.
Class groups show how they think it would end – two tableaux, one showing success and one failure.

Bibliography and Sources

Minoans
A Closer Look at ... *MINOANS* (J. Heath, London, Hamish Hamilton, 1979).
Palaces – Amazing Buildings (P. Wilkinson, London, Dorling Kindersley, 1993).
The Mediterranean (P. Wilkinson and J. Dineen, Limpsfield, Dragon's World Ltd, 1992).
The Knossos Labyrinth (R. Castleden, London, Routledge, 1990).

Leonardo

A useful Leonardo website which gives a list of artwork of inventions is
www.museoscienza.org/english/leonardo/invenzioni.html
Leonardo and the Flying Boy (Laurence Anholt, London, Frances Lincoln Ltd, 2003).

Books for the legend

Daedalus and Icarus (P. Farmer, London, Collins, 1971).
Heroes and Monsters (J. Reeves, London, Piper, 1993).
Greek Myths and Legends (J.Snelling, Hove, Wayland, 1987).

'The Snow Queen'

A drama based on the story by Hans Christian Andersen

Learning objectives

Pupils will understand:

- how to create new versions of a well-known narrative
- how to create oracy related to a traditional story
- the poetry structure called a cinquain
- the use of symbolism in poetry

Roles

	Role	Signifier
Teacher	Chief Superhelper Gerda Kai Signifier The Snow Queen	Clip board Shawl Hat Map Crown
Pupils	Superhelpers	N/A

Research and preparation

- A map showing the Land of Ice and Snow
- A picture of the Snow Queen
- An overhead of the letter from Gerda

Structure

1. Negotiate doing drama

Contract

Set the rules with the pupils. Have they been Superhelpers before? Set the children up as people who help children who are in trouble ... Discuss what does it mean to help people?

Set up the agency offices ... What would it be like? Each group has their own area ... What does it look like? What happens there? Have them show themselves working on problems.

2.   TiR as Chief Superhelper

TiR sets up the problem

Calls them to his (or her) office to hear about a letter he has received.

TiR: *I want you to hear this.*

Reads the letter.

Dear Superhelpers

I am very worried. I know you have helped people before and I need your help now.

I cannot write down what is wrong. I need to talk to you. We need to meet here in the Land of Ice and Snow. But it is dangerous.

I have a special rhyme to keep me safe:

> Dream of sun and warmth and light
> Think of fire and heat
> You will then survive the night
> Have drink and food to eat.

Anyone who comes here must have one. Could you please make one about the things that keep you warm?

You must not tell anyone about your visit and you must not enter the Land without me. I'll be waiting at the bridge that crosses the Great River in two sleeps' time. You will know it is me because you will recognise my chant.

> Yours Faithfully
>
> Gerda

TiR: *What a mystery! I do not know what this means but I want you to tell me what it means. What must we do before you set out to help?*

3.   ToR: They discuss what they need to write to protect them

Writing to build belief

All the poems must have the theme of keeping warm and opposing the cold.

Depending upon the level and experience of the class, there are three possible approaches:

Approach 1: Have a pre-written poem in which the class have to finish two of the lines. For example,

> Keep away the snow and ice,
> Make us feel warm and …
> To help us safely on our way,
> Protect us night and …

Approach 2: Make a class poem using four lines – rhyming or not

Approach 3: Use the structure of a cinquain

5 lines
> 2 syllables
> 4 syllables
> 6 syllables
> 8 syllables
> 2 syllables

For example:

> Keep warm,
>
> Light a good fire,
>
> Feed it with clean, dry wood,
>
> Wrap up with clothes against the cold,
>
> Stay safe.

Work on the rhyme and practise chanting it together.

4. TiR as Chief Superhelper

TiR sets
context

You gather the Superhelpers around and tell them you have researched some information about the Land of Ice and Snow.

I have been looking at an old book and there is story of the Land the note speaks of. I think it might help us.

The Land of Ice and Snow was not always like that. Before the great cold came life in the Land was simple, where people lived off the land, where crops sometimes failed but not often, where people were experts at tending animals and were successful farmers.

Then suddenly came the great freeze bringing perpetual winter.

OoR: *What were the effects? The people were very clever. How did the people adapt?*

You may want to use a picture of the Snow Queen and talk about what kind of person she seems to be.

5. Map of the Land of Ice and Snow

Context
building

As a class you can create a map on a piece of paper. (You can have one prepared already if you wish to include certain content and to speed the drama up.) This will contain the information from the letter and the position of the Snow Queen's castle.

Two pupils will be given the task of holding the map and the poem on the journey.

6. Set up the bridge

OoR: *Are we ready to go to the bridge? What must we remember as we set out?*

Repeat the poem.

Narrate: *The Superhelpers made their way to the Old Bridge by the waterfall. Across the bridge they could see the Land of Ice and Snow. They stood and waited on their side of the bridge.*

Use two chairs to create the bridge and place a chair on the far side to mark where the Superhelpers will meet Gerda.

OoR: *How will we know it is her? What do we need to listen for? OK when she has finished the poem you must chant yours – but quietly! Who is going to hold the paper with the poem on? Who is going to look after the map? You are now going to meet Gerda.*

Raising tension

Move across the space and stand on the far side of the bridge. Narrate the story so far.

Narrate: *The Superhelpers looked and in the distance they could see a figure.*

7. TiR as Gerda

Stand, head bowed, on the other side of the bridge. Gerda says her poem very quietly.

> *Dream of sun and warmth and light*
> *Think of fire and heat*
> *You will then survive the night*
> *Have drink and food to eat.*

TiR honours their work

Wait for the class to respond with their poem.

Gerda whispers for them to cross the bridge very quietly.

She tells them of the problem.

Nearly a week ago my brother, Kai, went missing. It is not unheard of for people to vanish around here. SHE is very powerful. We try to keep safe by putting our poem on the door at night but if ever we forget we may be in trouble ... if Kai forgot that night he went missing SHE might have taken him.

As she is listening and talking to them she freezes as if she has seen someone.

8. Meeting the Stranger

TiR sets up the first challenge

OoR: *Why do you think she has stopped? What does she look like?*

She has seen someone approaching. I want you to look at him. He is not near enough to talk to yet. This is what you would see if you were looking at him through binoculars.

TiR as Stranger approaches looking lost, checking his map and looking around.

ToR: *How was he behaving? What do you think the problem was? He is going to approach. Are you going to speak first? If so what are you going to say to him?*

ROLE BRIEF

The Stranger

He will not reveal who he is. He is just a traveller. He approaches them very positively and if they ask he says he has not seen any travellers on the route so far. How will they deal with him? They may lie and send him on his way or they may accept him and keep him with them.

TiR: *I am relieved to meet you and would like to travel with you if that is all right. It would make me feel safe, especially travelling through the forest. Where are you going?*

Before they can answer come OoR and discuss what is happening and what they understand and need to do. There are 3 possibilities:

(a) The children accept him – in which case he will ask them if they are travelling with anyone else. When he finds out about Gerda he will change his mind about going with them.

I may be a burden to you. I will carry on alone.

Discuss why he might have changed his mind and report back to Gerda.

(b) The children accept him – in which case move the drama on 3 days.

Narrate: *It was late, the Superhelpers were getting into their sleeping bags for the night. The Chief Superhelper was supposed to be keeping watch but he had fallen asleep.*

The Stranger starts to move suspiciously to the pupil carrying the map.

The Stranger had waited his moment. He crept towards the map, but just as he was about to steal it some of the Superhelpers awoke and gave the alarm.

Stop the drama. Discuss what happened.

(c) If the children reject him, he will go on his way.

9. Opening the mysterious box

They sit down together with Gerda and report back to her what happened. Gerda then tells them about her dilemma.

Use of
symbol to
focus the
drama

TiR Gerda: *People have disappeared. My brother is one of them. I must find him. I feel that I can now trust you and must seek your help. Late last night I heard a scuffling sound outside and after leaving a short gap, because I was afraid, I ventured outside and found something left for me to find and saw marks in the snow where some creature, like a dog had been. I could see nothing.*

Gerda produces a box wrapped in cloth. Carefully, and to raise tension, unwrap the cloth to reveal the box.

I am afraid to open the box. I hope it brings us something to help us, but I fear it might it be bad for us.

Will you help? I am afraid to open it but I know you are experts.

When someone takes on the responsibility, open the box to reveal a letter and an object. The object can be anything that connects Kai with his sister, e.g. a photograph, or one earring and she has the other, or some piece of jewellery that matches a brooch on the shawl.

That's Kai's! What does the note say?

The note:

> Dear Gerda,
>
> You do not know me but I tell of someone you hold dear.
>
> He is with SHE who is all powerful that is clear.
>
> In stronghold high within HER walls
>
> Your brother is held and hear his calls.
>
>   A friend

I wonder who sent this? It must be genuine as they have … [whatever object of Kai's is in the box].

10. Narrative action

Narrative action

OoR: *In the next part of the drama we are going to make pictures of the dangers the Superhelpers and Gerda had to overcome on the journey. What kind of dangers might they meet? In our pictures we are going to see how the Superhelpers saved Gerda from a danger.*

A whole class tableau(x) showing a danger they overcame on the journey.

11. The Snow Queen's castle

Use two chairs to represent the width of the door.

Building the context

OoR: *We are outside the Snow Queen's castle. Can you use your drama eyes to describe what this door looks like?*

As the class make suggestions, repeat and join their ideas in a word picture. These ideas will be useful in writing that follows up the drama.

We need to find a way into the castle but we will have to get past the guard. What tactics could we use? Remember we cannot fight them. We are outnumbered and they are far too powerful for us to fight. We must be cleverer than that. What should we do? We need a plan to get in. How can we trick the gatekeeper? Why would they let us in? Who can we say we are? Can we be convincing?

Pick up on pupils' ideas. Take the role of the gatekeeper. Challenge them until they come up with an interesting deception.

12. Prepare to talk to Kai

Set up the chamber where they discover Kai. There are several alternatives as Kai; it very much depends upon what learning objects you have. We have included several possible Kai roles for this drama in an appendix. Here is one suggestion.

The main challenge

Kai is sitting eating sweets and reading. The children look at Kai. *What do you notice about him? How can we help him? How do we approach him? How can we get to speak to him?*

Listen to the pupils' ideas and having discussed them let them try them out.

13. Task – persuading Kai

ROLE BRIEF

> ## Kai
>
> He does not want to leave. It is not the ice in his heart, as in the original story, but just that he is impressed by the Snow Queen as she has promised so much to him Their job is to persuade Kai of the Queen's evil (Task 1) and to think of a way to rid the land of her (Task 2).
>
> Kai must have the possibility of being persuaded to leave with Gerda and return home but, as Kai, you are not going to make it too easy for them.

During this conversation you stop the drama and tell the class that while they are persuading Kai a visitor comes into the room.

14. TiR as the Snow Queen

Raising the tension

TiR: *Well done, Kai. You will be rewarded with all the books and sweets you require.*

OoR: *How are you going to deal with her? What do you need to say to Kai?*

The class must deal with the Queen. She will assure them they cannot escape and soon, like Kai, they will be under her spell. The class may use their poem at this point and if they do the Queen will leave but vow to return.

15. Forum between Gerda and Kai

Forum theatre

TiR as Kai and class as Gerda. The class as Gerda can use their influence to remind him of his forgotten childhood and the folly of living in isolation, albeit with all the books and sweets he desires. Again, as Kai your role is to be persuaded but not to give in too easily. The pupils must exercise their skills in persuasion.

16. Images of the fall of the Queen

Symbolising success

Having persuaded Kai of his folly the class will either make one class image of the fall of the Queen or several images in groups. This will depend upon the experience and maturity of the class.

Structure summary

1   **Negotiate doing drama.**

   Have they been Superhelpers before? Set the children up as people who help children who are in trouble. Discuss what does it mean to help people?

   Setting up the agency offices.

2   **TiR as Chief Superhelper.**

   Reading the letter from Gerda.

3   **Approach 3: Make a class poem using five lines – 2,4,6,8 and 2 syllables.**

4 **TiR as Chief Superhelper.**
  More information about the Land of Ice and Snow.

5 **Creating or introducing the map of the Land of Ice and Snow.**

6 **Setting up the bridge and moving into the drama to meet Gerda.**

7 **TiR as Gerda.**

8 **Meeting the Stranger.**

9 **Use of symbol.**
  Opening the mysterious box and finding the letter from Kai.

10 **Narrative action.**
   Whole class tableau(x) – dangers on the journey to the castle.

11 **Building the context – the Snow Queen's castle.**
   Word pictures – describing the castle gates.

12 **Preparing to talk to Kai – setting up the context.**

13 **Task – persuading Kai.**

14 **TiR as the Snow Queen.**
   Increasing tension and setting the dilemma.

15 **Forum between Gerda and Kai.**

16 **Images of the fall of the Queen.**

Appendix: other possible Kai roles

All are victim roles and under the spell of the Queen, but in different ways, with different challenges for the class and therefore different learning possibilities.

The Opposer Kai who is a danger

When the Superhelpers enter his room he is absorbed in the activity of lighting a fire and his responses to being approached can be:

Hi, come and warm yourselves here and throw more wood on the fire.

Help me make it as big as we can.

Look at that ice melt … Excellent.

If challenged about the safety of this in an ice palace he replies:

I want to do this … Yes, of course, it will all melt. That's the idea.

Why, am I doing this? Because I want to, because I can.

I don't see why I should stop. I want to see a big melt-down.

The logic is that the Snow Queen has created a monster who thinks only of self and what he wants. The class have to take strong action to challenge this and one of the key ways is to face Kai with the isolation he is in, how he can never have any friends if he behaves like this.

Of course, the Snow Queen has to be made to face the monstrousness of him, maybe to see the need to release him (if he does not succumb himself to the need to change).

Kai as enjoying being there

This is demonstrated by the figure being found with a table with a chess game on it and with a chair either side as he plays one move for each side in turn. He is chuckling with delight and muttering about always winning.

The key issue for PSHE learning is how can there be real pleasure in only having yourself to play against. Kai must be made to see the problem of his position and maybe how Gerda feels about having lost him.

Kai as a servant of the Queen

The Superhelpers find him busy rushing round the room wiping walls with a cloth:

I must make sure it is all smooth with no cloudiness and no icicles hanging down.

What are you all doing here? I haven't had any instructions that you were coming and what to do with you.

Please don't breathe so much. Can't you see your breath is freezing on the walls and clouding it and forming ugly bulges. She won't like that and I must please her at all times.

Maybe you want to be taken to her? Is that what I am supposed to do.

He continues to polish.

If told not to do this ...

I must ... Don't you want me to?

If it is pointed out that he doesn't have to, he can put the cloth down and heave a sigh of relief.

The key for the class is to try to reassure this subservient Kai that life is not just to please others. He must think of himself and what he might want as well. He must realise that the Queen is imposing on him. They want him to reclaim his life, which includes his sister and his past.

'Charlie'

A drama based on *Voices in the Park* by Anthony Browne

Learning objectives
Pupils will understand:

- about the characters and attitudes in the story – Literacy – viewpoints and character
- more about prejudice and class

Roles

	Role	Signifier
Teacher pictures	Volunteer Co-ordinator	Clip board and folder of pictures
	Charles	Diary and pencil
	Charles's Mother	Copy of *The Times*
	Smudge's Dad	Woolly hat
Pupils	Volunteers who help to look after the park	N/A

Research and preparation

- If you don't already know it, read the story *Voices in the Park* by Anthony Browne
- Pictures of litter and areas of a park
- Charles's diary with the cover notice 'Secret Diary, KEEP OUT – Charles'
- The piece of writing from his diary that he throws away, which is a hand-written copy of Charles's 'Voice 3' from the storybook

Structure

1. **Negotiate doing drama**

2. **TiR as Co-ordinator for Volunteers**

   TiR sets context

   Meet the class as the Co-ordinator for volunteers who come to help with looking after the park.

   I was pleased that so many of you could turn out today to help. We seem to have had quite a lot of litter left around the park. So the first job really is to tidy up. We need to divide the litter up. Paper and cardboard and plastic can be recycled so that needs to be put in separate bags.

OoR: *What is going on here? Who are you? Tell me what sort of park this is and the places you know in it.*

Use pictures of different areas in the park to help define the space and show litter as a problem.

3. Set up the class as volunteers

Occupational mime

Occupational mime of the litter collecting and sorting. Indicate there is an imaginary set of bins for different sorts of litter to help recycling.

What would the different sorts of bins be?

Possibles – paper, cardboard, plastics, glass, rubble, non-recyclable litter.

4. Narration

Narration

Soon the park looked very tidy and the recyclable materials were being organised to be taken away when the volunteers noticed someone who has come to sit on a bench.

5. TiR as Charles

ROLE BRIEF

> ## *Charles*
>
> He is upset that his mother will not let him meet Smudge, not let him play properly, but he is afraid of his mother and will not confront her. At this stage he is reluctant to talk to anyone about his feelings as he is struggling with them. He will begin to open up to the class as the drama progresses. See the cues for that at each stage.

TiR sets problem

Charles walks to a seat and sits all hunched up.

He is clutching a little writing book, labelled 'Secret Diary, KEEP OUT – Charles'. He tears a page out of it and throws it on the ground.

What do the children do? Do they object? Do they pick it up?

(In every run of this drama members of the class have tackled him about the piece of paper, being upset that someone is ignoring what they are doing to keep the park tidy. They also usually pick up his piece of paper spontaneously and are interested in looking it at.)

You may have to go OoR in order to deal with whether to pick up the paper or not.

6. Dealing with Charles

If they approach Charles, he does not want to talk to anybody. Eventually he gets up and leaves: *Leave me alone. I'm not very happy.* But he leaves his little book behind.

Moral issue – privacy

Do they try to get a look at the book?

OoR: *What about 'Keep Out' on it? Is it private?*

If they do look inside it contains some thoughts on different pages:

> *I like Smudge*
> *She goes fast*
> *Next week is Smudge's party – cool!*
> *What shall I wear?*
> *What shall I get her as a present?*
> *I want to be like Smudge.*

Use of text from book

If they have not already looked at the paper, make sure the class discover the thrown away paper.

OoR: *This looks interesting. What do you think it's about? Does the paper tell you anything?*

Discuss the content: *What do you think?*

(NB: One class decided to look at the paper and not the notebook because the paper was thrown away and not 'private'. They got what they wanted from the paper and did not pursue the notebook.)

How do they tackle him?

7. Groups

Tableaux of attitudes

Tableaux of four characters, Charles, Smudge, Charles's Mum and Smudge's Dad, and what they think of each other.

8. TiR as Charles returns

Moral issue – privacy

Charles returns and catches them with his notebook.

What are you doing? What have you found out? All right nosey parkers …

Charles begins to talk to them. Gradually the other facts about the party come out:

- He has not told Mother.
- He hasn't got money for a present but wants to go.

Class take on responsibility

The class may try to tackle him about Smudge and encourage him to find her or they may encourage him to tackle his mother.

Charles must fend off talking to Mother at this stage so you can move the drama straight on to structure point 10. He continues to be very upset and sad:

It's not fair. I'll never get to play with Smudge.

9. (*Optional*: Role on the wall)

Role on the wall

For Mother and/or Charles, looking particularly at attitudes and opinions of others and themselves.

10. Smudge's letter

While they are sorting this the Co-ordinator returns with a letter. The helpers are called together.

TiR: *A little girl has just given this to me to give to Charles. Then she ran away. She said we can look at the letter. She said, 'You can read it if you want. If you think you can help Charles, I would be grateful.'*

The letter:

New
stimulus to
further
involve the
class with
Charles

> *Dear Charlie,*
>
> *I'm really sorry about this, 'cos I really wanted you to come to my party. I was really looking forward to you coming, but you can't come now, my dad says.*
>
> *He says he doesn't want anybody coming who looks down on our family.*
>
> *He says your mum's really snobby. She was really snobby about the dogs playing together in the park and she told my dad off for letting the dogs run and play together, which he didn't.*
>
> *Really sorry,*
>
> *Smudge*

What do they do about the situation? They have to give the letter to him but how to soften the blow?

11. Possibilities

Tackling the
issues

Do they talk to Mother, explain to her?

Do they approach one of the other characters?

What advice do they give to Charles?

Whoever they decide to go to see, Charles asks them to do the talking for him: *I'm too scared. I don't know what to say.*

So he goes with them – one of the class carries his cap.

Because you negotiated for them to talk for Charles, you are able to become the role they decide to tackle. They could go straight to Mother or, as one class did, tackle Smudge's dad and ask him to let Charles go to Smudge's party. He will only do that if Charles's mother apologises to him, so that means they have a real task on to get her to apologise.

12. Forum theatre of key issue (one or more?)

Forum
theatre

It must end with the class taking on the role of Charles and tackling Mother. Before that one do we see forums of

    Charles and Smudge?

OR Charles and Smudge's dad?

Finish with Charles and Mother.

ROLE BRIEF

Mother

She needs to portray her prejudice towards Smudge. This is largely based upon the fact Smudge comes from a council estate. She does not want Charles to play with her or to go down there because he is mixing with the wrong kind of people. She had an argument with Smudge's dad about the dogs. Their dog 'looks common' and she doesn't want her 'pedigree' mixing with 'that dog'. She wants the best for Charles because she knows what's best for him. She never listens to him.

ROLE BRIEF

Smudge's dad

He is really very tolerant, but he can't stand stuck-up people who are richer than him. He thinks Charles is like his mother and looks down on them. He doesn't want his daughter being looked down on by someone posh.
He can't help it that he hasn't got a lot of money. He's sure that if Charles comes he will bring some posh present that will show up his own present to his daughter.

Structure summary

1 **Negotiate doing drama.**

2 **TiR as Co-ordinator for volunteers.**
Meet the class as Co-ordinator for volunteers who come to help look after the park.
Use pictures of different areas in the park.

3 **Set up the class as volunteers.**
Occupational mime of the litter collecting and sorting.

4 **Narration.**
Soon the Park looked very tidy ... the volunteers noticed someone who came to sit on a bench.

5 **TiR as Charles.**
He walks to a seat and sits all hunched up.
He tears a page out of his book and throws it on the floor.
What do the children do? Do they object, do they pick it up?

6 **Dealing with Charles.**
He won't tell them anything and gets up, but he leaves his little book behind.
Do they try to get a look at the book?
Make sure the class discover the thrown away paper.

7 **Tableaux of attitudes.**

8 **TiR as Charles.**

He returns to catch them with his notebook.

The class may try to tackle him about Smudge or they may encourage him to tackle his mother (move the drama straight on to structure point 12).

9 **Roles on wall – Mother and/or Charles (*optional*).**

10 **Smudge's letter.**

11 **Possibilities.**

Tackling the roles.

12 **Forum Theatre of key issue.**

Charles and Mother.

'The Maasai Boy'

Learning objectives

Pupils will understand:

- aspects of Kenya
- issues to do with tourism
- viewpoints about heritage and change

Relates to SMSC Curriculum:

- **Spiritual**   The individuals and group can gain insights into their own values, beliefs, ideas through the values examined in the fiction.
- **Moral**   Difficult choices can be presented.
  Is it right to break rules if we want to save someone?
- **Social**   The work is based in interaction and can explore social organisation.
- **Cultural**   What beliefs, values customs do we show of other cultures?
  How representative are they? Whose view of another culture is it?

Research and preparation

- Maps of the world, Africa and Kenya
- Facts, figures and pictures about Kenya and village life, e.g. tourism to the Maasai Mara
- Find resources available from Development Education Centres, the warrior statue
- We used other objects from Kenya, like the lamp, brush and toy, the more authentic the better

Roles

	Role	Signifier
Teacher	Exhibition Organiser Kilesi, the boy who has sold the statue	Clip board Sweeping brush, lamp made out of cans, toy made out of recycled materials
Pupils	Exhibition advisers, who can advise on how to best cater for pupils	N/A

Structure

1. Negotiate doing drama

2. Narration

Narration

Outline the situation at the beginning of the drama.

This drama takes place in a hall where there is an exhibition about Kenya in Africa.

Imagine we are in the room now.

What is it like? What are you looking at?

3. Tableaux

Exhibition tableaux

If the drama is used at the beginning of the project, this section is valuable for diagnosing what ideas of Africa and Kenya the pupils bring to the topic, what misconceptions and stereotypes, etc. need to be addressed. For example, with two classes tigers featured, which is a common mistake for many people, not only pupils, as tigers are not found in Africa.

If the drama is used to consolidate knowledge, then it will show what they know and what they still might misunderstand as they have to use the knowledge.

Organise the pupils working in threes or fours to set up a whole group still picture of people in an exhibition looking at an exhibit.

What is the exhibit you are standing in front of? What does it show? Does it have objects, pictures, models, written information? What size is it? What part is each of you looking at? Are you talking to each other about it? What is your reaction?

They create the idea of being in an exhibition and move into drama (pretending) mode.

If I touch you on the shoulder tell us all what you are seeing and thinking about the exhibit.

Discuss what they show themselves doing and what the tableaux show about being in an exhibition.

You will now find out who you are going to be in the drama because the Exhibition Organiser will enter and you need to listen carefully to what is going on in the exhibition.

4. Pupils' role – 'Mantle of the Expert'

TiR and Mantle of the Expert role

Enter in role and gather them to tell them how pleased you are to have them there as experts in pupils and exhibits and that they have only a half an hour more before they must present a report on how well the exhibition caters for pupils and how it might be improved.

OoR to discuss who they are and what they might have been looking at and what they might put in their report.

5. The statue

OoR set up one particular exhibit.

Look at this exhibit and tell me what you see. It is in the final room of the exhibition.

Set the statue of a Maasai warrior, in a glass case. (Standing it in a plastic fish tank will do.)

There are also two labels on the plinth on which the glass case stands.

Maasai Warrior
(Maasai, Kenya, East Africa)

The Maasai are a pastoral (cattle herding) tribe in East Africa. Their warriors were important both in protecting their cattle and acquiring new cattle, upon which their survival depends.

(purchased from a dealer in Nairobi and lent to the exhibition by Mr L Torrance)

Do not touch.
This case is protected by an alarm.

What do you notice about it? What does it show?

End of Part One

PART TWO

6. OoR

Are you ready to begin our drama? As the experts on child-friendly exhibitions, you are looking round the room where the statue is. You are looking at the exhibit you were in front of before and deciding whether pupils will be able to use it. Then we will see what happens. Let's see how the drama starts. I will narrate what is going on.

Narrate: *It was a wet day and the people had been coming in and going out all day, lots of them. By five o'clock the exhibition keepers were tired and wanted to close up. There was still half an hour to go.*

The group of exhibition advisers was still looking round and had just reached the room where the statue was. Then it went very quiet and still, the lights seemed to dim and then become bright again. The group noticed a young black boy hiding behind one of the cases. He was carrying a brush of some sort and was dressed in a tee shirt and shorts even though it was January.

(The narration sets the scene and the tone, helps the pupils focus and raises expectations.)

7. TiR as Kilesi – the Kenyan boy

> ## *Kilesi*
>
> The issue centres around the injustice Kilesi feels at being punished, as he sees it, given menial tasks to do rather than properly looking after the cattle, with the men, because he unknowingly sold the original carving of the warrior to Mr Torrance, an American tourist, when he was running the family's stall near the Game Reserve.
>
> He is eager to get it back when he finds it in the exhibition and puts pressure on the pupils as the advisers to let him have it, gradually shifting the responsibility onto them to negotiate its release to him.
>
> The magical appearance in the exhibition from his home yard is a drama convention pupils can understand and respect but it needs negotiation.
>
> Crouch as though hiding and give the signals of being very wary. He will not come out.

At his appearance, briefly go out of role and discuss what the pupils understand to be happening.

As Kilesi, give signals that he thinks the class look different and other clues as to the unusual nature of the situation:

TiR: *Where has the sun gone? When I was doing my jobs I was outside in the sunshine. Now I cannot see the sun and this seems to be some sort of building.*

You must raise the pupils' interest through the uncertainty of the situation but must make it possible for them to begin to take initiatives, to see that they are required to try things out.

He tells of what has happened to him, responding to the questions.

Two days ago I was working on the family stall in the Trading Centre in our village selling carvings to the visitors to the Tsavo Park and sold quite a number of statues. One of the statues is very important apparently and I should not have sold it. My grandfather carved it. My father was very angry and has punished me, making me stay home and sweep the yard and not take the cattle out to the Chyulu Hills. I am fed up doing this girl's work and must get the statue back. I was wishing I could find it and suddenly felt odd. I found myself here and I don't know why.

Why am I here?

8. Kilesi's statue

If the pupils show him the statue in the case that's fine. If they do not he must begin to examine it himself.

He moves towards the case as though to take the statue out.

If the pupils do not tell him to stop, freeze in the act of reaching for the case and come OoR to discuss what will happen and what they should do.

The boy can plead with them:

*Give me the statue. It is **mine**. Well it belongs to our family. Why is it in that thing? I know I sold it but it really doesn't represent our people anyway. We just make hundreds of these to sell to tourists. That thing is about the past and makes us look like ignorant savages ... We will never be part of the twenty-first century if we let you all carry on thinking about us like that.*

Do you know how it feels to be laughed at? If I can take it back they will let me look after the cattle again.

Do they give him it or not?

This is where we set the heart of the dilemma for the pupils. In having to look at this they have to consider: *What is the purpose of the statue? What is the exhibition meant to show?*

If they decide NO then they have to give him good reasons to persuade him to go back without the statue.

However, if he tries to go back he finds he cannot. Some way has to be found to allow him to explain to his father before the 'place-warp' will open to take him back.

If they decide YES, how do they get the statue?

If they do not suggest fetching the Organiser and they just go to take the statue from the case, TiR enters as the Exhibition Organiser and challenges them. They can not take it.

The Organiser, of course, cannot 'see' Kilesi if they give the real explanation. The purpose of the Organiser's 'blindness' to the boy is that the responsibility of dealing with the boy cannot be shifted onto the Organiser but must stay firmly with the pupils.

TiR hands over responsibility

9. The Organiser's position

TiR: *This does not even belong to the exhibition. It belongs to Mr Torrance. He has kindly lent it to us and it cannot be given to someone else.*

10. Who owns the statue?

Forum theatre resolution

The pupils will want to put the case to Mr Torrance. He is in another place and they have to phone him. Set up a forum theatre with TiR as Mr Torrance facing away from the participants, miming use of the phone.

The class have to present the best case they can.

OoR discuss this with them first. *What is the point here? Who owns the statue? How did Kilesi come to sell it? What right does he have to it?*

What is its value? ... to Mr Torrance? ... to the family?

Do they find a way to persuade him to let them give Kilesi the statue or do they tell the boy he cannot have it?

If the pupils come up with a compromise then the owner can accept that. OR If he can be persuaded of the rights of Kilesi and his family, perhaps he can offer to pay the family for the proper value of the statue or offer to return it to them after the exhibition.

11. Mr Torrance's request

Finale
tableau

Either way, TiR as Mr Torrance says: *I would like to see this person and you, as I haven't met you. Make sure you take a photograph of you all with the statue.*

Set up a whole group tableau where a pupil takes over Kilesi's role and holds the statue, where the objects are each held by different pupils.

Whatever the resolution, the pupils must be allowed to 'win' and then debrief the issues:

Distant place ... meeting someone out of their culture and trying to understand it:

Why do we have exhibitions of other cultures?
How do we decide what should be in them?
What does it mean to say that the statue is just made for the tourists?
Why do we keep traditions from the past – for the Maasai or for the tourists?

Ownership:

Who owns the artefacts in exhibitions?

Structure summary

1 **Negotiate doing drama.**

2 **Narration.**

   This drama takes place in a hall where there is an exhibition about Kenya in Africa. Imagine we are in the room now.

3 **Tableaux.**

   Organise the pupils working in threes or fours to set up a whole group still picture of people in an exhibition looking at an exhibit:

   If I touch you on the shoulder tell us all what you are seeing and thinking about the exhibit.

   Discuss what the tableaux show about being in an exhibition.

4 **TiR as Exhibition Organiser.**

   Pupils' roles – 'Mantle of the Expert' gathers them to tell them ... as experts in pupils and exhibits.

   OoR to discuss who they are and what they might have been looking at and what they might put in their report.

5 **The statue.**

   Set the statuette of a Maasai warrior, in a glass case. Two labels on the plinth. *What do you notice about it? What does it show?*

                        [End of Part One]

PART TWO

6 **OoR.**

   Recap Part One and re-establish the exhibition room where the warrior statue is.

   Narrate: *It was a wet day ... a young black boy hiding behind one of the cases.*

7 **TiR as Kilesi the Kenyan boy**.

Where has the sun gone?

8 **Kilesi's statue**.

The statue in the case is pointed out or found.

The boy moves to take the statue out of the case.

*Give me the statue. It is **mine**. Well, it belongs to our family.*

Do they give him it or not?

If NO, then they have to give him good reasons to persuade him to go back without it.

If YES, how do they get it?

9 **The Organiser's position**.

This does not even belong to the exhibition. It belongs to Mr Torrance. He has kindly lent it to us and it cannot be given to someone else.

10 **Who owns the statue?**

The pupils will want to put the case to Mr Torrance.

Set up a Forum Theatre with Mr Torrance.

11 **Mr Torrance's request**.

Set up a whole group tableau photograph for Mr Torrance.

'The Governor's Child'

A drama based on *The Caucasian Chalk Circle* by Bertolt Brecht

Learning objectives

Pupils will understand:

- the nature of community
- the power of a child
- ideas of choice and democracy

Roles

	Role	Signifier
Teacher	The Villager The Soldier	Sack or agricultural tool Battered military coat
Pupils Volunteer	The mountain villagers Maria	N/A Blanket rolled as baby

Research and preparation

Read Brecht play
Plan how to draw the village and mountain map

Structure

Contracting

1. **Negotiate doing drama**

2. **Drawing and setting scene**

Setting the context

A village in the mountains where life is fairly primitive but comfortable, away from the bustle of the city.

Take a felt-tip pen and a large sheet of paper. Without saying much draw an outline of a mountain range with a village nestling below the tops. A road over the mountain though a pass and field pattern below the village in the valley. Ask the class:

> *What have I drawn? What would life be like in this village? How would they live?*

> *What would the houses be made of?*

> *Any questions? What do you need to know to set up the village?*

> *How is everyone called to the centre of the village if there is an emergency?* (possibly an imaginary bell)

3. Narration

Narration

It was late on a winter afternoon and the sun was setting. The village families were getting ready for the end of the day. There was the threat of heavy snow to come.

In groups, pupils create still pictures of the villagers finishing their work.

4. TiR as Villager

ROLE BRIEF

Villager

A villager returning from a day spent in the lower pastures.
The purpose of the role is to bring immediate focus on the key situation of the woman in need of help. He must not ask if they want to bring her in, but emphasise how serious her situation is and how it is his and their duty.

When she is brought in and the role taken by a volunteer pupil he must be with her and support her in the hot-seating.

TiR stimulus

He rushes in, rings the bell (or other signal) and calls villagers together.

He speaks to his family (whom you have chosen beforehand while they are making the tableaux).

I am sorry I am late but I should have been here an hour ago. I was slowed down on my return from mending the walls in the fields below. I have just met a girl travelling on the road over the mountains. She seems to have come a long way and is very tired. That's why I was so slow coming up. She is in need of shelter and I asked if she wanted spend the night with us. I am sure that she will die out on the mountain if the threatened snow comes. What makes it worse is that she has a child with her, a baby, who will also die. I know this is sudden and I wanted to let you know that I want my family to take her in. I for one cannot leave her to her fate. She says she will come if I can bring something to her to show her our good faith and kindness.

OoR: *What has happened here? How do they show their good intentions to her?*

Gifts? A symbol?

5. The girl (Maria) comes to the village

Choose a volunteer from the class to take the role of Maria.

Pupil takes lead role

The class as villagers prepare questions to hot-seat the role. How is she made welcome? What is said?

Prepare the villagers for hot-seating her.

The family who take her in would talk to her, but for the drama, you are all going to gather round her and talk to her as though you are in the house where she is staying. How would they talk to her as she is so tired? Now think of what you would want to try to find out.

I am going to brief [name of volunteer] who is going to be Maria. While I am doing that I want you to draw up a list of questions to ask her. One of you can write these down.

Teacher briefs the pupil taking the role separately.

The girl is called Maria. She is fleeing from the capital with the Governor's son, Michael. She is running from the rebellion where the Governor has been killed by the rebels. She was the maidservant to him and looked after his baby son, whom she has rescued from the soldiers. His mother ran away. But she needs a story to tell the villagers because she cannot tell them the truth … She must not tell them this or they will not take her in and they might tell others. She must be very quiet and answer only in one word. Her cover story is that she is fleeing with her baby over the mountains from the fighting in the capital city. She is going to her brother's house over the mountains, to safety because of the riots in the city. Her husband was killed in the fighting.

You can own up to the truth if you feel you need to at any point, but remember you don't have to answer every question. If you are not sure, just stay silent.

Set up Maria with the baby entering the village – representing the baby by folding and rolling a cloth in front of the group. It is important to negotiate the meaning of the roll directly in this way.

6. The entry of Maria

Use your drama eyes. How would the girl look? We will create the idea of her entry together. She goes to the house of her host's family.

7. Hot-seating Maria

You must help handle the hot-seating, stopping to discuss with her if she needs help.

8. Sociogram of attitudes to her

Sociogram

The class as villagers take position according to how they feel.

9. Narration

Narration

They all settle down for the night and it passes peacefully. The next morning as Maria is preparing to leave and continue her journey, and the villagers are getting ready for the day, something happens.

10. TiR enters as the Villager (rings the bell)

I have just been to the pass to check if it is possible for Maria to get over and it is possible despite the snow-fall. As I returned I saw armed soldiers, two on horseback, approaching from the valley, heading up the track to the pass. They are riding fast and look as though they may turn off for the village.

OoR: *What is happening? What do the villagers do to save her and the baby from the soldiers?*

The class usually decide to hide the girl and behave as if they have not seen her.

11. TiR as the Soldier

TiR
stimulus
and tension
creator

Who is in charge here? I need to speak to everyone.

The villagers gather.

I am searching for a girl with a baby. I know you up here in the mountains, so far from the capital, have not been affected by the rule of the old Governor of the Province, the high taxes, the killings by his soldiers, but he is dead now and the revolutionary guards have taken control. We want the Governor's nurse-maid and his son that she has saved and taken with her. They were reported coming in this direction. You must realise how we suffered and we want no one left who could return the province to the old ways.

OoR: *How do they get him out of the village so they can decide what to do?*

The Soldier shows belief in them and says he'll carry on searching further up the mountain, but if he finds no bodies, he will be back. He leaves and gives time to think as he is going to seek her on the trail, but if he does not find her and the baby, he will be back.

12. Sociogram about Maria

Sociogram

Compare to the first.

What can they do now?

Villagers decide what they are going to do.

Action leading to consequences.

13. The Soldier returns

TiR: *I have not found her. You must have seen her. I think you are lying.*

Responds to whatever the children offer at this point.

If they offer good ideas a novice group can be allowed to win and get the Soldier to leave.

OR

Starts to search ... threatens to burn a house.

OR

I will take the children one at a time and kill them.

This last is only used to push a very strong and experienced group.

14. Group tableaux

Possilble
endings

Each group prepares two tableaux: one of the ending the villagers would want and one of the ending the villagers fear.

Share and discuss the endings.

Structure summary

Split the drama over two or more sessions

1 **Negotiate doing drama.**

2 **Drawing and setting scene.**

   A village in the mountains where life is fairly primitive but comfortable.

3 **Narration.**

   It was late on a winter afternoon and the sun was setting. The village families were getting ready for the end of the day.

4 **TiR as a Villager.**

   Returning from a day spent in the lower pastures, he rushes in, rings the bell and calls villagers together. News of Maria.

   OoR: *What has happened here?*

5 **The girl (Maria) comes to the village.**

   Brief the volunteer to take role of Maria. Class plan questions.

6 **The entry of Maria.**

7 **Hot-seating Maria.**

8 **Sociogram of attitudes to her.**

9 **Narration.**

   The next morning as Maria is preparing to leave ...

10 **TiR enters as the Villager and reports the impending soldiers.**

11 **TiR as the Soldier.**

   Enters the village and demands Maria and the baby.

12 **Sociogram about Maria.**

   What can they do now?

13 **The Soldier returns.**

14 **Group tableaux.**

   Possible endings good and bad.

Other possible work to develop this drama or as separate work

Viewpoints and pre-text

1 Revisit the moment in the Governor's Palace when Maria took the baby.

   Recreate the chaotic moment as a whole class tableau and constrain it by asking for it to be shown from Maria's point of view.

   Where is the mother? What is she saying? What threat from the soldiers is shown?

2 Revisit the moment when the Soldier was ordered to pursue and kill Maria and the baby.

   He packs his kit and supplies for the journey – thought-track him. How does he feel about the orders? What are his thoughts about Maria and about the Governor and his wife?

   He remembers the death of his brother at the hands of the Governor. How did it happen? Recreate that moment. Was the Soldier there?

3 An overheard conversation between the Governor's wife and Maria when news of the revolution arrives at the Palace.

'The Highwayman'

Based on the poem by Alfred Noyes

Learning objectives
Pupils will understand:

- themes of 'The Highwayman', such as love and responsibility
- the function of 'The Highwayman' as a narrative poem
- the roles
- the idea of the author's voice

Roles

	Role	Signifiers
Teacher	Mr James, the current landlord Tim the Ostler Bess Highwayman Possibly Innkeeper	Clip board with research materials Riding crop or horse brush Ring on a ribbon Cape Old tankard
Pupils	Historians researching the history of 'The Highwayman Inn'	N/A

Research and preparation

- Find and photograph pictures of the two sign boards, one 'The Highwayman', one of a mail coach for the 'before' sign. There are Internet sites and books of inn signs
- Research the history of highwaymen for some facts and figures, especially if you are intending to compare the poem to the reality of the lives.
- Prepare A3-sized outlines of the old inn, plan view and front view. (See below, structure point 3.)

Structure
(*Note*: as with all the dramas, it will take at least two sessions and you should choose where to make the break or breaks. A suitable break might be after point 10. The next session could start with a recap where the historians report their research to the Landlord, Mr James.)

1. Introduce the poem:

Poem – drama focus

Introduce the first part of the poem, up to:

Then he tugged at his rein in the moonlight, and galloped away to the West

using interactive whiteboard or hard copies of the poem.

This is going to be the focus for our drama work so we just need to read it through to start with.

Read it. Do not discuss it at this stage.

2. Meeting of the historians and the present landlord

TiR setting research context

TiR as Landlord: *Welcome to the inn, our focus for the project that really gets under way today. I know you have already done some preliminary research into this inn, but I know we are going to do so much more now that I have your expert input. The Brewery are keen to back us and can see how the project will help us move forward with the business. People are very interested in the older parts of this building and want to know more.*

Picture stimulus

To start with I want to know why the inn name changed from this – [show picture of 'The Quicksilver Mail' sign] *'The Quicksilver Mail', the name we know the inn had back in the 18th century – to this* [show picture of 'The Highwayman Inn' sign].

We know there is a legend attached to the change, but what is the truth and why was it changed?

OoR: *So what is the situation here? Who are you, where are you and why does he say you have gathered there?*

Discuss their understanding of the project.

He says you have already some knowledge. Let's look at your research. If the poem is the legend about this inn, what does it tell us?

3. Back into role

TiR: *What might the layout of the inn have been at this period, considering what is described in the legend?*

Hand out the plans of the old inn.

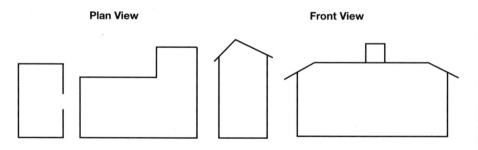

Plan View   **Front View**

This is the lay-out of the oldest parts of the inn as we know them and the probable place of the stables. We don't know of other buildings. From your research you can probably fill in some detail of what the place looked like.

The researchers now look at the poem and mark on physical details they can glean from the text.

Possible areas: The Inn Yard cobbles, the inn door, the window, the stables and the stable wicket, the moor, trees.

They report back to the Landlord. To develop this lay-out they could add:

Who are the characters in the legend and where would they be situated if we placed them on our plan?

4.   Narration

Narration
Time shift

As the historians worked at the site of the inn on their plans, the lights suddenly dimmed and there was an odd feeling They became aware of a figure sitting in the corner who had not been there before.

5.   TiR as Tim the Ostler

TiR contact
role

He sits with his head bowed, holding a riding crop in his hand.

OoR: *What has happened? Who might this be?*

Their task is to get him to speak to them.

He reluctantly talks of his worry.

TiR as Tim: *I have a real problem and I don't know what to do. You look like sensible and official people. Can I trust you?*

Go out of role to discuss this with the class.

OoR: *How can you find out more? This is a unique opportunity for the historians that can only happen in a drama. You can talk to one of the people from that time. I wonder what his problem is?*

6.   They hot-seat Tim

ROLE BRIEF

> ### Tim
>
> They must learn quickly that he is Tim and not the Highwayman, who they usually think he is. These are several issues you have to raise as the role:
>
> There are soldiers now arrived at the inn and he wants to know why they are there.
>
> A secret – this comes out more as they probe him; groups usually ask him about the Highwayman.
>
> He knows of a Highwayman who will be coming to the inn that night. Should he tell the soldiers he's coming, because he's a man wanted for many crimes committed on the highway?
>
> However, he doesn't want to get himself into trouble and there are other people to consider: people who are close to the Highwayman, people who would protect the Highwayman and therefore risk their own freedom if he were to tell.

During the hot-seating the group will raise Bess's name even if he tries to keep her out of it. He is shy of talking about her. This part of the drama can help look at the love theme from the poem in a serious and thoughtful way.

Signifier and symbolic object

Use the riding crop:

This is not mine you know. It belongs to him. He broke it and gave it to me to mend. He doesn't care for any horse he rides. He whips them to save his own skin.

He shows them his hand.

Yesterday I patted the horse and it felt damp, I thought it was just sweat, but it was blood. Soaked in blood from being whipped! What sort of a man is that?

7. OoR

Who is he? What is he on about? What should they do?

Could he help them with the history of the inn? What advice to give him? Do they tell him what else they know?

We are going to create more about this role now.

8. Create Tim's room over the stables

Define the Space

The class tell you what they think it will contain and look like and you write down with a felt-tip pen on pieces of paper, which label particular areas: for example, *bed straw mattress* was one input from a class. They usually show considerable understanding of the historical context at this point. Then one of the class volunteers to represent Tim in the room.

After everything is in its place a note is produced which the children put in an appropriate place.

> I will need a new horse when I get back tonight. Make sure it is the best and there will be a reward for you. I will come on foot from the copse at the back of the inn.
>
> A friend

9. Children become the walls of the room

One thought one action

The children participate in the one thought, one action strategy. This is in response to Tim, who is deliberating over the note and its contents.

Wherever the final thought or movement places Tim, the next issue is that he hears someone coming, and through the door comes …

10. TiR as Bess

TiR raise tension

Switch roles by placing the riding crop where Tim is. The class might have recommended he hide for example.

ROLE BRIEF

> ### *Bess*
>
> She has come to seek Tim's help to cover for her this evening as she will be leaving the inn. She does not say why initially but hints at a wonderful future. When tackled her attitude to any criticism of the Highwayman must start as: *I don't believe he means any harm. He is a wonderful man, full of excitement and charm. I love him.*
>
> If the note is produced by the class: *This note could mean anything.*

Forum Theatre

OoR: Immediately after she explains what she wants:

Where is she going? Of course, she is going to flee with the Highwayman.

What does Tim do? How does he stop her going and ruining her life?

Discuss possibilities.

The class now take over Tim's role. They must try to get across to Bess what the Highwayman is really like. She resists and then they provide evidence.

11. Tableaux

Tableaux to embody argument

The children create images of what the Highwayman does in order to inform Bess of the true nature of the man she professes to love. They show them to her. She should show some unease but does not want to hear this view of the Highwayman and rejects their version of his personality. She leaves to go to prepare for the Highwayman's arrival.

OoR: *Why is Bess so difficult to convince? Why doesn't she believe what you are saying? How does her reluctance to 'tell on' the highwayman compare/contrast to Tim's reluctance? What are the differences? What should Tim do?*

They must decide whether they as Tim tell the soldiers about the Highwayman or not.

Narration: *The Highwayman is coming. Having left his horse in the trees at the back, he approaches the stables very cautiously. He has met Bess as she leaves the stables.*

12. Overhead conversation

Narrate: *Tim listened and heard the Highwayman speaking to Bess.*

TiR as Highwayman: *We must leave quickly. Tim will fetch us a new horse. There is no time to waste. You must come with me now. Get what you need and meet me here in 10 minutes.*

OoR: *What happened there? What did Tim overhear and what does it mean?*

13. Thermometer line of whether she should go or not

(*Optional*: Set up the class to thought-track Bess.)

14. Forum of Tim with the Highwayman

Forum Theatre 2

Beforehand discuss with the class what Tim might want at this point and what he might want to say to the Highwayman.

ROLE BRIEF

The Highwayman

He has had a narrow escape on his hold-up today and is nervous.
He begins to show how much he is thinking of himself first and his fear of being caught.
He loves Bess and wants her with him.
He is very afraid when he hears of the soldiers.
There is the possibility of Tim persuading him to leave without her if he wants Tim's help.

---

15. Tableaux

Two tableaux of the ending as each of the groups think it might be. First tableau to show the best outcome and a second to show the worst.

This is how legends are made.

The poem shows a different picture.

Read Part Two of the poem and compare.

Structure summary

1   **Introduce the first part of the poem.**

2   **Meeting of the historians and the present landlord (TiR).**
    Show pictures of *The Quicksilver Mail* and *The Highwayman* signs.
    OoR: *So what is the situation here?*

3   **Back into role.**
    What might the layout of the inn have been?
    Hand out the plans of the old inn.
    They report back to the inn Landlord.

4   **Narration.**
    As the historians worked, the lights suddenly dimmed. They became aware of a figure sitting in the corner ...

5   **TiR as Tim the Ostler.**
    OoR: *Who might this be?*

6   **They hot-seat Tim.**
    Go out of role to discuss this with the class.

7   **OoR.**
    Who is he? What is he on about? What should they do?

8 **Create Tim's room over the stables.**

A note is produced.

9 **Children become the walls of the room.**

Children participate in the one thought, one action strategy.

Tim hears someone coming and through the door comes …

10 **TiR as Bess.**

Where is she going?

The class now take over Tim's role.

11 **Tableaux.**

The children create images of what the Highwayman does.

OoR: *Why is Bess so difficult to convince?*

They must decide whether they as Tim tell the soldiers.

Narration: *The Highwayman is coming.*

12 **Overheard conversation.**

Narration: *Tim listened and heard the Highwayman speaking to Bess.*

TiR Highwayman: *We must leave quickly.*

OoR: *What happened there?*

13 **Thermometer line of whether she should go or not.**

(*Optional*: Set up the class to thought-track Bess.)

14 **Forum of Tim with the Highwayman.**

15 **Two tableaux of the ending.**

One to show the best outcome and a second to show the worst.

Postscript

There is the possibility of taking the drama and then turning it into a performance piece. Possibly for an assembly?

It could be the video made by the historians for showing at the inn, to show how the inn got its new name.

Decide on the key moments of the story as they have developed it and turn them into six or seven short sharp scenes, pages from the history. Use expanded tableaux.

'The Victorian Street Children'

Learning objectives

Pupils will understand:

- the ideas, beliefs, attitudes and experiences of men, women and children in the past
- the social diversity of the late Victorian period
- how to ask and answer questions, and to select and record relevant information relating to past

Roles

	Role	Signifiers
Teacher	Edward Fitzgerald (Dr Barnardo's assistant)	A lamp
	Thomas Barnes (a photographer)	A case for carrying his equipment
	A wealthy gentleman (could be a lady)	A cape or top hat
Pupils	Social historians	N/A
	The five boys in the photograph	N/A
	Street children	N/A

Research and preparation

Use the photograph from the Barnardo's collection or the version from *Drama Structures* by Cecily O'Neill and Alan Lambert

Read the chapter 'Barnardo before and after' from Blake Morrison's book *Too True* (Granta Books, 1998)

It is also interesting as a follow-up activity to look at other pictures of street children and open up a discussion about the power of images and the values embedded in them

Structure

Contracting

1. **Negotiate doing drama**

2. **Key questions to introduce the drama**

    What is a historian?

    What is a social historian?

    What do historians do?

    What skills do they need to be successful?

3. Looking at a photograph

'Five boys and a man with a lamp'

Whole class interactive whiteboard activity.

Using photographic evidence to frame the historical perspective.

The analysis of the photograph is constrained by the givens, those elements of the analysis that are non-negotiable. The 'givens' are:

- genuine photograph – *c.*1874
- five boys
- man with lamp is called Edward Fitzgerald (he really existed, as did Thomas Barnes, but our use of the roles is entirely fictional)
- photograph was taken in front of derelict buildings
- in Stepney, London.

What do we know? Facts	What do we think we know? Hypotheses	What do we want to find out? Questioning
The non-negotiable elements – the givens: genuine photograph – *c.* 1874 five boys man with lamp – called Edward Fitzgerald photograph was taken in front of derelict buildings in Stepney, London		

The class offer suggestions to expand upon what they already know.

4. TiR as Edward Fitzgerald

ROLE BRIEF

Hot-seating

Edward Fitzgerald

He answers questions about his work.

He is employed to find children who live rough on the streets.

He encourages them to return with him to the new home 'the Good Doctor' has set up. Many of the children are in a dreadful state. They are 'tired and listless'.

We get some food in their belly. Get them some learning. Learn them their letters. Teach them their Bible.

His attitude is patronising but concerned for them. He wants to help them but *you have to be firm with some of these ... they're rough.*

During this dialogue it is important to come out of role and clarify meaning and understanding. The children's task is to make sense of the attitudes being hinted at and what this says about attitudes towards homeless children at that time.

5. Establishing the task

Negotiate with the class five volunteers to take on the role of the boys in the photograph.

We are going to remake this photograph as a tableau, a still image. While five of you will be in the picture with me the rest of you will take the role of people who are writing a report about street children. You are trying to find out the truth by talking to all those people who are involved with their welfare. Your investigations may be the basis of a newspaper article.

This picks up on the work of Henry Mayhew, writer, journalist and co-founder of *Punch* magazine. He devoted some of his writing to social issues and articles were published in *London Labour and the London Poor*. This can give the class a perspective and purpose in their investigations.

6. Setting up the tableau/questioning of the boys

This needs to be done in two parts.

Part One – brief the boys

The five pupils who are taking on the role of the boys. They need time to structure a history and identity for themselves, no more than 15 minutes. To do this they need to decide on several things:

- **Their names.** They should avoid any names of other pupils in the class and they should look at common names for boys at this time. They were often biblical (e.g. Samuel or Joseph) or royal (e.g. Albert or Edward)

- **Their history.** How did they end up on the streets? Life at home, perhaps, too many mouths to feed?

- **Their relationship.** Are any of them blood relations? Or do they stick together like a family?

- **Are any of them ill?** This can be a point of tension or their reason for going back to the home with Fitzgerald.

- **Who is the boss?** Is there one member of the group who speaks for the others? To whom they defer?

Non- negotiable – fear of Fitzgerald

A key element in making the next part of the drama successful.

It must be negotiated that the boys are afraid of Fitzgerald. Not only does this give the improvisation authenticity, as many children were afraid of physical chastisement, but it acts as a constraint for the teacher. Without this the pupils may take it as an opportunity to say what they like to the teacher! Not only would this lose authenticity and tension it would become difficult to manage the learning.

Not all of the boys have to speak or answer all the questions. If the pupils want to raise the tension they can keep silent after certain questions. They can give each other looks which then will have to be decoded by the questioners.

Pupils take on roles

Part Two – Setting up the questioners

Those asking the questions can view themselves as researchers or journalists in the style of Mayhew. They are interested in finding out about life on the streets. They are relatively wealthy and educated therefore they have more power in this situation than Fitzgerald. If they find Fitzgerald's presence too intrusive for the boys to answer the questions, he can be asked to leave, although he will only do this reluctantly. This should only happen when as teacher you are happy the role-play is taking on a life of its own. It means that you move to an OoR position to stop the drama and reflect upon what is happening.

They must be given time to prepare questions and this can be done as a whole class with the pupils in role as the boys listening to their preparation.

Finally, the tableau is set up with the whole class by making reference to the photograph and trying to get the positions of the boys as close to the original as possible. It helps to tell the boys not to look at anyone in the class in the first instance and for the class to maintain a serious tone to the questioning so as to help them create a solemn atmosphere.

Hot-seating the boys

During this section of the drama it is important to come in and out of role as Fitzgerald. Your presence will model the serious attitude of taking on a role and will open up the opportunity to see if your presence as Fitzgerald effects the nature of the dialogue with the boys. The questioners may ask you to leave.

TiR: *I am not sure that is a good idea, ladies and gentlemen. You can't always trust them. They are rough sorts.*

You will, of course, be persuaded to leave and this will allow you to move to your OoR function to manage the questioning and reflection by the class.

7.   Add the information gained to the 'What do you know…?' chart.

8.   Question the photographer, Thomas Barnes

Hot-seating
the
photogapher

The photographer Thomas Barnes offers a view of the street children that is full of prejudice.

I don't have too much time for these do-gooders. To me it's a job and pays regularly. I'm thankful Fitzgerald is there, he keeps them in order. They're pretty rough some of them. You have to keep them still. [He counts to ten] *Ickerty-pickerty one, ickerty-pickerty two … You see they have to keep still and some of them can't do it. What with fleas, an' all. Mind, Fitzgerald keeps them straight.*

ToR examines with the class the implications for our view of the Victorians that the slow technology of early photography imposed upon the evidence – serious expressions and posed positions.

9.   Whole class sculpture and thought-tracking

Whole
class
scultpture

Gather the class together and negotiate that they are all going to be representing the street children in the next part of the drama. They must make a whole class sculpture showing children gathered together on a winter's night in 1874. The sculpture is part of an exhibition in a museum of the future; the exhibit is entitled 'Street Children in the Victorian City'.

The pupils choose a position they can hold still. They must concentrate on their hands and feet. It will help them not to look at anyone else in the group and just concentrate on themselves. The idea of a fire is introduced and issues such as who gets closest to it, who keeps it alight and is there someone to keep look-out?

When they have done this ask half the group to remember their positions and stand away from the others. They are going to be visitors to the museum and you will take the role of their guide.

TiR: *Ladies and gentlemen, welcome to our new exhibit on the theme of children in the nineteenth century. In the next room we have an interactive exhibit, a sculpture of children who were known as street children. When I touch the shoulder of the sculptures they are able to speak and say what they are thinking at this moment in history. Sometimes they say nothing. Some of them are too cold to speak.*

This process is repeated with the second half of the class as the visitors and the first half taking up their positions as the children.

10. Meeting the wealthy gentleman

OoR negotiate that you are going to take the role of a wealthy gentleman who accidentally comes across the scene of the street children around the fire. The sculpture will come to life after a short narration and the class must answer his questions as best they can. OoR, move to one side as the class remake their sculpture and when they are quite still and listening begin to narrate the scene.

From still image to improvisation

Narrate: *It was a bitterly cold December night. A wealthy gentleman had been waiting for a cab to take him back to his large London house. His patience had run out and he decided to take a short cut through the damp foggy night to his mansion. It was then that he came across a scene that appalled him. A scattered bundle of rags huddled around the dying embers of a fire. He realized these were children and went straight to his house and organised soup and bread to be brought to them. He sat down amongst them.*

OoR: *Pick up your bowls. Cup your hands and think of the warmth and sustenance this is going to give you. Just concentrate on **your** bowl, ignore everybody else and imagine you have a crust of bread to dip into the soup. Mime dipping the bread into the soup. Decide whether you are going to eat it slowly, and make it last, or greedily and quickly.*

Narrate: *As they sat there enjoying their unexpected good fortune, the gentleman began to question them.*

TiR as the rich gentleman: *What are you doing out here? Have you no home to go to?*

The questions continue. *Where do you live? Where are your parents? ...* and crucially *How do you survive?*

This is usually responded to with, *We steal.*

You steal! Do you not know your Bible? Do you not know your Ten Commandments?

The questioning and reasoning about their behaviour can continue and the gentleman will offer a place at the workhouse where he is a governor. This is usually received with some indignation and their perception of life in the workhouse will be revealed. The old gentleman will tell them that, as a governor of a workhouse, he has never seen the cruelty they talk of and he will be especially vigilant in the future.

11. Class discussion

Reflection on attitudes expressed in drama

The class discuss the attitudes of the various roles and go back to their chart of 'What do we know...' etc.

The drama can lead into the drama about the workhouse or to sharing literature (possibly Dickens) and written evidence of the time (Mayhew, etc.).

Further discussion can focus on the street children of the twenty-first century: 'Where do we still see children living on the streets?'

Structure summary

1 **Negotiate doing drama.**

2 **Key questions – what is a historian?**

3 **Looking at the photograph of the man with the lamp.**
Decide and record 'what we know', 'what we think we know' and 'what we want to find out'.

4 **TiR as Edward Fitzgerald.**
Attitudes toward the poor and what needs to be done with them.
OoR: *What is his attitude to the boys and how does he see his job?*

5 **Establishing the task.**
We are going to remake this photograph ...

6 **Setting up the boys to be questioned.**
Contracting their fear of Fitzgerald.
The class question the boys with TiR as Fitzgerald. Be prepared to be asked to leave so that the class can question without Fitzgerald's presence.

7 **Add to 'What do you know?' chart.**

8 **Questioning the photographer, Thomas Barnes.**
His attitude and issues of technology and photography.

9 **Whole class sculpture and thought-tracking.**
Split class in half and view each half as if a museum of the future.

10 **Meeting the wealthy gentleman: living through drama.**

11 **Whole class discussion on the issues raised.**
Are there any street children now in the world?

'The Workhouse'

Learning objectives

Pupils will understand:

- the conditions of the workhouse
- issues of power, justice and fairness
- the concept of reform as it related to the workhouse

Roles

	Role	Signifiers
Teacher	Crimmins, employee at the workhouse	A cap
	Mards, the Workhouse Master	A stick
Pupils	The commissioners	N/A
Volunteer	Martha – a new inmate	Rolled blanket as baby
	Inmates of the workhouse	N/A

Research and preparation

- Picture of a workhouse – Abingdon, Oxfordshire is a good example as it exemplifies the oppressive nature of workhouses
- If possible, find where the local workhouse was and research for a local picture and Workhouse Rules
- It is interesting as a follow-up activity to look at other pictures of workhouses, many of which do not look oppressive, and open up a discussion about power of images and the values embedded in them
- The website at http://users.ox.ac.uk/~peter/workhouse/ is very good for background information and images

This drama benefits from two separate sessions. The first or preliminary session is to set up the roles, establish the context and introduce the role of the Workhouse Master.

Structure

1. Negotiate doing drama

Contracting

We will all have some part to play in the drama. There will not be an audience. There will not be any script or learning of lines. We will stop the drama every now and again to talk about what has happened.

2. Introduce the focus of the drama, the workhouse

Picture stimulus

Show a picture of a workhouse, e.g. the drawing of the Abingdon workhouse.

What sort of place does it look like? Who would go there? Why?

Let's begin to answer some of these questions:

- In the nineteeth century there were places called workhouses.

- They were the last place a person would go to if they had nowhere to live.

- Every town would have a workhouse; some larger towns and cities would have several.

- Towards the end of the nineteenth century many important people, people in the government, church leaders, people with power, were not happy with the treatment of people in workhouses.

3. Role for the class

OoR: *To find out what workhouses were like, you are going to be members of a Royal Commission enquiring into them.*

Key question: *What are Royal Commissions?*

Royal Commissions are set up to find out the truth about something and there were several Royal Commissions to look at the conditions of the poor in the nineteenth and early twentieth century.

As members of a Royal Commission you are powerful people. What you ask to see you must be shown. You are also fair people, you may have heard a great deal about the workhouse but you will only judge on what you see and hear. You must find out the truth, what conditions are like.

Key question: *If you are members of a Royal Commission what are you going to be good at?*

Who will you need to talk to?

What sort of things will you want to find out about?

Now you will meet the Workhouse Master and other people who live and work in the workhouse. Your job is to make a report on the workhouse.

4. TiR as Mards, the Workhouse Master

> ### *Mards*
>
> Mards suspects all of the inmates of the workhouse, he believes them to be work-shy, lazy and in need of rules, discipline and reform. His rule book is his Bible and he uses phrases such as 'a tight ship' and 'cleanliness is next to Godliness', 'the devil finds work for idle hands', etc.

As a way to introduce the drama you are going to have a chance to meet briefly the Workhouse Master, Mr Mards. He is going to talk to you and you will have a chance to ask him a couple of questions. We don't have long this morning but you will be able to make a more detailed investigation in the next part of the drama.

Mards introduces the rule book he has to ensure the workhouse is run fairly and efficiently.

The class question the Workhouse Master. The role does not give too much information but hints at his attitudes and view of the workhouse inmates without being too specific.

The interview is brief, five or six questions long, and is enough to interest the class in their role as commissioners.

End of Preliminary Session

MAIN SESSION

5.   Task – visualising the workhouse

Have the picture of the Abingdon workhouse for the class to see. Place two chairs to represent the door of the workhouse. Stand the class in a group facing the chairs.

Using your drama eyes

OoR: *I want you to use your drama eyes and imagine we are approaching the workhouse. Look at the picture of the workhouse. Now look at the door represented by the two chairs in front of you. Tell me words and phrases that describe what you see. What is this door made of? How big is it? How is it opened? How do people outside the door make known to those inside they want to come in?*

Manage the ideas; where there are differences, try to combine them in one idea. For example, if one pupil says the door is metal and another says it is made of oak you can combine the ideas with: *It's a huge oak door with strips of iron to strengthen it and iron hinges and a great metal bolt with a chain attached to it.*

Then continue with a non-negotiable element of the picture: *In one door is a small shutter. This can be opened by anyone wanting to see who is at the door.*

Discuss how they will get in. Is there a bell? They are not expected. *This is a surprise visit. What would be the advantage of visiting unannounced?*

They are going to meet Crimmins. He works for the Workhouse Master. He used to be an inmate of the workhouse but is now employed there. How did he get to be chosen to work for the Master? Why would the Workhouse Master want to employ him?

I am now going to be Crimmins. He will come to the door and speak first then you can speak to him. What are you going to say?

6.   TiR as Crimmins

TiR contact role

Crimmins approaches ...

TiR: *Who are you? What do you want? Are you looking for the Town Hall? I hope you're not charity do-gooders again. We want no charity here! The Master's very busy. Be off with you! Go and do good somewhere else!*

Listen to the response of the class. When they say who they are there is a change in Crimmins's attitude.

I am most humbly sorry. I thought you were the charity people poking their noses in. I didn't realise, what with ladies being in your party. Do come in.

Perhaps a glass of something, some supper after your journey from London?

I will get the Master.

OoR look at the change in Crimmins's demeanour when he realises who the visitors are, and his attitude to Mards.

7. Setting up of Mards's office

Defining the space

OoR: *We are going to make the Master of the Workhouse's room and I want you to tell me what is in there. I will make labels of the objects you decide are in there and you will decide where you want them.*

As the class decide upon different objects, table, chair, wine cabinet, etc., get them to explain why they think those objects are in there. Are there differences between this room and the rooms for the inmates? What are those differences and why?

I want you to stand around the room and you will hear the voice of Crimmins talking to Mards. Listen to him then we will stop and talk about what he has said and what we understand is going on.

8. TiR as Crimmins

Overheard conversation

TiR: *They're here, Master, the inspection trouble-makers.*

And there's a new one arriving. Shall I tell them to wait till we get her out the way?

OoR: *What is his attitude to the Commissioners? How will you be towards Crimmins and Mards during this visit?*

TiR as Crimmins: *Mr Mards would like you to partake in a glass of sherry in his office. We've got a new one arriving ... young woman by the name of Martha ... and her baby. We'd like to get her in here, so Mr Mards can explain the rules. So you'll have to wait here till he's finished with her. Is that OK?*

OoR: *Why is he asking you to wait? What does he not want you to see?*

If the class say they wish to witness the induction of Martha into the workhouse then that is set up. If they do not, then negotiate with them about what would be the value for the Commissioners to see the induction. What would they learn from it?

9. Thought-tracking Martha

Conscience alley

The class return to the door of the workhouse. They make two lines facing each other, like a corridor leading to the door. One of the pupils is going to be Martha. She holds a blanket wrapped to signify a baby. She does not have to speak and all she has to do is walk slowly towards the door of the workhouse with her head down. She must not make eye contact with the class.

Introduce the idea of a conscience alley, the opportunity to hear what someone is thinking as they approach a difficult situation. Before she begins walking to the workhouse door say to the class:

Martha is going to walk towards the great gate of the workhouse. She doesn't want to go there but she has a baby and nowhere else to go. It is her last resort. As she approaches the door we can hear her thoughts, her fears, her worries. You do not have to speak if you can't think of anything to say or if someone has already voiced your thoughts.

The pupils voice the thoughts of Martha.

We will now listen to what Mards is thinking. Martha will walk again towards the door where he stands to receive her.

The exercise is repeated, this time with the class listening to the thoughts of Mards as Martha approaches.

TiR as Mards: *Another waster. Another scraggy baby to feed. I hope she's a good worker. She and that baby better not be ill. Don't want her bringing her disease in here. I'll take that baby off her straight away. Maybe wait till this lot have gone. Must impress the inspector do-gooders while they're here. Can get back to normal when they've gone.*

When Martha stands in front of Mards, he speaks to her:

TiR: *We've got special visitors, right! So say as little as possible and you'll get in. Speak and we'll have no room!*

10. Forum theatre – Martha

The class make a horseshoe shape around a chair. Martha sits on the chair with her baby. The class will speak for Martha or swap in to sit in the chair to answer questions.

For this to work they must agree two things:

- She is frightened of Mards
- She has a baby and desperately needs to get into the workhouse

Collectively the class will give Martha a history. Why has she ended up with nowhere to go? What has happened to her? What does she know of the workhouse?

This having been considered and agreed, move to the forum.

Place another chair opposite Martha's. This is where TiR as Mards will question her.

11. TiR as Mards

Mards will read the first rule of the workhouse to her.

Rule One
ORDERED, that all Persons upon their admission deliver up such household furniture, linen, and clothes as they are possessed, to the Master in order to be cleaned and made useful for the service of the house; that they be clothed if necessary, and have their proper apartments and employments assigned them by the Master; and if such persons be likely to be discharged from the house, their old clothes are to be kept until they be discharged, and then delivered to them to wear, in exchange for the clothes found by the house. (Cumbria Record Office)

So what goods have you got to hand over? Anything of any value?

Your baby will be taken to the older women to look after it. You'll work in the washhouse. Is that clear?

You will wash and be given a workhouse uniform.

The class are constrained by Martha's need to get shelter with her baby and the contract to apply the givens.

Mards insists on her compliance to all the rules.

Sidebar notes:

Setting up the induction of Martha Forum theatre

Givens

Building Martha's role

Use of historical primary source

The induction of a new inmate

Class take the role of the commissioners to question Mards

12. The commissioners have a chance to speak to Mards about the induction

OoR: *What questions or things do you want to say to Mr Mards at this point?*

TiR as Mards will try to justify why he does things that way ... put her to work, make her useful, etc.

13. Introducing the research section: turning the workhouse rules into tableaux

Using authentic materials on which to base narrative

The class will now shift role to inmates of the workhouse. To this set this up they will use the rules of the Kendal workhouse. The language of the rules has been modified to make them more accessible. Using rules from a local workhouse can be part of the research part of the pre-drama activities.

ToR: *In the next part of the drama you are going to take the role of the inmates in order to look at life in the workhouse from their point of view.*

This will begin as a group activity. The class is divided into four groups and each group is allocated a rule. The rules can be discussed as a whole class initially. The fifth rule will be a whole class activity.

The tableaux are to show each rule being broken. The text of the rule can be put on the interactive board.

The groups of pupils will then make an image of the moment the rule is broken. They may add one line each and one movement to the picture.

Rule One
ORDERED, that all Persons upon their admission deliver up such household furniture, linen, and clothes as they are possessed, to the Master in order to be cleaned and made useful for the service of the house; that they be clothed if necessary, and have their proper apartments and employments assigned them by the Master; and if such persons be likely to be discharged from the house, their old clothes are to be kept until they be discharged, and then delivered to them to wear, in exchange for the clothes found by the house.

Rule Two
That no person go out of the prescribed bounds without leave from the Master or Mistress, and to return in good order at the time appointed, or be denied going out for a considerable time afterwards.

Rule Three
That the slothful and idle, who pretend ailments, to excuse themselves from work, be properly examined; and if it appears they have been impostors and have made false excuses, then they shall be punished, by restricting their allowance of diet, or by confinement in the dungeon.

Rule Four
That a book be kept wherein the names and surnames of every grown person shall be set down and called every Sunday evening, and if any of the said persons are missing or any other offence be committed by any in the house the name shall be noted, in order that the offender be examined and punished. (Cumbria Record Office)

Look at the pictures and what they demonstrate about rules.

14. 'Infamous liar' rule – whole group tableau

For this rule the whole class make a still image of Rule Five.

ToR: *In this final tableau you all need to decide who you are in the workhouse and how you ended up there. Listen to the rule and then we will make some decisions about how we can show the rule being broken.*

> Rule Five
> *Persons convicted of lying, to be set on stools in the most public place of the dining room, while the rest are at dinner, and have papers fixed on their chest, with these written thereon, 'infamous liar', and shall lose that meal. (Cumbria Record Office)*

Focus upon the 'infamous liar' rule as a whole class activity

ToR: *Martha has been stealing food – she is so hungry and has to feed the baby four times a day. The workhouse master has discovered this and has hung the label 'infamous liar' around her neck ... not for one day but for all week ... with bread and water rations. Not only that but all the inmates have been given half rations until the stolen food has been paid for.*

They are thought-tracked as to how they feel about Martha's punishment. They then make a circle around Martha and voice her thoughts as she stands with the label 'infamous liar' hanging around her neck.

ToR: *In the next part of the drama Mards, the Workhouse Master, is going to speak to Martha, so I want you to watch and listen then we will stop and talk about what he says.*

15. TiR as Mards

Introducing a dilemma

TiR: *Right you need to get down from there. One of those busybody visitors is coming back. If he comes through here I don't want him seeing you up there on that stool. Get off the stool. Give me that label and mind your tongue if he speaks to you or there'll be trouble when he's gone!*

OoR: *How are you going to deal with the Commissioner? What are the risks you take if you tell the truth?*

What are the consequences if you don't use this opportunity to say how things really are in the workhouse?

16. TiR as Commissioner

Tir raises the tension

He picks up the 'infamous liar' sign from beneath the chair.

What's going on here? Who is the liar?

The class have to deal with him. They have to decide whether to tell the truth about Mards or say nothing.

If they say nothing TiR comments what a well-run, fair and just place this is and how lucky they all are being placed under the care of Mr Mards.

Alternatively they may wish to tell the Commissioner how it really is in the workhouse, in which case they need to decide how they avoid retribution when the Commissioner has gone.

Forum theatre to deal with Mards

17. Forum theatre with TiR as Mards

The class return to their role as commissioners to confront him with what they have seen.

Mards is defensive and eventually shows his deep-seated dislike of the inmates.

18. Workhouse reality

Images of life in the workhouse

Divide the class into groups to show the inspectors what life is really like.

The class make pictures to show how harsh it is in the workhouse. While each group show their pictures the rest of the class, as the commissioners, will take Mards around to show him and ask for an explanation.

19. Setting an agenda for reform

Whole class activity

The commission draw up a list of changes that must happen and confront Mards. Do they sack him? Or is he able to reform the workhouse? They must decide and tell him.

Structure summary

1 Negotiate doing drama.

2 Introduce the focus of the drama; the workhouse.

3 Role for the class.

4 TiR as Mards, the Workhouse Master.

End of Preliminary Session

Main Session

5 Task – visualising the workhouse.

6 TiR as Crimmins.

7 Setting up of Mards's office.

8 TiR as Crimmins.

9 Thought-tracking Martha.

10 Forum theatre – Martha.

11 TiR as Mards.

12 The commissioners have a chance to speak to Mards about the induction.

13 Introducing the research section.

14 'Infamous liar rule'.

15 TiR as Mards.

16 TiR as Commissioner.

17 Forum theatre with TiR as Mards.
Class in role as the commissioners confront him with what they have seen.

18 Workhouse reality.

19 Setting an agenda for reform.

'The Egyptians'

Learning objectives

Pupils will understand:

- that ancient Egypt provides us with stories and views of the world that were different than our own
- the concept of absolute rule

PSHE – the over-arching theme of family and relationships

- the idea of ambition and its effect upon others
- the concept of selfishness and ambition
- the issue of accepting or disagreeing with choices made by family members

Roles

	Role	Signifier
Teacher	Expedition leader High Priest's servant, Hathor High Priest Servant, Geb Wife, Selquet	Clip board When running this drama we made simple distinguishing sashes to represent the different status of the roles
Pupils	Archaeologists Geb and Selquet in the final conscience alley	N/A N/A

Research and preparation

- Pictures of the inside and outside of a pyramid in Egypt
- Pictures of a Pharaoh and a High Priest or Priestess
- A map of the Nile Delta

Structure – preliminary session

1. Negotiate doing drama

Contract

- introduce the way of working and the content
- introduce their role in the drama – archaeologists
- introduce pictures of the tomb and the pharaoh

2. OoR introduce the idea of an expedition

The expedition is going to the Nile Valley to explore a pyramid in the early part of the twentieth century. Introduce the class role of archaeologists.

What do archaeologists do? What tools do they use?

3. TiR as Head of British Egyptology Expedition

TiR sets the
context

Good morning, ladies and gentlemen. I have some important news. I have just received a letter from our sponsor, Lord Bryant.

Dear Society of Egyptologists

Regarding the expedition I am sponsoring. I have just received confirmation from the Governor of the Al-Minya region that we will be given four weeks to explore the site on the eastern bank of the Nile, 20 kilometres south of the city of Al-Minya.

The licence will last until the 20th of August and you must leave the site in good condition. Anything you find must not be taken out of the country, although drawings, photographs and replicas may be taken from the site. Please respect the religious nature of this site and the indigenous peoples of this land.

Lord Bryant of Stafford

---

4. Current knowledge and misconceptions

Exploring
what the
class know

Out of role draw up lists from the following three questions about the subject of ancient Egypt and the pyramids:

What do you know?

What do you think you know?

What do you want to find out?

Having made an audit of the class's current knowledge and understandings, as well as their misunderstandings, you can do some research with the class outside the drama to increase their content knowledge in preparation for the main session.

Structure – main session

5. Recap on preliminary session

Who are you in the drama? What was the letter you received, who was it from and what was it telling you? What is your task?

OoR: *In the first part of the drama the archaeologists are working in the tomb of the Pharaoh.* Negotiate working in the tomb, what does it look like? (Look again at the picture.) *What jobs would you be doing? What is your special skill?*

Set up the room with some chairs or a table to represent an altar.

When the class have decided what tasks they are doing in the tomb, get them to make a whole class photograph of the work going on.

6. Introducing the idea of a shift in time

Class sets
the context

OoR: *I am going to narrate what happens in the story and I want you to bring the picture to life while at the same time listening to the story to know what is going to happen next.*

Narrate: *The team were working hard. They knew they hadn't got long before they would have to leave. They needed to work efficiently. They made measurements and drawings, took photographs and examined vases and artefacts. As they worked the lights dimmed.*

TiR as Chief of the Expedition:

Look, we seem to be having problems with the generator. We're going to have to work by flame-lit torches. Can you light a torch where you are working and put it on the stand? I will go and see what the problem is.

7. TiR as the High Priest's servant

TiR shifts the focus – back in time

Immediately go into role as Hathor, the High Priest's servant: TiR: *I am glad to see you have lit the sacred torches. The High Priest has approved the story. The life of the Pharaoh is ready and your work may begin. The walls of the tomb must be ready by the New Moon. Gather around and I will give you your tasks, your part of the wall decoration.*

ToR: *Who is this? Do we know his name? And what has happened?*

The fact they have gone back in time is negotiated.

What are the implications for us in the story? How could this be a great opportunity for the archaeologists?

We will now go back to the story to listen to the High Priest's servant.

The class gather round the High Priest's servant.

TiR: *The High Priest has decreed you must create five pictures of the great Pharaoh Chephren's life in this new tomb.*

He hands out scrolls.

The first picture is of his childhood and the time it became known he was indeed the God Horus in human form.

The second is of his great strength and ability as an athlete.

The third is his power and magnificent cruelty – no human can challenge him.

The fourth is how he has created wealth and the largest pyramid known.

And the final picture is of his journey to heaven with Re, the Sun God, accompanied by his most faithful servants.

You must have them ready soon, for the High Priest will be here to inspect our work – and as you know he is powerful and we must please him or we will suffer his wrath. I don't want to be sacrificed to the evil God Seth!

ToR: *Have you any questions for the High Priest's servant?*

This is an opportunity to clarify issues through the role. There may be questions about the High Priest or why the walls are being decorated. The High Priest's servant answers their questions and then leaves.

8. Group task – making the tableaux

Building
belief and
using the
research

Tell the class to discuss what they have to do – the pictures they must make. It is best to gather ideas and interpretation as a whole class initially then move into groups for the creation of the pictures.

The pictures must be made with these considerations:

- They must be in positions that can be held still for some time.
- This can be helped by telling the pupils not to have eye contact with anyone.
- They might use labels/pictures to help us know what is in the picture.
- Rehearse making all the pictures together – each title is read out for each picture.

9. TiR as the High Priest enters to inspect the work

TiR
honours the
class's
work

TiR: *Let me see the room as it will look for our great Pharaoh Chephren. Let me see the life of our God King.*

OoR: set up the room as it will look, two pictures down either side of the room and one behind the altar.

TiR as the High Priest is complimentary about their work. He looks at the last picture:

Good, I am glad the favourite servants of our Pharaoh are in this – this will please him.

He then turns to the class:

Get the ritual ready. When I return I want the blessing of the pictures to be rehearsed and read. Each picture must be blessed with gifts. No mistakes do you understand? I want a blessing ritual fit for the Gods. Now I haven't got time for this, get it ready now!

He walks out.

10. Creating a ritual

OoR: *What does the High Priest mean – we need to have the ritual of the blessing?*

Discuss the meaning of the word ritual. When do we have rituals now? Footballers lining up at the beginning of a match, birthday parties, etc. It is useful to have a structure for this in which the pupils' ideas are added.

We need to work out a ritual, a blessing ceremony. Any ideas? Sounds movement, etc.

Where does it start? It ends with making the pictures ... each in turn.

This is done as a whole class activity. It is almost like a procession to the altar to present a gift or bow, and then each group moving into their tableau and then watching the others as they do the same. The pupils' ideas can be related to the sounds, chants, percussion, etc. This can be done as a separate activity to be taken to the drama when ready.

When the ritual is finished and during the final rehearsal for the High Priest, stop the drama and say: *While the servants were practising the ritual, a man stood at the side and watched.*

I want you to watch and to listen and then we will stop and discuss what happened and what was said.

11. Setting up the entrance of Geb

The pictures have been made at this point.

Narrate: *At the end of the blessing a figure moved into the tomb. He had been watching.*

TiR as Geb, the Pharaoh's favourite servant, approaches and kneels down in front of the altar, beginning to pray aloud:

Anubis, God of embalmers, thank you for making me the Pharaoh's favourite. I will be chosen to accompany him, to row him across the sky.

Geb looks up and sees the last of the pupils' pictures, gets up and moves to the last picture and sees himself.

This is truly wonderful! This is me! I AM to be chosen.

Geb returns to the altar and kneels to pray.

TiR presents the dilemma

12. Hot-seating Geb

The pupils have a chance to talk to Geb. The class question Geb as to why he is there.

ROLE BRIEF

Geb

Geb believes he was to be chosen to accompany the Pharaoh on his last journey to be sealed in the tomb with him. He is very proud of his position and the privilege it gives him. He thinks little about anything or anyone else. If the class raise the issue of how others feel about his sacrifice he is dismissive but may mention in passing that he has a wife and small child.

This is a great honour. It means my name will live on forever. I will be famous, known throughout the land. Geb, the favourite of the Pharaoh Chephren! The High Priest is jealous of me. He doesn't like the way the Pharaoh treats me, asking me for advice and not him. Me, a mere servant!

13. Return of TiR as the High Priest

As Geb, you stop to look around as if someone has just arrived. Stop the drama and ask the class what they think has happened.

ToR: *Why has Geb stopped speaking? Why did he bow?*

Negotiate that someone has arrived in the tomb and you are going to take that role. The class must imagine Geb is still there and place Geb's sash on the chair (or whatever signifier you are using for him).

Narrate: *As the archaeologists were talking to Geb, the High Priest returned.*

Raising the tension

High Priest (to the signifier as Geb): *What are you doing in here? You know you are not allowed in here, not until the day of the ceremony. Not only are you stopping these people working, you are desecrating this tomb by your illegal presence here. I will have you arrested.*

OoR tell the class they must deal with the High Priest as if they were Geb:

Anyone of you can speak for Geb as the High Priest questions you.

The High Priest will not accept any defence. It is obvious he has found something to accuse Geb of and will take this information to the Pharaoh.

14. Thought-tracking Geb

Thought-tracking

Discuss the implications for Geb. Get the class to stand around the chair with his signifier on and thought-track them.

15. TiR as Geb asks for their help

The responsibility for the class

Now I have lost everything. Will you do one thing for me? Will you go to my wife and tell her what has happened. Her name is Selquet. She thinks I am at work at the Pharaoh's palace. I cannot leave here. The guards will be here soon.

OoR: *You are now going to meet Geb's wife, Selquet.*

ROLE BRIEF

Geb's wife

She is sad because her husband is selfish. He cares only about his job and his ambition to be buried with the Pharaoh. She has to manage everything herself – the house, her baby. He works long hours and has little time for her and the child and now she receives this information.

OoR: *What is she to do? I want you to look at her and see how she is before you talk to her.*

16. TiR as Selquet

Selquet sits alone with a piece of cloth to represent her baby. She is reading and a scroll and looks sad. On the scroll is written a message:

IT IS DECREED BY THE KING GOD

OUR GREAT

PHARAOH CHEPHREN

THAT THE SERVANT

GEB

SHALL ACCOMPANY HIM TO THE AFTER-LIFE

HONOURED ARE THOSE THAT ARE SEALED IN THE TOMB

Negotiate with the class what they must say to her. How do they tell her about what has happened?

The class find out more about Geb

TiR as Selquet: *Geb is only interested in himself – in fame – in being immortal.*

The edict would have meant he would leave me on my own. And now he is in disgrace it will be the same. And what of me? The child? What can you do to help? Can you appeal to the High Priest? Will not the loss of his ambition be punishment enough?

OoR: *Where do your sympathies lie? With whom?*

17. To whom do they wish to speak?

Possibilities the class may choose:

Key choice for the class

(a) Speak to the High Priest

If they wish to speak to the High Priest to try to persuade him to change his mind, he is adamant the punishment is fair and according to the law of Egypt.

(b) Speak to the Pharaoh

The Pharaoh regards the event as a test. Geb has failed. He forgot his place. He lacks humility. To make the Pharaoh distanced from the human form, he answers all his questions with questions. For example, *Is not humility the test of worthiness? Does not the High Priest speak for you humans? Can we gods be involved in such trivia?*

(c) Forum wife and Geb

Class to take the part of Geb's wife and TiR as Geb.

18. Final picture and conscience alley

The class remake the picture from the tomb of the boat journey across the sky with a pupil representing Geb in it.

The rest of the class form two lines leading towards the picture. The High Priest (TiR), followed by a pupil taking the role of Geb's wife, walk down towards the picture and the pupils voice the wife's thoughts.

The High Priest ties rope around Geb's wrists, takes him from the picture and leads him back down the lines.

Geb's wife stays at the picture.

The class voice the thoughts of Geb as he is taken away.

Exploring the class's position

19. Sociogram of Geb and Selquet

Two chairs, one representing Geb and the other his wife. They must choose whom they stand close to and this will represent their feelings. The class are then thought-tracked as to why they have chosen the place where they stand.

Structure summary

Prelimary session

1 Negotiate doing drama.

2 OoR introduce the idea of an expedition to the Nile.

3 TiR as head of British Egyptology Expedition.

   Read letter from Lord Bryant.

4 OoR diagnosing current knowledge and ironing out misconceptions.

Main session

5 OoR recap on prelimary session and negotiate working in the tomb.

6 Introducing the idea of a shift in time moving into narration and TiR as Chief of the Expedition.

7 TiR as the High Priest's servant.

   Building the context and introducing a narrative-building exercise.

8 Group task – making the tableaux.

9 Inspection of the pictures by TiR as the High Priest.

   He demands a ritual to accompany the service.

10 Creating a ritual.

    Setting up the context for the entrance of the Pharaoh's favourite servant.

11 Setting up the entrance of TiR as Geb.

12 Hot-seating Geb.

13 Return of the High Priest and threats to Geb.

    Class must handle the High Priest.

14 Thought-tracking Geb.

15 TiR as Geb tells them of his wife, Selquet, and asks for their help.

    Setting up the meeting with Selquet.

16 TiR as Selquet.

    The class find out more about Geb.

17 To whom do they wish to speak?

    To the High Priest or the Pharaoh? Or do they wish to forum Geb and Selquet?

18 Final picture and conscience alley.

19 Sociogram of Geb and Selquet.

    For whom do you have the most sympathy?

'Macbeth'

A drama based on *Macbeth* by William Shakespeare

Learning objectives

Pupils will understand:

- issues about *Macbeth* and Shakespeare's language
- about tackling someone who abuses power.

Roles

	Role	Signifier
Teacher	Steward Macbeth	Staff of office Sceptre
Pupils	Servants at Macbeth's castle	N/A

Research and preparation

- Refreshment reading of the play
- Preparation of the extracts from the play, the letter (see structure point 10)
- Pictures of Elizabeth I or Henry VIII and an Elizabethan banquet
- Preparation of symbols like candle, red cloth

Structure

1. **Negotiate doing drama**

2. **Introduction**

   OoR: *What must it have been like to be a king 500 years ago?*

   How glorious it must have been to be a monarch at this time ...

   Look at a picture of Elizabeth I or Henry VIII and an Elizabethan banquet. The class define the power the king must have had and what the banquet might have involved – food, decoration, entertainment.

   The King is holding a great banquet to entertain all his friends since he has recently become King. You are the servants set to organise this event. Lay the room out. He intends to make a speech to his guests so make sure the room is set up for it. See to all the food and entertainment.

   They are instructed to work together as a class to set out the banquet room. Give them some gold cloth to use to show which place is the throne.

Show what the servants are doing on the great day.

Mime loop

Create the jobs in action for servants to represent work being done for the banquet.

Use a mime loop.

In groups create an occupational mime but represent it in four to six stages. Then organise it so that you all finish where you can start the same sequence again easily and seamlessly and loop them until stopped.

Look at them and what they show.

(Later, see structure point 12, when Macbeth's guilt is recognised, the loop will be revisited and changed as the activity would now be seen through Macbeth's eyes, coloured by his guilt and his evil ... e.g. chopping vegetables becomes a stabbing motion.)

3.   The focus of the drama

TiR as the Chief Steward to the King:

TiR Steward
establishes
tension of
expectations

I felt I had to come to warn you. You are the most trusted servants. As you know this is the most important banquet that has happened for a long time. He has invited all great people to celebrate this most important time in his life now that he has become king. However, it's important that you know that he's not in a good mood this morning. Make sure that everything is prepared, everything in its place and everything done in the right way. He is sure to come down to check on things. We have known each other for a long time. We must look after each other, protect each other's backs. He will be looking for me – I must go. Be careful! He's wanting it all to be just right.

4.   TiR as Macbeth

TiR
Macbeth
raises
tension

The group go back to the representation of the activities. During the preparations enter TiR as Macbeth in a foul mood ... walk through the activity stopping and staring but not speaking. Look towards the chair set up with the gold cloth on the throne. Survey it ... silence. If they have only covered one chair, which is fairly certain, you declare, *Where is the place for my great Queen? I shall assume that you have not got to the point of putting it in yet ...*

Look at the servants and see if any apologise and set to remedying the situation. If they are too awestruck, come OoR and negotiate what they think they should do/say to cover the mistake.

ROLE BRIEF

> ## *Macbeth*
>
> The main focus for the role is the paranoia and the guilt that the play works on.
>
> This behaviour by Macbeth is represented by his oppression of the servants. There is no way they could be expected to have created two thrones and the teacher does not tell them to, but that only reinforces how Macbeth is.

Exit Macbeth.

5. **Sociogram – showing reaction to Macbeth at this stage**

6. **TiR as Chief Steward returns**

Gather the servants round. *Has he been in? What was he like?*

Introduce the story of the chambermaid:

I have grave news, which only serves to show how difficult the time is for us and how uncertain his behaviour.

The Queen's chambermaid was slow in clearing her mistress's chamber this morning and he visited to check the room. Unfortunately there were remnants of her Majesty's supper; there was bread and wine left on the table. There were crumbs and spilt wine and a used knife left lying in the spilt wine. He saw it and, according to the girl, who arrived then, he went livid white and cried out that it should be removed at once. He is vowing to punish the girl for her idleness. He said he will have her hand cut off. I hope I can intercede for her but we all must be very careful now.

There is the need for us all to keep an eye on the King.

End of Part one

PART TWO

7. **Recap last session**

8. **After the banquet**

Narrate: *The next morning the servants gathered round the great table to be addressed by the steward.*

TiR Steward: *We have to think about what happened last night. Your work was excellent and the banquet was a credit to you all. It was not your fault that things went wrong.*

As it was reported to me, because I was not in the room at the time, some of you will have seen it, our Lord was not himself. He was the last person to come to the banqueting hall, his was the only seat empty. The assembled company were all expectation as he approached the table. And then he stopped and as it was reported to me ...

Describe the report of Macbeth at the banquet. Use language from the text, but mediated in the delivery because it is as reported rather than as delivered in an acted speech by Macbeth, so if the teacher stumbles it does not matter because the Steward is trying to remember.

He looked at the empty throne and then he said:

> *Thou can'st not say I did it ... Never shake*
> *Thy gory locks at me ...*

Then he paused and seemed to remember himself and turned to the guests and said:

> *Do not muse at me, my most worthy friends:*
> *I have a strange infirmity, which is nothing*
> *To those that know me.*

But again he turned to the throne and, his face ashen, he cried out:

> *Avaunt and quit my sight!*
> *Let the earth hide thee!*
> *Thy bones are marrowless, thy blood is cold.*

At this point the Queen seemed to recognise that all was not right and intervened drawing him away and urging the rest of the company to finish the meal without them.

It was a sorry meal with much speculation by the lords and ladies present and they dispersed early.

9. Servants discuss what they have seen with the Steward

What does this mean? What has he seen?

The class need to be led through what the words might mean (either in role as the Steward or out of role). What does he mean by 'gory locks'? What is on the throne, etc.? They may know the play in which case they may add from this knowledge. They do not need to know the play and will work their way towards the idea of someone having been killed. Classes have suggested he killed the previous king, which is useful. They do not need to work out that it is the ghost of Banquo on the throne, as in the play.

Even if they only get a vague idea that Macbeth is mad and guilty that is fine.

10. The Steward provides more evidence

TiR: *I have received other evidence that something is amiss. The Queen's chambermaid, who is under threat from the King gave me this. She found it in her lady's chamber. If you cannot read I will tell you what it says.*

He produces the letter sent by Macbeth to Lady Macbeth at the beginning of Act 1 scene V. Copies can be handed round, one between two or three, written out in a suitable hand.

TiR introduces further text from the play	They met me in the day of success: and I have learned by the perfectest report, they have more in them than mortal knowledge. When I burned in desire to question them further, they made themselves air, into which they vanished. Whiles I stood rapt in the wonder of it, came missives from the king, who all-hailed me 'Thane of Cawdor'; by which title, before, these weird sisters saluted me, and referred me to the coming on of time, with 'Hail, king that shalt be!' This have I thought good to deliver thee, my dearest partner of greatness, that thou mightst not lose the dues of rejoicing, by being ignorant of what greatness is promised thee. Lay it to thy heart, and farewell.

Discuss what this shows.

(*Optional*: In groups OoR design a tableaux to show what they think was happening at this moment and what this shows about Macbeth.)

If the servants suggest they suspect 'murder' the Steward can introduce a note of scepticism:

I cannot believe that our King could have done such things. How can we be sure? We are in great danger if we are right or if we are wrong.

How do we cover up and pretend nothing has happened? What do we do for ourselves? See what ideas you can come up with. I must get about my business. I will talk to you later tonight.

He hands the letter to one of them and leaves them to discuss their next step.

11. The servants are threatened with discovery

TiR presents a challenge for the group

As they are discussing, change roles to TiR Macbeth and stand far across the room from them as though you are in another room, looking about and walking up and down.

There are no servants? Why is the palace empty? Why should I be shouting for servants? You should be here to see me now.

The servants have to deal with this moment. Go OoR if they struggle to overcome the shock of the challenge and negotiate how they might get round it.

As an example: in one session as the class all stood tense and unsure of what to do, one pupil took the initiative, strode quietly over to Macbeth and said, *Sorry, your Majesty, but we thought the banquet was such a success, we were planning the next one.*

The TiR Macbeth was able to relax and reply, *Your loyalty is admirable but you should not all be unavailable* and exit.

There was an audible sigh of relief from the class.

12. Repeat mime loop and develop

Mime loop revisited

Now, when Macbeth's guilt is recognised, repeat the mime loop and redo the original but work on it to change it as the innocent activity would now be seen through Macbeth's eyes, coloured by his guilt and his evil, for example, chopping vegetables becomes a stabbing motion.

Start the loop normally and show how it changes as Macbeth enters.

13. Macbeth comes looking for the letter

TiR challenge to the servants

TiR: *Gather all you servants. I have serious business. My lady is missing a letter from her chamber. One of you must know of this. It is deadly secret and if you know you must return it, telling no one of its contents. I will be very angry if it is not found at once.*

Do you all understand? I will return shortly.

OoR: *What do they do? Return it secretly to where it belongs?*

14. Set up the Queen's bedchamber

Define the space technique

Choose a volunteer servant to return the letter.

One thought, one action direction of the returnee from the door of the room. At a critical moment TiR Macbeth enters. Forum theatre is used to deal with that moment.

15. Ending possibilities

Theatre form to embody ending

OoR: *This King is not worthy of leading the country and he threatens us all. The servants all rise up against him. How do we show his overthrow?*

The class work to find a theatrical form to symbolise the end of Macbeth. Introduce symbols that can be used in the representation; the themes and symbols in the play suggest possibilities – the gold-covered throne/candle in a candlestick/a red cloth.

Possibilities

- Five movements and single statements using the symbols.
- Tableau with captions.
- 30-second scene involving figures important in Macbeth's downfall – Macbeth, a 'weird sister', his wife, the dead King, the servants.
- Sociogram of the servants showing them surrounding the body of the dead Macbeth.

A whole group tableaux at the coronation of the new King, with an image of the overthrown Macbeth involved somewhere.

Structure summary

1   **Negotiate doing drama.**

2   **Introduction.**

OoR: *What must it have been like to be a king 500 years ago?*:

Look at a picture of Elizabeth I or Henry VIII and an Elizabethan banquet.

They are instructed to work together as a class to set out the banquet room.

Create the jobs in action for servants to represent work being done for the banquet. Use a mime loop.

Look at them.

3   **TiR as the Chief Steward to the King.**

I felt I had to come to warn you. It's important that you know that he's not in a good mood this morning.

4   **TiR as Macbeth in a foul mood.**

Where is the place for my Queen?

5   **Sociogram to show thoughts about Macbeth at this point.**

6   **TiR as steward returns.**

Has he been in?... What was he like?

Introduce the story of the chambermaid.

End of Part One

PART TWO

7 **Recap last session.**

8 **After the banquet – the next morning.**

   The report of Macbeth at the banquet.

9 **Servants discuss what they have seen with the Steward.**

   What does this mean?

10 **The steward provides more evidence.**

   The letter sent by Macbeth to Lady Macbeth.

11 **They are threatened with discovery.**

   As they are discussing, change roles to TiR Macbeth: *There are no servants?*

12 **Repeat mime loop and develop.**

13 **Macbeth comes looking for the letter.**

14 **Set up the Queen's bedchamber.**

   Choose a volunteer servant to return the letter.

   One thought, one action direction of the returnee from the door of the room.

   At a critical moment TiR Macbeth enters. Forum theatre dealing with that moment.

15 **Ending possibilities.**

   The class work to find a theatrical form to symbolise the end of Macbeth.

   Sociogram of the servants showing them surrounding the body of Macbeth.

   A whole group tableaux at the coronation of the new King, with an image of the overthrown Macbeth involved somewhere.

Appendix: The Witch

An optional piece of drama that can be inserted instead of the letter section, or added before the finale to develop the drama further, or as a separate piece having set the class up as Macbeth's servants.

1. An arrival at the castle

Narrate: *Later that day they are all clearing away the banquet when there came a loud knocking at a side door to the castle.*

OoR: *Have the servants been told to expect anyone?*

Who answers the door? Visualise the door. What does it look like? Is it a heavy door to open?

Set up a volunteer or volunteers to open the door, assembling the rest of the class as observers.

They 'open' the door to find a hooded figure (TiR), holding a package, something wrapped in sacking.

Witch TiR (speaking in the sort of gnomic way of the Witches in the play): *Ah, thank you for letting me in. You have need of me. Are you ready to be the saviours of your land?*

Are you thinking of the health of the King and therefore your good fortune?

I hear the King is troubled?

What can the future hold?

What do I bring?

Can we see through the gift I bring?

Do you want what I bring?

At an early point go OoR to discuss their perception of the Witch.

Give them the opportunity to question the newcomer, who will never call him/herself a witch: *I am a seer, one who knows the inner desires of those I meet.*

The aim is to get the servants to open the package/take the mirror and see what they think it all means.

2. Set up the ritual

Standing in a circle

The Witch holding up the mirror for each volunteer

OR

Passing the mirror from person to person.

In either case, the servants are looking to see what the future might bring according to each one.

Witch: *Take – hold out – look deeply beyond the reflection.*

Each servant does so in turn.

You must take this to the King so that he clearly sees his future. He will know the meaning of the mirror and who has brought it.

The Witch leaves after this.

3. Reflecting on the moment

After the meeting with the Witch, the Steward comes back and asks what has happened and what they have found out.

4. They take the mirror to Macbeth

He becomes frightened by what he sees in it.

Did they give you this? What know you of them? Why are you working with them? All they have done is evil. What are you trying to get me to do?

He sends them away so he can study the mirror.

Arrange the class as an invisible wall.

They watch as he stands transfixed by the mirror.

Class thought-track him to reveal what they create as his imaginings.

They use one thought, one action to show what he does as a result of this event.

This leads to his end and links to the endings in the drama above.

'Ebenezer Scrooge'

A drama based on *A Christmas Carol* by Charles Dickens

Learning objectives

Pupils will understand:

- the relationship between how we see ourselves and how others see us
- some of the themes of Dickens's *A Christmas Carol*

Roles

	Role	Signifier
Teacher	Editor Bob Cratchit A Carol Singer Ebenezer Scrooge	Clip board Scarf Black cap Walking stick
Pupils	Journalists on *The London Chronicle*	N/A

Research and preparation

- Prepare the letter from Scrooge to the editor of *The London Chronicle* (see structure point 9 below for text)
- Either a list of the main features of an obituary or an unfinished version, this will depend upon the ability of the class

Structure

Contract

1. **Negotiate doing drama**

2. **Negotiate the role for the class**

   Newspaper journalists – 150 years ago, in Victorian times.

TiR sets up the drama

   TiR as editor of the newspaper *The London Chronicle: We just heard that Ebenezer Scrooge, a local businessman, has passed away. We must write an obituary. Apparently he had a lot of money and no one knows whom he left it to.*

   OoR discuss what an obituary is and how we get the information to go into it.

   Set them to research and write an obituary.

We are going to interview two people who knew him: Bob Cratchit, Scrooge's clerk, and a carol singer who once went round to his house.

3. TiR as Bob Cratchit

ROLE BRIEF

Hot-seating
Bob
Cratchit

> ### *Bob Cratchit*
>
> He is a kind family man. He tries to see the best in everyone and in terms of Ebenezer Scrooge this is quite a challenge. He has heard through a newspaper journalist that Mr Scrooge has died and has come to help provide some information about his former employer.

TiR: *I don't mind doing this. But I don't want my name in this. Since you just told me that Mr Scrooge has passed on, I'll have to get another job and I don't want to make no enemies, 'cause I want to tell the truth. I don't want to tell lies. I mean, I tell my kids, 'Don't tell lies', I says.*

The key information he brings is:

Scrooge never takes his eyes off Bob Cratchit when he is at work copying letters.

Scrooge had a very small fire; mine was so very much smaller that it looked like one coal. If I tried to get some more coal Scrooge would threaten me with the sack! I put on my white comforter, and tried to warm myself at the candle.

On Christmas Eve Bob had asked for the next day off. Scrooge was not happy and grudgingly allowed him the holiday on condition he was *extra early into work on Boxing Day.*

4. Role on the wall

Role on the wall

OoR: *We can gather the information we have got from Bob Cratchit on this diagram. What words would describe the person you have heard about so far?*

What have we learned about Scrooge?

We are now going to meet someone else who has met Ebenezer Scrooge. She/he is a carol singer.

5. TiR as the Carol Singer

TiR: *I went carol singing to raise money for the church because it holds a party for the poor children. I went to Scrooge's and sang, I sang my best. 'God rest you merry, gentleman! May nothing you dismay!' I knew someone was in but they didn't answer when I knocked on the door. So I asked politely through the keyhole, 'Can I have sixpence for the poor children's' party?' He flings the door open and shouts, 'Bah, Humbug! Christmas! Be off with you!' and shakes his stick!*

6. Role on the wall

What more have we learned about Scrooge?

The class add to the role on the wall.

7. Tableaux

Discuss what other incidents show us how mean Ebenezer Scrooge can be.

Groups make a tableau of another incident in Scrooge's life that illustrates his personality or alternatively they show how Scrooge was when he was a child. Was he always mean?

8. Whole class writing of obituary

The role on the wall of Scrooge is the source of information for the obituary. It provides a summary of the meetings with those who knew him and the incidents the class have imagined. Now the class move on to write a class obituary using a template of the key elements required.

OBITUARY OF EBENEZER SCROOGE

We are announcing the death of Ebenezer Scrooge, who departed from this world on the 24th of December 1835.

He will be best remembered as a local businessman who was …
(Complete this section with words that describe him.)

In talking to some who knew him we learned that he …
(Complete this section with what we learned from Bob Cratchit.)

Others who had dealings with him told how he once …
(Complete this section with the incident told by the Carol Singer.)

The world has lost a man who …

---

9. TiR as Editor
He tells the class that there has been a grave error made, which could cost them dear, and he reads a letter from Scrooge.

13, Park Lane,
Borough of Walworth,
London.

Dear Sir,

I was shocked and distressed to discover that rumours of my death had spread to such an extent that an obituary had appeared in your newspaper under the heading 'Ebenezer Scrooge – Died 24th December 1835'.

I was even more horrified when I read this disgraceful account of my life, in which the likes of employees of mine and strangers off the street (a money-grabbing carol singer) claim I was less than the careful, frugal, hard-working businessman that I truly am.

I must defend myself against this slander, and so, gentleman, expect to see me at eleven o'clock this morning to register my complaint.

Yours faithfully,
Ebenezer Scrooge

Immediately after reading the letter TiR as Editor leaves, saying he must see the Editor-in-Chief.

10. TiR immediately returns in role as Scrooge

TiR raises tension

TiR: *Humph, what is all this, eh? I have already been to see my lawyer (cost me enough money just to talk to him) but he says I'm owed at least a front page apology and MONEY! But I am prepared to hear what you have to say before I go to law. I never like to waste money.*

The class must deal with Scrooge. He does not accept their view of him.

OoR: *What evidence have you got to say these things? He cannot deny the evidence they present but is unwilling to accept their description of him.*

How can we show Scrooge what he is really like? In the original story he is taken on a journey through his past. If we remake the pictures you made earlier you can show him these and so convince him that the obituary you have written is fair.

11. The class remake the pictures of Scrooge's life

Tableaux as evidence

TiR as Scrooge is shown the pictures. You may wish to add one line, one gesture, to the pictures or thought-track them to show what people thought about his behaviour. Scrooge will begin to see the error of his ways and ask the class how can he become a more likeable person.

12. Tableaux of a reformed Scrooge

Contrasting tableaux

You could set different contexts: at work, at Bob Cratchit's Christmas dinner, opening the door to carol singers, etc.

You might also forum Bob Cratchit or the carol singer with Scrooge listening to their opinions and telling them how he will behave from now on.

Structure summary

1 **Negotiate doing drama.**

2 **Negotiate the role for the class.**
   Newspaper journalists – 150 years ago, in Victorian times, working for *The London Chronicle*. TiR informs them of the death of Ebenezer Scrooge.

3 **TiR as Bob Cratchit.**
   Pupils in role as journalists question Bob so as to learn more about Scrooge.

4 **Role on the wall.**
   The picture of Scrooge is recorded.

5 **TiR as the Carol Singer.**
   Presents more information about Scrooge.

6 **Role on the wall.**
   Information gained from the Carol Singer is added.

7 **Tableaux.**

The class embellish the history of Scrooge with their pictures of his behaviour.

8 **Whole class writing activity.**

An 'obituary' of Ebenezer Scrooge.

9 **TiR as Editor reads a letter from Scrooge.**

The dilemma is set up.

10 **TiR as Scrooge.**

Threatens legal action unless they can explain themselves and apologise.

11 **The class remake the pictures of Scrooge's life.**

TiR as Scrooge is shown the pictures. He debates their view but eventually sees the error of his ways.

12 **Tableaux of a reformed Scrooge.**

How will he be in the future?

Multiple context of a reformed Scrooge.

'Christopher Boone'

A drama based upon *The Curious Incident of the Dog in the Night-Time* by Mark Haddon

Learning objectives

Pupils will understand:

- the nature of adults' interpretation of children's behaviour
- the meaning of being inclusive

Research and preparation

- Read the book
- Create a logo for the Worried Parents Organisation
- Create six labels: 'The road', 'The pavement', 'The grass verge', 'A dog', 'The dog is dead', 'It is still warm'

Roles

	Role	Signifier
Teacher	The head of the WPO Christopher Boone Mrs Shears Mrs Boone	Clip board Melvin's bag Apron Shopping bag
Pupils	WPO personnel	N/A

Structure

1. Negotiate doing drama

Contract

I am going to introduce the drama we are going to do today. I am in it and you are in it. I know how it begins but I don't know how it ends and your input will affect that.

Is that OK?

2. Set up the office of the Worried Parents Organisation

Setting the context and the pupils' roles

(Overhead of logo – 'Worried about your child? We can help')

OoR: *What are the people who work here going to be good at?*

What does the office look like?

What sort of jobs will the people who work here do?

Worried Parents Organisation

Worried about your kids?
WE CAN HELP?

3. Introduce the case

Narrate: *It was another busy day at the Worried Parents Office. Phones were ringing, faxes and emails were being received.*

TiR as Head of WPO: *Can you gather round, I've got an urgent fax here.*

Read letter to class:

Dear WPO

My name is Mrs Boone and I live at 44 Bower Street.

I am having some problems with my son Christopher.

I know he thinks differently from the other children but he gets very upset at some of the things that happen to him. I would like to see if you could help.

Yours Sincerely,

Mrs Boone

OK. I've arranged for Mrs Boone to come and see us. I not sure what this is about because she doesn't give us much detail.

Do you have any ideas? What do we need to ask her?

4. Prepare some questions for Mrs Boone

| TiR sets context |

TiR as Mrs Boone: *I hope you don't mind me coming. I've heard you're very good with children who are going through a hard time. The thing with Christopher is he doesn't think like other children do and it gets him into trouble. I mean he's not stupid, he knows lots of things. But he does have to have a special teacher working with him at school.*

I mean this morning he said he knew every country of the world and all the prime numbers up to 227 and I don't even know what a prime number is!

He might shout out or laugh at something very loudly. In the library if he finds a funny book – he doesn't realise other people are wanting quiet.

5. OoR write up the issues

| OoR summarise the features of Christopher's behaviour |

He gets into trouble:

- When he gets frustrated
- If you ask him too many questions
- If you shout at him
- If you touch him, even if it's friendly.
- If something unexpected happens

6. Interview with Christopher

| Setting the context – listening for clues |

The class have a chance to watch Christopher having an interview with his new teacher. There are two chairs, one with a clip board on it to represent the teacher and the other for TiR as Christopher. The class will ask the questions, either from an overhead or a handout. They are set questions that teachers ask each of the pupils.

OoR: You are going to witness Christopher being interviewed by his new teacher. One of you will ask the questions and the rest will listen to the answers very carefully then we will stop and talk about them.

- *How old are you?*
- *Do you have any family?*
- *Who are they?*
- *What is your mum's phone number?*

ROLE BRIEF

> ### *Christopher*
>
> Christopher is very pedantic in all his answers. He is exact in his date of birth, name of his mother and phone numbers. He also notices things in the room, size, etc. All these things demonstrate particular features of his personality.

What is your name?

TiR: Christopher John Anthony Boone.

How old are you?

I am 8 years 311 days old. 30th of August 1998.

Do you have any family?

Yes I do.

Who are they?

I have a mum called Alice Dawn Boone neé Deane. I don't have a Dad. I have an Uncle Terry who lives in Gosford, Cheshire at 4 Whitefield Lane and a Grandma who is in a home called 'Autumn Leaves'.

What is your mum's phone number?

She has two phones, one for home and one if she is not at home. 0158226399 and her mobile is 07893 423576.

This is a nice room. It is approximately 2 metres wide by 2 metres in depth; therefore it contains 8 cubic metres of air.

Role on the wall – what we know now

7. OoR discuss their understanding of what was said

Make a role on the wall to summarise what we know about Christopher.

8. Tableaux of the problems for Christopher

OoR setting up the pictures:

Pupils add to the narrative

We are going to look at two situations where Christopher might be misunderstood.

The playground, then

A school trip.

We are going to make a still image of the moment when Christopher is misunderstood or is finding it difficult to cope. I am going to take the role of Christopher and you are going to put me in the situation. You must tell me exactly how I must stand and look.

Thought-
tracking

The class look at and discuss the pictures. Each picture is then thought-tracked.

The setting up can be done as a whole class having given a short time to discuss what they want to show.

9. The incident of the dog in the night-time

Main focus

OoR: *Something happened last night. We are going to look at it.*

Put the class in a large circle

In the circle is a piece of material, a black or brown cloth. There are some labels on and around it:

'The road'
'The pavement'
'The grass verge'
'A dog'
'The dog is dead'
'It is still warm'

OoR: *Christopher found the dog by the side of the road and this is what he wrote in his diary.*

The teacher reads a page from Christopher Boone's diary.

It was 7 minutes after midnight. The dog was lying on the grass verge by the pavement in front of Mrs Shears's house. Its eyes were closed. It looked as if it had been running on its side, the way dogs do when they think they are chasing a cat in a dream. But the dog was not running or asleep. The dog was dead. I knelt beside the dog. I put my hand on the muzzle of the dog. It was still warm.

The dog was called Wellington. It belonged to Mrs Shears who was our friend. She lived on the opposite side of the road, two doors to the left.

TiR as Christopher moves into the space and picks up the dog.

Oh no! Poor Wellington.

He rocks back and forward holding the dog.

OoR: *I want you to tell me as I go round the circle what Christopher is thinking. Say it as if it were Christopher's thoughts. Remember you might just want to listen to Christopher's thoughts and not say anything. That's fine.*

Go round and touch each child on the shoulder to indicate they can speak if they want to.

Now I want you to watch what happened next.

10. Confrontation with Mrs Shears

TiR as Mrs Shears: *WHAT HAVE YOU DONE TO MY DOG? I knew there was something wrong with you. There is no use talking to you, lad. I'm going to speak to your mum NOW!*

Move across to the dog, pick it up and say:

TiR as Christopher: *I didn't do anything, Mrs Shears.*

Christopher puts the dog down, backs away and on his knees buries his head in the ground and puts his hands over his ears. He says:

The grass is wet and cold and it's nice.

OoR: *Why would Christopher say that? Discuss what it all meant to the class.*

11. Mrs Boone's response

TiR as Mrs Boone is on the phone in her kitchen.

So tell me again. Wellington was knocked down by a car and Christopher might have seen it. Well, where is he now? You don't know? But where is he now? Yes, I am very worried.

OoR: *Who was Mrs Boone talking to? What do you think the police officer was saying? What do you think might have happened to Christopher? Who is on her way here now? What does she think has happened?*

I am going to be Mrs Shears and you are going to take the role of Christopher's mum. Anyone can speak for her and you are going to have to deal with Mrs Shears. She is going to speak to you first.

12. TiR as Mrs Shears

Well, your Christopher has done it now hasn't he? I knew there was something wrong with him, now he's gone and killed my dog. Well, I'm going to make sure he has to move from round here.

OoR: *How does she seem? Why is she behaving like this? What do you need to tell her?*

Mrs Shears will eventually realise her mistake. She offers to help find Christopher.

13. Rescuing Christopher

The class set up where they think Christopher is hiding. TiR as Christopher. He does not wish to come out. The class have to reassure Christopher and suggest ways they can deal with Mrs Shears.

TiR: *That Mrs Shears thinks I hurt Wellington. She will tell my mum and I'm in trouble.*

Eventually Christopher will be persuaded to come out of hiding when he thinks he is safe from Mrs Shears.

Margin notes:

TiR to raise the tension

Overheard conversation

Identifying with the key role

Forum theatre	**14. Forum Mrs Shears and Mrs Boone** TiR as Mrs Shears and class as Mrs Boone
Tableaux	**15. Tableaux** A good week for Christopher at school – in the classroom. A good week for Christopher at school – in the playground.
Summarising the learning	**16. A list** of things that the teacher, the pupils and Mrs Boone can do to help Christopher.

Structure summary

1 **Negotiate doing drama.**

2 **Set up the office.**

   Overhead of logo – 'Worried about your child? We can help.'

3 **TiR as Head of WPO introducing a case to be examined.**

4 **Prepare questions for Mrs. Boone.**

5 **OoR write up the issues regarding Christopher's behaviour.**

6 **Interview with Christopher.**

   TiR as Christopher class to use structured interview form as his teacher.

7 **OoR to discuss pupil's understanding.**

   Role on the Wall to summarise what we know about Christopher.

8 **Tableaux of the problems for Christopher.**

   In the playground and on a school trip.

9 **The incident of the dog in the night-time.**

   Defining the space.

10 **Confrontation with Mrs Shears.**

   Raising the tension.

11 **Mrs Boone's response.**

   Overheard conversation

12 **TiR as Mrs Shears.**

   Dealing with misunderstandings.

13 **Rescuing Christopher.**

14 **Forum Mrs Shears and Mrs Boone.**

   TiR as Mrs Shears and class as Mrs Boone.

15 **Tableaux.**

   A good week for Christopher at school – in the classroom.

   A good week for Christopher at school – in the playground.

16 **A list of things that the teacher, the pupils and Mrs Boone can do to help Christopher.**

'The Dream'

A drama based on *A Midsummer Night's Dream* by William Shakespeare

Learning objectives

Pupils will understand:

- who the key characters in the play are, their attitudes
- the opening of the play and its themes of:
    parents/children and obedience
    love versus duty

Research and preparation

- Find a suitable coat of arms for Theseus
- Prepare group folders for the advisers with the letter in them

Roles

	Role	Signifier
Teacher	Philostrate	Staff of office
	Theseus	Sceptre
	Egeus	Law scroll
	Hermia	Lysander's ring on a ribbon and a letter from him
	Possibly Lysander and	Letter for Hermia
	Demetrius if called on	A ring for Hermia
Pupils	Council of Advisers to Theseus	N/A
	Possibly role of Hermia or Lysander	Take over the signifiers

Structure

1. **Negotiate the opening** and them listening to a role

Contracting

TiR as Philostrate: *I have come to warn you that the Duke is coming down here to talk to you. You know you've been given all these tasks to do to prepare for his wedding, the celebrations, his speech to the people.*

Setting the context – listening for clues

I can see that you're getting on very well at these. He does trust you very much. You're the people whose advice and ideas he looks to all the time. However, he is not in a very good mood this morning. He seems to have had some news of some sort. I don't know what, but I know he's coming down here to ask you about it, to get your advice about it. I don't think it's anything to do with the wedding, but I don't know for sure. I thought I'd come down to warn you to make sure that you don't get yourselves into trouble.

What do you think you should be doing when he arrives?

2. OoR – setting the context

Discuss who that is, what he's told them and what they think their role is.

Establishing
pupil roles

What do advisers do, what skills do they possess?

You're going to be the Council of Advisers to a great Duke who rules over the important city-state of Athens in Ancient Greece.

How would you behave to him?

This is the council chamber. What does it look like? He is about to enter to talk to you. What tasks are you engaged on in preparation for and your planning of the wedding?

Discuss their division of tasks where they work in groups. Each of the six or so groups is dealing with a different task. They will come up with the list but it is likely to include: wedding lists and invitations, design décor and flowers, food and seating plans, transport, speeches, entertainment.

3. Set out the room and where the tasks are going on

Explore how the Council of Advisers will be feeling having heard from Philostrate.

4. TiR as Theseus

The Council are busy about their tasks in preparing the wedding when TiR enters as Theseus.

TiR
stimulus

I'm pleased to see you getting on so well with the preparations for the wedding. It is a worrying time for all of us, but we're all looking forward to it as well.

Pause to look at them all.

Well, I was looking forward to it until this morning, when I received this. I'm sorry to interrupt, to stop what you're doing, but I'm afraid I have to call a Council meeting urgently. I need your advice and ideas about this straight away. Please gather round for the meeting.

ROLE BRIEF

> **Theseus**
>
> His attitude is that Egeus is wrong to do this, but that it is the law of Athens that a father has ownership over his daughter and she must obey his will. Egeus has a right to invoke this. He, Theseus, cannot change the law when it has been invoked and Egeus is a very clever courtier who will attack him in the courts if he is seen to be trying to undermine the laws as they stand. He will seek to change it later to avoid any such further cases but for now it is impossible.

Hand out official folders with the coat of arms on. The folders contain a letter from Egeus.

I would have you listen very closely to what this says. It presents us with a difficult problem.

Read the letter.

My noble lord,
Full of vexation write I, with complaint
Against my child, my daughter Hermia.
Demetrius hath my consent to marry her.
Lysander hath bewitch'd the bosom of my child: given her rimes,
And interchang'd love-tokens with my child;
By moonlight at her window sung,
With feigning voice, verses of feigning love;
And stol'n the impression of her fantasy
With bracelets of his hair, rings, gawds, conceits,
     messengers
Of strong prevailment In unharden'd youth;
With cunning he hast filch'd my daughter's heart;
Turn'd her obedience, which is due to me,
To stubborn harshness.

And, my gracious Duke,
Be it so she will not before your Grace
Consent to marry with Demetrius,
I beg the ancient privilege of Athens,
As she is mine, I may dispose of her;
Which shall be either to Demetrius,
Or to her death, according to our law
Immediately provided in that case.

                Your most vexed, humble servant,
                      Egeus

I really didn't need this at this time. The man seems determined to confront his daughter in this way. What do you understand the problem to be? I'm not sure I understand it fully.

5. The character relationships

Out of role to discuss the meaning of the letter. Use large name sheets for the key characters to map out the relationships on the floor so that the class can see the issue. It should look like this:

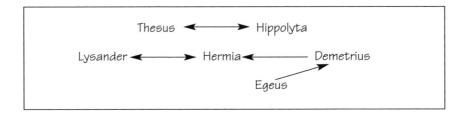

Decide what the advisers would need to say to Theseus. Do they have any suggestions for him?

Discussion with Theseus about the letter. Do not let them question Theseus too much.

When they have interpreted the letter for him, Theseus directs them:

I need advice on how to handle this. I need to avoid invoking the Athenian law which still exists about a father's right of life over disobedient children, but which has not been used for a long time. If he insists on his rights, I will have to have her put to death. It is the law after all. I need you to sort this out so I don't have a problem. I don't even want to think about it in the week leading up to the wedding.

6. Identifying with Theseus

Thought-tracking

Advisers stand around Theseus and thought-track him.

OoR class decide how the advisers should approach sorting this out.

What do they need to know? Whom do they need to interview to be able to give Theseus advice?

7. Possibilities – choices for the advisers

TiR as Hermia

Dynamic set-ups for meeting TiRs

If they choose to approach Hermia, they find her standing outside her father's house, reading something, which she folds away quickly and tries to hide.

They have to discover what she is reading, which turns out to be a letter from Lysander referring to *an arrangement* they have made. *What does it mean?*

> Dearest Hermia,
> Things have become very difficult for us, I realise.
> Now is the time to take action.
> You must be brave, my sweetest girl.
> I know you will be because you are very strong to stand against a father as you have done.
> Let us do what we planned when we last met. Let tonight be the night.
> I must write no more.
>
> The luckiest man

TiR – Egeus

If they choose to approach Egeus they find him shouting after a servant who has just left him: *I know you are lying. I know you gave her a letter from him. If I find out you have I will ... Ah, the Duke's advisers! Servants – you can't trust them. That one is her personal servant and she is covering up for her. I know it.*

His attitude is that these advisers should be enforcing the law and he assumes they are his allies. He shows them the letter: *This man keeps after her and I won't have it. It proves I am right in what I am doing. What self-respecting man behaves like this with a young girl?*

He asks the advisers,

What are you and the Lord Theseus going to do about it?

I swear I will have the law on her if she does not reject this man.

I want you to keep an eye on her.

8. What do we know? What do we think we know? What do we need to know?

On paper the advisers write down what they know so far and what they think is going on.

OoR: *How would they keep an eye on her? What do you think is going on? She must be meeting him somehow.*

They decide how to watch Hermia.

Reflecting on the situation

9. The advisers hide to watch Hermia

She creeps out of the house and they confront her.

Does she reveal the elopement plan?

If so she begs them not to tell. She will be out of the way and there is no death, no interruption to the wedding plans.

TiR creates tension

10. OoR discuss what the advisers do at this point

Do they tell Theseus? How do they deal with Egeus?

Do they confront Lysander?

Do they try to deal with Demetrius?

Whose side are they on?

11. The report

Theseus sends a request for the advisers to report.

They prepare a set of pictures to show what is happening and to advise him what to do.

In four groups they are each given a tableau.

Two groups are given picture A – how they understand the situation of the four people at the moment. One of these groups shows it from Egeus's point of view, the other from Hermia's.

One group is given picture B – what the consequences will be if Egeus insists on the marriage he wants.

One group is given the task of showing the consequences if Hermia and Lysander elope.

The ideas contained in this material are discussed, including how they want to see the outcome, and Theseus instructs them to tackle Egeus and Demetrius.

Tableaux of information and advice

12. Dealing with the problem

Forum theatre

Possibles ... Forum theatre

Hermia – Egeus
Hermia – Demetrius.
The class take over Hermia's role.

Structure summary

1 **Negotiate the opening and them listening to a role.**
TiR as Philostrate.
I have come to warn you that the Duke is coming down here.

2 **OoR – setting the context.**
Who that is, what he's told them and what their role is.

3 **Set out the room.**

4 **TiR as Theseus.**
The Council get busy about their tasks in preparing the wedding.
Theseus: *Please gather round for the meeting.*
Hands out official folders with a letter from Egeus. Read the letter.

5 **The character relationships.**
Out of role to discuss the letter – map out the relationships on the floor.
Discussion with Theseus about the letter.

6 **Identify with Theseus.**
Advisers stand around Theseus and thought-track him.
OoR class decide how advisers should approach sorting this out.

7 **Possibilities for the advisers.**
If they approach Hermia, they find her reading something, which she folds away.
If they approach Egeus he has the letter, which a loyal servant has brought to him.

8 **What do we know? What do we think we know? What do we need to know?**

9 **The advisers hide to watch Hermia.**
She creeps out of the house and they confront her.

10 **OoR discuss what the advisers do at this point.**

11 **Theseus requests a report.**
The advisers prepare a set of pictures to show what is happening.

12 **Forum theatre.**

References

Alexander R. (2000) *Culture and Pedagogy: international comparisons in primary education*, Oxford, Blackwell Publishers.

Alexander R. (2004) 'Talking to Learn', in *Teacher, The Times Educational Supplement*, London.

Alexander R. (2005) *Towards Dialogic Teaching: rethinking classroom talk*, York, Dialogos UK.

Baron-Cohen S. (2003) *The Essential Difference*. London, Penguin.

BBC (2004) 'Life on the Streets: children's stories', translated from BBCHindi.com Rajan, Delhi, India. http://news.bbc.co.uk/1/hi/world/4026855.stm.

Bolton G. (1979) *Towards a Theory of Drama in Education*, Harlow, Longman.

Bolton G. (1984) *Drama as Education*, Harlow, Longman.

Bowell P. and Heap B. (2001) *Planning Process Drama*, London, David Fulton.

Browne A. (1998) *Voices in the Park*, London, Doubleday.

Chambers (1972) *Chambers 20th Century Dictionary* (A.M. Macdonald, ed.), London, Chambers.

Clark J. and Goode T. (eds). (1999) *Assessing Drama*, National Drama Publications, London, The Gulbenkian Foundation.

Cooper H. (2006) *History 3–11, a guide for teachers*, London, David Fulton.

Cumbria Record Office *Kendal Workhouse Rules* (ref WD/CU/78).

DfEE (1999) Circular 10/99 Social Inclusion: Pupils Support, Chpt 3: Groups at Particular Risk, London, DfEE.

DfES (2005) *Primary National Strategy Excellence and Enjoyment: social and emotional aspects of learning new beginnings*, London, DfES.

Fines J. (1997) 'Truth and Imagination – a little investigation in three fits', in D. Davis (ed.), *Interactive Research in Drama in Education*, Stoke on Trent, Trentham Books.

Goffman E. (1975) *Frame Analysis*, London, Peregrine Books.

Haddon M. (2003) *The Curious Incident of the Dog in the Night-Time*, London, Red Fox Definitions.

Heathcote D. and Bolton G. (1995) *Drama for Learning*, Portsmouth, NH, Heinemann.

Johnson, L. and O'Neill C. (eds). (1984) *Dorothy Heathcote: collected writings on education and drama*, London, Hutchinson.

Morrison B. (1998) *Too True,* London, Granta Books.

Ofsted (2006) *Evaluating Educational Inclusion: Guidance for Inspectors and Schools.* www.ofsted.gov.uk.

O'Neill C. (1989) 'Ways of seeing: audience function in drama and theatre', *2D magazine*, vol. 8, no. 2.

O'Neill, C. and Lambert, A. (1982) *Drama Structures*, London, Hutchinson.

QCA (2000) *Personal, Social and Health Education and Citizenship at Key Stages 1 and 2*, London, Qualifications and Curriculum Authority.

QCA (2002) *Citizenship: A scheme of work for Key Stages 1 and 2: Teacher's guide*, London, QCA/DfES.

QCA (2003) *Speaking, Listening, Learning: working with pupils in Key Stages 1 and 2*, Handbook, London, Qualifications and Curriculum Authority.

QCA/DfES (2000) 'The History National Curriculum', National Curriculum Online www.nc.uk.net.

Reader W.J. (1974) *Victorian England*, London, Batsford.

SEAL (2006) www.teachernet.gov.uk/teachingandlearning/socialandpastoral/sebs1/seal/.

Sendak M. (1970) *Where the Wild Things Are*, London, Penguin.

Toye N. and Prendiville F. (2000) *Drama and Traditional Story for the Early Years*, Abingdon, RoutledgeFalmer.

UKLA (2004) *Raising Boys Achievements in Writing*, Hertfordshire, United Kingdom Literacy Association.

Bibliography

Baldwin P. and Fleming K. (2003) *Teaching Literacy through Drama: creative approaches*, Abingdon, RoutledgeFalmer.

Bolton G. (1992) *New Perspectives on Classroom Drama*, London, Simon & Schuster.

Bowell P. and Heap B. (2001) *Planning Process Drama*, London, David Fulton.

Dickinson R. and Neelands J. (2006) *Improve Your Primary School through Drama*, London, David Fulton.

Fines J., Nichol J. and Verrier R. (1997) *Teaching Ancient Greece*, London, Heinemann.

Fines J., Nichol J. and Verrier R. (1997) *Teaching Life in Tudor Times*, London, Heinemann.

Fines J., Nichol J. and Verrier R. (1997) *Teaching Primary History*, London, Heinemann.

Heathcote D. and Bolton G. (1995) *Drama for Learning: Dorothy Heathcote's Mantle of the Expert Approach to Education*, Portsmouth, NH, Heinemann.

Kitson N. and Spiby I. (1997) *Drama 7–11: developing primary teaching skills*, Abingdon, Routledge.

Neelands J. (2001) *Structuring Drama Work*, 2nd edn, Cambridge, Cambridge University Press.

Toye N. and Evans D. (2006) 'How Can Children Connect to a Distant Place through Drama?', in H. Cooper, C. Rowley and S. Asquith (eds), *Geography 3–11*, London, David Fulton. (This relates to 'The Maasai Boy' Drama.)

Winston J. (2004) *Drama and English at the Heart of the Primary Curriculum*, London, David Fulton.

Index